# Unmoored

# UNMOORED
*Coming of Age in Troubled Waters*

## J. R. ROESSL

Essex, Connecticut

An imprint of Globe Pequot, the trade division of
The Rowman & Littlefield Publishing Group, Inc.
4501 Forbes Blvd., Ste. 200
Lanham, MD 20706
www.rowman.com

Distributed by NATIONAL BOOK NETWORK

British Library Cataloguing in Publication Information available

**Library of Congress Cataloging-in-Publication Data**
ISBN 978-1-4930-6995-8 (hardback: alk. paper)
ISBN 978-1-4930-6996-5 (electronic)

♾ᵀᴹ The paper used in this publication meets the minimum requirements of American National Standard for Information Sciences—Permanence of Paper for Printed Library Materials, ANSI/NISO Z39.48-1992.

*For Vivien*

*"Now we fish together again."*

*"No. I am not lucky. I am not lucky anymore."*

*"The hell with luck," the boy said. "I'll bring the luck with me."*
—ERNEST HEMINGWAY, THE OLD MAN AND THE SEA

# Contents

# Prologue

"Now, close your eyes and imagine water so blue you can't tell where the ocean ends and the sky begins. . . ." So began Mother's bedtime story. It was always the same tale and the one, starting at age seven, I'd never tired of because it was about us. Night after night, my mother wove a wonderful tale of our life and the adventures we'd have aboard our magical ship. I'd drift off and fly like Peter Pan, following the second star to the right toward Neverland, where I'd play all day and never go to school. A big, red-and-yellow parrot would ride on my shoulder and Grandma, half-hidden under a large floppy hat, would sit in a chair perched on the cabin top and cheer me on as I flew through the air fighting Captain Hook and his motley crew. My sisters and I would get along, and best of all, my father would never yell. After a dinner of peanut butter and jelly sandwiches and chocolate milkshakes, we'd count the stars in the Milky Way. Together we'd sail the seven seas and around the world ten times over and never go home again.

# I
# SHAKEDOWN

# Departure

### Alameda, California

**DECEMBER 5, 1969**

My father paced up and down the dock. "Goddammit, where the hell are they?"

"I'm sure they'll be here any minute," my mother said, placing her hand on his arm.

Ignoring her, he punched the air with his fist. "Incoming tide's less than thirty minutes."

Well, this is a great start to our trip, I thought. We hadn't even left the dock and already my father was in a bad mood.

The professionals he'd hired to accompany us on our shakedown leg to San Diego were hours late. We should have been well on our way, motoring out on an ebbing tide, with enough light to guide us out of the Oakland Estuary, across the Bay, and safely under the Golden Gate Bridge, but now, if and when they showed, we'd be leaving under the cover of darkness, like fugitives fleeing the scene of a crime.

"Is it at all . . . ?" Before my mother could finish, my father cut her off.

"No! We're leaving tonight. With or without them."

Why did my mother even try, I wondered. At sixteen, I knew better than to reason with my father. It had taken him nearly a decade to reach this moment and nothing, short of keeling over and dying, was going to stop him from leaving. Even Grandma's sudden passing had not delayed our departure. While my mother, sisters, and I were still reeling from my grandmother's death, my father had moved on. For him, the start to our three-year, round-the-world adventure on our forty-foot schooner, *Heritage,* lay on the *other* side of the Golden Gate and "come hell or high water," he was heading there tonight.

My father slammed his hand on the railing and growled, "Just wait 'til these guys show up. I'm gonna rip them some new . . ."

"Why don't we go over the schedule?" my mother gently suggested.

He coaxed one of his favorite Salem cigarettes from the pack nestled in his shirt pocket, lit up, and after a couple of long drags, settled down. "I'm figuring it'll take six days to make it down to San Diego. . . ."

Apart from a single day-sail in the Bay, this was to be *Heritage's* maiden voyage testing California's winter waves and weather against her virgin timbers. While I, my father, my thirteen-year-old sister, Gayle, and the two hired crew, sailed *Heritage* down the coast, my mother, eighteen-year-old sister, Pam, and four-year-old sister, Nancy, would drive south in our family's old Bonneville. After a brief stay with my paternal grand-parents in Burbank, they would then rendezvous with us in San Diego.

"I'm gonna make one more call," my father said, glancing at his watch.

My mother linked her arm in his. "I have to check on the girls." Tired of waiting, Pam and Nancy had returned to the car to stay warm.

I watched my parents walk away and wondered if my father thought what I thought: His professionals had bailed.

Years of catechism classes taught me when the going got rough, and all else failed, the tough got going by begging for help from above. I slapped my palms together, recited three Hail Marys, two Our Fathers, and for good measure invoked the Holy Trinity with the promise I'd be nice to my sisters, if only these guys would show up before my father totally lost it.

Gayle leaned against me, fast asleep from our perch on the cabin top. I closed my eyes and tried to ignore the numbing chill that rose straight from the boat's rime-frosted cabin top and into the cheeks of my butt. Even though I had on my new navy float coat, two wool sweaters, a turtleneck, and two pairs of thermals under my jeans, the cold seeped through and traveled along my skin and into my bones.

When I shifted back and forth to ease my sister's dead weight, she slipped off my shoulder and jerked awake. "Huh?" she mumbled. I felt guilty but was tired of being her pillow. It irritated the crap out of me that my sister could fall asleep anywhere. True to form, she resettled and nestled against my jacket like a satisfied cat.

When my father returned, his grim expression signaled the crew was still AWOL.

Even with my father in a foul mood, sailing with him for a week on *Heritage* was far better than what Pam would face once she reached my grandparents' house. I couldn't stand my father's parents, who, through either hard-heartedness or willful ignorance, designated my sisters and me as the least desirable of their grandchildren. We spent two hellish weeks with them each summer, with every year incrementally worse than the one before.

I suspected, though, we were mere stand-ins for the actual culprit, my father. Although he rarely talked about his childhood, I knew that life under my grandparents' roof was no picnic. Growing up under the shadow of an older, more favored brother and an obedient and mallea-ble younger sister, my father chafed under my grandparents' Catholic conservatism.

But at fifteen my father found freedom in the Sea Scouts. When he discovered he could learn to sail on the Great Lakes, he forged his parents' signature on his application and used money that he'd saved to pay for it. The summer-long caper exploring Lake Michigan was the start of what my father believed would be an annual occurrence; he'd found something he loved—sailing. But as punishment for his streak of independence, my grandparents made sure he never sailed the Great Lakes again.

On *Heritage*'s launch day, a reporter from the *Livermore Herald and News*, interviewing my father asked, "Why take on such a huge project?"

I remember my father stood there, lost in thought, gazing out over the hills and vineyards beyond the barn, where we'd built *Heritage*. The reporter waited, pencil in hand and notebook ready, for my father to answer.

"Ever since sailing the Great Lakes as a teenager, I've dreamt of having my own boat . . . but with a wife and three kids . . . well, the only way was to build one, so two years ago I took the big leap. . . ." He'd spread his arms wide, and grinned. "And *this* is the result!"

I remembered his joyful expression and wondered if my father felt *Heritage* was his way to lay claim to that Lake Michigan summer. For my grandparents, my father's act of selling our house, giving away our pets, and pulling us out of school to sail the seven seas only bolstered their conviction he was an irresponsible dreamer and my sisters and I, along with our mother, his gullible minions.

\* \* \*

The sound of car doors slamming snapped me back to the present. Our crew had arrived. I swore I heard trumpets and a chorus of angels fill the air. I was glad someone up there had heard me, but now I was on the hook to be nice to my sisters.

"Hey there, Captain," said the younger of the two men. He set his large duffel bag on the main dock and walked onto the finger slip. He looked to be in his midthirties but already had the beefy thickness men develop in middle age, at least the ones I'd seen working around the marina. The exception, of course, was my father, who at forty-three, was as lean as a twenty-year-old.

Having cursed the hired crew to eternal damnation just moments earlier, my father grinned and clasped the younger man's hand as if he were a long lost relative.

"Denny, you've met my wife, Lorraine?" my father said, as my mother, returning from the car, reached the three of them.

Denny smiled as he shook my mother's hand. "Yes, great to see you again."

"It's a damn interesting time to leave, Jim," groused the older of the two. If he'd been on time, I thought, he wouldn't be complaining. He looked to be in his fifties, and in the moonlight his sour expression made him look as if he wanted to be anywhere but here.

Denny laughed. "Hey, Stan, if you didn't have something to complain about, I'd wonder what was wrong with you."

Not one for banter or small talk, my father shifted his weight, and took a long drag on his cigarette. "Well, I know it's kinda late, but if we leave soon, we can reach the Gate by midnight."

Why didn't he yell at them for being late, I wondered. And whatever happened to "ripping them some new . . ."

"Well, gentlemen, this is my cue to say goodbye," my mother said.

"Don't worry, Lorraine, we'll take care of the crew," Denny said, and with a slight nod and a wink added, "and the captain."

Climbing on board with both his and Stan's duffel bags, Denny smiled at us. "You girls look frozen. Why don't you get underneath the dodger while Stan and I help your dad cast off?"

Maybe these guys are okay, I thought.

Gayle and I climbed over the coaming and into the cockpit, where we made ourselves comfortable beneath the shelter of the dodger. I watched as the men worked quickly, checking the bow and aft, and port and starboard lights, and felt my heart pounding. Was I excited or afraid? What had sounded exciting and adventurous in stories was very different in reality. We were heading out into deep ocean when we'd barely explored the waters of the Bay. Our weekends should have been spent learning how to sail, and not sanding and varnishing at the dock.

Whether it had simply been the monumental upkeep required of wooden boats, every choice we'd made after *Heritage*'s launch had revolved around her maintenance. No longer hidden in the womb-like environs of the barn, she'd demanded as much attention as a giant newborn. Not even the addition of our new baby sister and construction of our house in the Oakland hills stopped our family from tending to *Heritage*. We'd spent every weekend at the marina, where my sisters and I learned to pump and clean her bilge, remove the never-ending tarnish from her copper and brass fittings, and wipe away the daily soot staining her decks and railings black. Added to those chores, my father had assigned maintenance of *Heritage*'s masts to the only family member not afraid of heights. From the age of ten, I'd welcomed this assignment, strapped in my safety harness high above with the world spread out below. Straddling the spreaders with my paint can and brush, I discovered I could view the world from a place no one else on board could reach and claim it as my own.

I thought about how many times, since then, I'd scrambled up the ratlines to the topmast to spend time alone. My fearlessness guaranteed I'd always have my spot high in the sky.

I glanced over at Denny, who was kneeling on the dock trying to unknot the bowline. I could see he was struggling, but I wasn't about to tell him that the line had remained untouched in the five years since *Heritage*'s first and only sail across the bay to Tiburon.

\* \* \*

June 1964. San Francisco Bay. It had been a year since *Heritage*'s launch when my father moved her from the shallow, muddy slip at the Aeolian Yacht Club to the more upscale Pacific Marina on Alameda's estuary side. With her newly bleached decks, polished fittings, and freshly painted hull, *Heritage* was ready for action. What better opportunity for my father to impress his older and more successful brother and to prove his rightful place beside the family's golden boy, than with an invitation to join us on *Heritage*'s first spin on the Bay?

A few weeks later, my aunt and uncle drove up from their home in Los Angeles, showing up in snappy, matching, yachting whites, a sharp contrast to our ragged cutoffs and the bulky, bright-orange life vests my father insisted we wear since, apart from me, no one could swim. Fortunately, the glorious June morning and anticipated departure offset our embarrassment.

As my father started the engine and my mother, sisters, aunt, and I settled in the cockpit, my uncle volunteered to man the bow and spring lines from the dock.

"Okay, Chuck, cast off!" my father called out, sounding like the jovial skipper on *Gilligan's Island*. "When the bow clears the finger, nose her over, and climb on board." Easier said than done, my uncle soon discovered.

Whether it was the pressure from gawkers who had lined the dock to witness *Heritage*'s maiden departure, or just a simple miscalculation, my uncle grabbed the stanchions at midships, and swung his right leg over the railing while his left leg remained firmly planted on the dock. My father throttled forward, and my uncle executed a perfect split into the oily harbor to a rousing round of guffaws and applause.

"So that's how you treat your guests, Jim," said Harry, a big burly guy who owned a little cutter three slips down from us. "Remind me never to accept an invitation from you!" The men all guffawed again and nodded their heads in agreement.

Several men pulled my uncle out of the water and back onto the dock. My father, red-faced, brought the boat back into the slip, so that my uncle, whose boating whites were now soaked and oil streaked, could board.

On our second attempt, Harry helped guide the boat out, holding onto the spring and stern lines before throwing them to us once we'd cleared the slip. Angry and embarrassed, my father refused to acknowledge Harry's salute as we passed out of the harbor, but we three girls gave him a shy wave when my father wasn't looking.

After the hour motor ride along the estuary to the Bay's entrance, my father suddenly barked out an order, sending Pam and me scurrying up the deck.

"Raise the mainsail, girls!"

Pam grabbed the first thing that caught her eye and asked in a panicked voice, "Dad, is this the rope?"

"Line! Not rope. It's called a line! And there's two of them, the throat and peak halyards. How many times have I told you girls?"

Pam and I frantically searched for the two lines, finally locating them.

"You gotta pull them both together!" Without waiting for a reply, my father turned the boat into the wind.

Pam and I tugged on the halyards, barely raising the sail. Even with the two of us pulling, we weren't strong enough and needed more leverage. While Pam held onto the lines from below, I leapt like a monkey from the cabin top, grabbing the halyards above her and yanking them as hard as I could.

"I'll do it, Jim," we heard my uncle offer.

"Thanks, Chuck, but they need to learn," my father said, and then hollered, "Put some muscle into it!"

When the sail was all the way up, my father yelled, "Get those lines belayed." Then he wrapped the line around the stern winch and yanked. Let's get the jib up!"

Pam and I raced to the bow, where several lines lay coiled on the deck. "Is this it?" Pam asked me, holding on to the end of one line.

"I think there's supposed to be a clip on the end," I said. I spied a second coil and grabbed it. "Like this one!" I snapped the shackle into the grommet sewn into the head of the sail. Pam and I pulled on the halyard as hard as we could and we both breathed a sigh of relief as the jib shot up and the wind filled its white canvas.

With two sails raised, we picked up speed and *Heritage*, with her sleek lines and deep draft, gracefully cut through the white-capped waves. My father's pride was palpable as we passed other boaters, who cheered and waved and blew their air horns in appreciation.

At eleven, I understood something wonderful had happened. I glanced at my uncle and aunt and realized, even with my uncle's unceremonious dunking, we had impressed them. All my envy over what I imagined was their glamorous life—a big house with a pool—and my two cousins, who were pretty and my grandparents' favorites, seemed to dissipate with each fill of the sails. As *Heritage* surged forward, I felt I was sailing toward a life belonging just to us and away from theirs.

But like anything involving my father's relatives, victory was short-lived. Without warning, Gayle lurched toward my mother. Her rosy cheeks drained of color and a green tinge spread under her skin like a jealous blush. Aware of an imminent eruption, my mother held Gayle over the rail.

"Mom!" Pam and I both shrieked, as we twisted our backs and braced for the onslaught. As the boat heeled over, we felt the first splats land on the backs of our life vests.

My father lunged toward my mother and Gayle. "Goddammit, Lorraine. You've got her over the windward rail!"

Pam turned to me and giggled. "She sure ate a lot of oatmeal this morning."

"Oh, fer chrissakes, it's all over me!" my father yelled, as he grabbed my sister and held her over the lee rail. The only ones spared were my aunt and uncle, who sat forward and upwind of us.

Upon reaching Tiburon's marina on the north end of the Bay, we pulled up to an available slip in front of the most popular wharfside restaurant, Sam's Cafe. While my father, aunt, and uncle made their way to an outside table, my mother herded us into the bathroom to rinse the rest of the regurgitated oatmeal out of our hair.

Refreshed and somewhat presentable, we joined everyone on the deck, where my father and uncle were sipping beers and my aunt, looking chic in her dark cat's-eye sunglasses and white chiffon scarf, sat between them, nursing a white wine spritzer.

"How's that crew of mine?" my father asked.

Still queasy from the sail over, Pam, Gayle, and I said nothing.

"Just fine and dandy," my mother cheerfully replied.

"What do you fancy, dear?" my father asked, as he pulled her chair out.

"Well, I guess I'll have what June is having," my mother said, enjoying the attention. "The girls want Coke, but I think we'll order a ginger ale for Gayle." The adults chuckled. I thought about my sister puking her guts out and didn't think it was all that funny.

Cocky after a few beers and fortified by a satisfying meal, my father announced that on our return we'd sail over and anchor at Angel Island. "After all, we've still got plenty of light and it's a great day. Who wants to go home so early?"

As we entered the cove on the northeastern side of the island, my father turned to my mother and said, "Ready with the anchor, Lorraine!"

She made her way forward, but sensing her hesitation, I followed behind her.

"Get a move on, will ya?" my father said, as he brought *Heritage* about.

My mother lifted the Danforth and leaned over the lifeline and poised, prepared to drop it over the side.

"Mom," I said, pointing at the anchor. "It's not attached. Don't . . ."

She glanced down at the pile of chain on the deck. "Oh, no!"

"Drop anchor!"

"Jim, the anchor is . . ."

"Now!"

"But . . ."

"Just throw it overboard!"

"But it's . . ."

"Now. Goddammit!"

I glanced at my mother. She looked back at me, shrugged, and then heaved the Danforth overboard.

The boat continued to move full speed ahead toward shore.

"What the hell?" My father leaped out of the cockpit and raced up the deck.

My mother stood next to the pile of chain. "I tried to tell you, dear."

Suddenly, the boat lurched and shuddered to a dead stop, running hard aground on the sandy shoal.

*Heritage's* "first time" had not been a tender one.

\* \* \*

"I'm having trouble getting this line free," Denny said.

"Take it off the cleat on deck," my father ordered.

Denny, determined to free it from the piling, continued to struggle with the knot. "It's good line. Are you sure?"

"Yup," my father replied. I knew he'd planned it this way; leaving expensive line heaped on the dock was his way of giving the middle finger to all the naysayers and weekend sailors who'd smirked and repeatedly asked, "That boat of yours ever gonna leave the dock?" I grudgingly admired my father's tactics, realizing the satisfaction gained in having the last word.

As my father threw the engine in reverse and *Heritage*, free of restraints, backed out of the slip, I felt an inexplicable urge to leap back onto the dock. After spending my entire childhood dreaming about the promise my father had made to me and my sisters that our *real* life would begin on this night, all I wanted to do was jump ship. The tenuous thread connecting me to the life I'd known was about to break. But before I could leap, Stan and Denny pushed the bow free of the slip and jumped on board.

As we motored out of the marina, I wondered if Stan and Denny were aware they were the only sailors on board. Even though I could name every line, sail, and rigging; scale the mast, work a ratchet, and countersink screws; and pass any tool to my father as efficiently as an operating nurse handing a scalpel to a surgeon—I knew absolutely nothing about sailing. Gayle knew even less than I did, and my father, with little more than a summer spent on the Great Lakes, was hard pressed to call himself anything but a day sailor. The truth was, we were landlubbers masquerading as seasoned sailors.

As Denny and Stan continued to check the lights and rigging, I was relieved my father hadn't left without them. Without experienced crew onboard, I wasn't sure we'd even make it past the Golden Gate Bridge.

"This is it, girls. We're on our way," my father said, as we entered the Oakland Estuary. I looked over at him, his hand steady on the wheel, and his ever-present cigarette precariously dangling from his lips. I wondered what he meant. It was hard to tell. Were we on our way to the glorious adventure he'd promised? Or did he mean there was no turning back to the life we'd known? I was afraid to ask.

Gayle leaned into me and moaned, "I don't feel so good." I knew I should go below and search for some crackers to settle her stomach, but the sickening smell of diesel fumes from the engine, combined with the wafting, acrid odor from my father's cigarettes, filled the cockpit.

Fighting off nausea, I worried I was going to get seasick before we even reached the Bay. I couldn't help but think maybe Pam had made the wiser choice, imagining that by now she was in her PJs, stretched out on a comfortable motel bed, watching TV.

"I'll go down below and get you something for your stomach in a few minutes," I said to Gayle, hoping my father would cut the engine and raise the sails, and I'd be able to navigate my way to the galley. In the meantime, I had to get away from the cockpit and its smell. Already my resolve to become the best sailor onboard was being tested.

Opting for the freezing salt spray against my face, I tried persuading Gayle to move forward with me, but she went below, so I made my way alone on deck toward the forward hatch.

As *Heritage*'s bow cut through the Bay's dark waters, I took a deep breath of the salty, frigid air. The Bay Bridge was now at our stern and the southeastern tip of Alcatraz was visible just beyond the bow.

High up, beyond the prison walls, tiny lights flickered like fireflies, a reminder of the American Indian Movement's protest occupying the island. As we passed the island's southern shore, a huge bonfire was blazing, its embers shooting high into the night sky.

When Alcatraz was just past our stern, my father had Denny raise the foresail and mainsail. With the engine off, *Heritage* pressed forward for the first time under sail power toward the Golden Gate. Soon we'd be crossing under its lighted span and into the dark waters of the Pacific.

I looked up at the star-studded sky and picked out the brightest one, hoping, and yes, even praying, that its twinkling was Grandma shining her love down on me. Throughout my childhood, I'd dreamed of my grandmother sailing away with us, but now I'd have to find her in the dark sky and stars above and in the shiny stack of silver dollars that lay nestled in my bunk drawer. "These are the first dollars I earned in America," she'd said, after placing the coins in my hand on my sixteenth birthday. "They will remind you that no matter what happens, I'll always be with you." I was my grandmother's favorite, and in return, I'd loved her with an unrivaled fierceness. Her sudden death had left me unmoored and lost, and as the bow nosed forward into the inky blackness, I wished those coins were in my pocket to remind me of her presence.

Just before reaching the Golden Gate, I made my way back to the cockpit. Gayle was still below, curled up in the quarter berth, and Stan and Denny were sacked out in the main salon, so my father and I were alone on deck. I looked up at him. With his face softened by the binnacle light and a slight smile forming about his mouth, he looked like a younger version of himself. I remembered a time in elementary school when he'd arrived to pick me up. My classmates had stared at him, wide-eyed, as if Superman had swooped in for a visit. Even my third-grade teacher, Miss Satter, fluttered about, fanning her face to cool the rising flush across her cheeks.

My father and I walked out of school that day, hand in hand, and as I looked up, he winked and grinned. In that singular moment, I transformed from a rough and tumble tomboy into an adored and happy princess.

I moved over and sat next to my father, and with one hand steadying the wheel, he put his other arm around me. Then he smiled and gave me a quick squeeze and said, "All the hard work's gonna pay off, Sport." I looked up at him, surprised and secretly pleased over his rare display of affection. As I leaned against him, a flicker of happiness rose in me. I stared up at the stars, winking and glittering in the dark night, and for the first time knew we were heading toward a new life. It was there, straight ahead, past the second star to the right.

# 2

# Straight on Till Morning

## San Francisco to Monterey

**December 5–8, 1969**

No sooner had we passed under the Golden Gate than the Pacific threw back her head and howled. *Heritage* was in for a rough ride. To maintain a safe distance from shore, my father steered west against the prevailing winds and into deep water. For five miles, *Heritage* rose and bucked through every trough and wave.

Within minutes after altering course and heading southward, the main gaff jaw broke. Denny scrambled up from below and helped me wrestle the mainsail down. Left with only the foresail, my father restarted the engine.

I headed below and made my way to the forepeak, taking care not to slip on the floorboards. Within a few hours, the ocean had worked its way through the planking, past every nail and screw, flooding the boat's shallow bilge with a noxious mixture of frigid seawater and leaking diesel fuel.

Hunkered down in the forward bunk, I lay fully clothed on my soaked and foul-smelling foam mattress. Hoping to catch a few hours of sleep before my 2:00 a.m. watch, I tried to ignore the sound of seawater sloshing up against the cabin walls as the boat heeled to port. *Heritage* slammed into wave after wave. I wondered if she was strong enough to withstand the pounding, or would her narrow planking finally give way and sink, sending us to the bottom of the sea? It was too bad, I thought, that fiberglass, with its easy maintenance, superior strength, and watertight properties, made its debut after we'd built her.

Of course, that hadn't stopped my father from experimenting. Like many boat builders who'd read how their wooden vessels could benefit from this new technology, he'd set about fortifying *Heritage*'s mahogany strip-planked hull. After covering the entire hull in resin-soaked fiberglass, he sat back and enjoyed his new watertight boat. But less than a year later, the strips had bubbled and peeled away like dead skin from a bad sunburn. He spent weeks with the boat dry-docked, grinding down the rest. I tried to console myself that unlike fiberglass, wood swelled and tightened in seawater, and that, in theory, the longer we sailed, the less she'd leak.

Gayle moaned from the quarter berth, but I was too ill to care. I had stopped thinking about how she felt, how my father was faring at the helm, or what Stan and Denny had found to eat. I lay curled in a fetal position in the forepeak, begging God to strike me dead, and I didn't care how. Just make it quick.

I thought about books I'd read by Steinbeck, London, and Melville, that were filled with stories romanticizing the seafaring life, and felt betrayed. There was absolutely nothing romantic about getting slammed from one side of my bunk to the other. To avoid further bruising, I wedged myself between the foremast and cabin wall and lay in the dark, concentrating with every fiber in me to control the dry heaves.

I closed my eyes for what seemed like seconds, when I felt a rough shake on my shoulder. I glanced up and recognized the outline of my father standing at the head of my bunk. When I didn't move, he leaned down, and over the roar of the engine, yelled into my ear, "Up and at 'em! Your watch starts in five minutes." His stale tobacco breath filled my nostrils, and another wave of nausea worked its way up my throat and made me gag. What had been a special moment between father and daughter right before we'd reached the Golden Gate was now replaced by a frantic, foul-smelling, ship's captain ordering a defiant, seasick crew member to "shake a leg and get the hell up on deck."

With one last skull-cracking smack to my head as *Heritage* bucked to port, I reluctantly rolled out of my bunk and pulled on my foul-weather gear. I leaned against the foremast, hoping to collect myself and force the saliva back, as I resisted the urge to hurl. It took everything I had not to crawl back into my bunk.

"I SAID, GET A MOVE ON!"

If ever there was a moment to consider patricide, this was it.

I made my way in the dark, passing the lumpy silhouettes of Stan and Denny and a small tight ball that was Gayle, and up the companionway. As soon as I stepped into the cockpit, my father, who I'd assumed was going to stay with me, at least until he felt I could handle my watch, pushed past me mumbling, "Gotta catch my forty winks. Hold her steady at 210 degrees southwest."

This was not what I had in mind when, at fifteen and a recent runaway, I'd negotiated a cease-fire, whereby I'd embrace a renewed commitment to obey my father's rules, for him granting me a few unsupervised hours away from boat work. How did the desire to hang out after school with friends result in my father's all too eager abdication and handing off of his captain's hat to me?

Alone on deck, with only the roar of the engine and the crash of waves for companionship, I questioned my father's judgment entrusting a green, inexperienced, seasick teen with the responsibility and safety of five lives. I had no fucking idea what I was doing! But he'd disappeared down below, exhausted, and seasick, and I knew if I forced him back up on deck, he'd lose it. Going it alone, I concluded, was far better than the alternative.

*All you have to do*, I repeated to myself, *is just stay the course, just stay the course, just stay . . . the . . . course.* For more than an hour, I maintained a death grip on the icy wheel. All feeling in my fingertips vanished, and I wondered if by the end of my watch, I'd be left with frostbitten stumps. Pointless, I thought, to have made such a fuss about bringing my guitar along.

I'd lobbied hard to include my brand-new guitar in what I could take on board. When my father eyed the guitar neck sticking out from the top of the bag, meant to be filled with clothes and personal items, he said, "That doesn't fit. If you take it, you'll have to sleep with it."

"Fine," I'd replied. "I'm not leaving without it."

"The salt air will ruin it. You won't be able to tune it, much less play it."

"I'll leave it behind, if you leave your cigarettes behind." I detested his smoking. A five-pack-a-day smoker, my father had bought enough cartons of his favorite Salems to fill the huge bin below the forward bunk.

The next thing I knew, my guitar had mysteriously found a home strapped to the ceiling of my bunk. Making it clear he still had the upper hand, my father mentioned my bag now had room for my schoolbooks. From his satisfied expression, I knew he assumed he'd evened the score; I'd just nodded and smiled, thinking about my secret stash of weed hidden in the drawer below my bunk.

As I gripped the wheel and the icy sea spray whipped my face, I tried to recall when I'd ever been as cold, wet, sick, or miserable. Not even the two times I'd run away and wandered terrified and alone at night on Telegraph Avenue in Berkeley were as bad as this night. At least there had been people and streetlights and solid ground underneath me, and the sense that if I walked long enough, I'd fill the emptiness inside of me. But here, aboard *Heritage*, engulfed in darkness, I had no sense I was running to or from anything.

The stars that had flooded the sky earlier had disappeared, and as the wind whistled through the rigging, a strange, high-pitched keening pierced the air. Rising above the sound of the engine and waves, the raw, ugly moaning increased. I twisted my head around, from starboard to port and back again. Something had to be making that horrible sound. I peered into the darkness, hoping to catch whatever it was; instead, nothing but the pitch black of night greeted me.

The wailing increased until I could feel myself vibrating. The sound issued forth, full-throated, as if it had a life of its own, howling into the black night. I didn't have to die to visit Purgatory; I was in it.

It was then that I realized it was not coming from the sea, but from *inside* of me.

Yet, strangely enough, it disturbed no one. As far as the comatose crew was concerned, an old salt was at the helm entertaining herself with a swig and a jig and a mighty heave ho! For me, though, it was all too real. Exhausted, frozen, and beyond terrified, I steered *Heritage* through the dark seas and prayed the wind would abate and the swells would lessen. If this night was a sign of what I was in for, I wasn't sure I'd make it to the next port. Counting the minutes to the end of my watch, I thought back to when *Heritage* was nothing but a hope and a dream, and how an old, dilapidated barn on the outskirts of Livermore had changed the course of my life.

\* \* \*

September 1960. Livermore, California. "This is it," my father said, as he pulled off the main road in our station wagon and turned into the dirt driveway. A huge, weathered barn leaning precariously to one side stood before us.

My mother peered through the windshield at the massive doors and murmured, "My, it's big."

"It's free," my father replied. "All we have to do is clean it out." Surrounded by fields and vineyards, the barn and the old farmhouse next to it were owned by Mr. Sessler, a friend and coworker of my mother's. Living alone on the outskirts of town, he'd offered the use of his barn, saying he was glad to help and welcomed the company.

"You kids stay here," my father said, as he opened the car door.

My sisters and I watched our parents disappear inside. Huddled in the backseat, we waited patiently as the minutes ticked by.

"I want to go home. I'm tired," my younger sister, Gayle, said.

"Stop being a baby," I said.

"I'm not a baby."

"Yes, you are."

"I'm four. I'm not a baby, I'm not a baby!"

"Now look what you've done," Pam said. She patted Gayle's back, then leaned over and gave me a hard pinch on my arm.

Two-peas-in-a-pod. Just like Grandma says, I thought. I opened the car door and slammed it behind me.

Hopping across the barn door's threshold, I made my way to the far end, where my parents were speaking in hushed voices. The smell of hay filled the air.

"Why aren't you in the car?" my father said when I sidled up next to him.

"They were picking on me."

"Dammit, why can't you kids get along?"

I hung my head but stood my ground. No way was I going back to the car. Hoping to skirt further criticism, I stood quietly off to the side. While they talked, I occupied my time by kicking around the loose hay scattered on the barn floor until I heard neighing. I made my way over to a stall where I discovered a horse. Sliding my hands through the slats, I rubbed its soft velvet muzzle.

"That's Mickey," my father said, coming up behind me. "He'll be sharing the barn with us." As the horse nibbled at my fingers, I felt a flush of pleasure, having discovered him before my sisters. My father pried me away, swinging me out in front of him. "C'mon, Sport, it's getting late."

I climbed into the backseat.

"What's in there?" Pam asked.

"Nuthin'," I said. I waited until the car pulled out onto the road, before I turned to her, grinning, ". . . except a horse."

"Mom! Why didn't you tell us there was a horse?"

My mother turned around, shook her finger at me, and then turned to my sisters and said, "Don't worry, we'll have plenty of time to see him." Gayle stuck her tongue out and Pam elbowed me in the rib, but instead of retaliating, I smiled and settled back in my seat.

Spreading the new blueprints out on our kitchen table a few weeks later, my father showed us the forty-foot-long Gloucester fishing schooner he wanted to build. It was narrow in the beam, drew a deep draft, and was gaff-rigged. With its four-sided sails and little ladders that rose to the top of the mast, it looked like a real pirate ship. I pictured myself climbing up and spying on Captain Hook or Tinkerbell, seeing things no one else could.

\* \* \*

"Jesus Christ, where's the food?" Stan yelled. I looked up from my barf pail just long enough to meet his glare, made more menacing in the gray light of dawn. "Aw, Christ," he growled, as he descended and brushed past me. He rummaged around in the galley for something to eat. "You're better off on deck," he said, ascending the stairs with a fistful of crackers.

In theory, my father's idea of hiring two experienced sailors was a sound one. Having professionals on board who were familiar with what could go wrong in rough winter Pacific swells would allow my father ample time to address and repair any issues once we arrived in San Diego. In a letter to his parents, my father described Stan and Denny as "both stalwart sailors with trans-Pacific experience."

"Stalwart" was the last word I would have used as I observed Stan and Denny's ashen faces peering down into the cabin during the early morning hours. Not only were we sick, but our "professional" sailors were definitely green around the gills.

While it was understood Gayle and I would act as "cooks," serving meals my mother had planned and packaged, no one considered the ramifications of what the French refer to as *mal de mer* and its equally debilitating partner, *ennui*. Better known in English as "seasickness" and its accompanying sidekick, "I-don't-give-a-shit," not even the threat of death could nudge Gayle from her fetal position, or make me care one whit whether the crew got fed.

The overpowering smell of bilge water and bile finally forced me out of my bunk and into the cockpit, where the sight of three sorry-looking men greeted me. My father looked the worst, clutching his false teeth in one hand and gripping the rail with his other, while he heaved over the side. I couldn't stop staring at him, mesmerized by the flapping sound his gums and lips made after each regurgitation. All I wanted more than anything was for him to put his damn teeth back in.

Stan and Denny didn't look much better. Although both had resisted the rail, they were as gray as the rainy dawn. Huddled in the cockpit, they munched on cheese and crackers. Stan was right, though. I felt better on deck; the crisp morning air and light rain on my face cleared my head. If I could just get back to feeling normal, I thought, this *Night of the Living*

*Dead* experience might eventually fade away. I clutched the rail, breathed in the salt air, and braced myself as the boat bucked from bow to stern.

By mid-morning, the seas had calmed. Layered in our damp clothing and heavy, blue float coats, and stretched out on the foredeck, Gayle and I lay side by side, like seals, warming in the sun. As we passed by the breakwater and entered Monterey's harbor, the pungent smell of seaweed and marine life hung in the air.

In one of his letters to a boating friend, my father wrote of our brief stop:

> *We pulled in for some rest and a meal at their Fisherman's Wharf, while we tried to regain our sea legs. After a meal eaten more out of necessity than desire, it was "off with the mooring lines" and pointing southward again.*

What I remember was that the floor swayed and undulated so much I had to grip the table to steady myself. I'd not yet gained my sea legs and had misplaced my land ones. As I picked away at the food on my plate, there was no escaping the queasiness. Glancing over at Gayle, I knew she felt the same. Getting back on board was something neither of us were looking forward to, so when my father announced that instead of a straight run to San Diego, we'd sail to Morro Bay, 125 miles away, Gayle and I were relieved and more than grateful about the change in plans.

Before we got underway, I wrapped up a dozen sandwiches, figuring I'd be useless as soon as we reached the outer harbor. Sure enough, *Heritage* was not five miles out when both Gayle and I took to the rail, giving up our expensive Monterey lunch to the sea. This time, however, we stayed above deck, choosing the penetrating cold over the oppressive smells down below.

If I had thought the swells were bad coming out of the Golden Gate, they were nothing compared to the ones along the coast near Big Sur. As *Heritage* slammed headlong into wave after wave, Gayle and I took turns holding each other over the side, emptying our already hollow stomachs. Spent and shivering from the cold, we huddled together for warmth.

By midnight, my father turned the helm over to Stan and stumbled past us and down below for some sleep. Meanwhile, Gayle and I remained in the cockpit, too sick to move. Somehow, we dozed off, more from exhaustion than any sense of comfort, only to wake to complete chaos in the cockpit.

"Shit! The steering's gone!" Stan yelled to Denny. "Get Jim up here, will ya?"

As if ousted from a foxhole, my father emerged looking exhausted and battle worn.

"The current's gonna sweep us right up on those rocks!" Stan said, no longer resembling the cocky sailor who'd boarded *Heritage* the night before. With an almost full moon, the silvery outline of Big Sur's cliffs and the ghostly phosphorescence from waves crashing against the rocky shore were easily discernable. It made me shudder, imagining what it would feel like to be smashed against them.

My father leaned over the stern rail with his flashlight and peered down at the rudder. "Something must have happened to the pin. We're gonna have to wait and jerry-rig it in the morning. In the meantime, I'd better send out an S.O.S."

He climbed below and emerged a few seconds later with a large pistol. Pointing it off the stern, he fired three times, each flare lighting up and coloring the sea, sky, and our faces a demonic red. With the boat hove to, the men payed out two hundred feet of chain along with our large sea anchor. Then Stan and Denny went down below to sleep while my father, Gayle, and I huddled in the wet cockpit. I prayed for dawn to poke its pale face over the dark cliffs.

The first light of morning took forever to appear. The muted grays of an overcast sky reflected in the drawn faces of the men and the chalky-colored waves lent an air of gravitas to an already dire situation. As the boat strained against the sea anchor, the men assessed the damage. *Heritage* was in trouble.

"One of you kids is gonna have to hang over the stern," Stan said. Although I was stronger and more agile, Gayle, being the lightest, was the obvious choice. As my father tied a line securely to her harness and cleated it off, I whispered, "Don't worry, both Dad and I are holding onto you real tight." She nodded and climbed up on the stern deck.

My father grabbed her by the ankles and lifted her upside down, lowering her head first over the transom. After I fed her a quarter-inch line, Gayle's job was to thread it through the shackle fastened to the rudder, located right above the waterline. Useless, Stan and Denny kept their distance at the far end of the cockpit.

Bracing myself between the binnacle stand and helm as the boat rose and slammed from wave to trough, I kept an iron grip around the line attached to Gayle's waist. After three failed attempts, my father prepared to pull her back up, when, on one last try, she succeeded. I grabbed the line with my free hand while my father pulled Gayle back up. As I helped her out of her harness, my father tied an overhand knot and brought the ends of the line under the counter to the winches and pulled them taut.

To everyone's relief, we were jerry-rigged.

With only thirty miles covered in a day and a half, my father decided to tack back up the coast with our damaged steering to Monterey rather than turning southward to Morro Bay. Notified by our distress signal, the ninety-foot Coast Guard cutter *Cape Wash* met us halfway and took us in tow.

As *Cape Wash* towed *Heritage* at breakneck speed, the two-inch line securing us to them stretched out and dug through the soft teak, disfiguring the rails and creating ugly gashes like open wounds. My father yelled and frantically signaled, pointing to the rail, but several of the young "coasties" just smiled and returned his hand signal with a thumbs up. All we could do was move to the far side of the boat to avoid getting decapitated in case the line snapped.

Finally, we arrived at the outer harbor, where *Cape Wash* passed our tow lines to a smaller rescue boat. The natural surge and narrow entrance required perfect timing for both vessels to make it safely through to the inner harbor. It appeared we were going to just clear it when the next surge swept both craft against the pilings. Our cleats, already loose from the strain of *Cape Wash*'s tow, ripped from their bolts, severing our tow line. When the next surge hit, it slammed us back into the rescue boat, creating a deep gash along *Heritage*'s midship. Close enough to the dock, we threw our lines to some fellow boaters, who helped guide *Heritage* into an empty slip.

As soon as we docked, I leapt off the boat, vowing never to set foot on her again. Right on my heels were the "two stalwart sailors," Stan and Denny, clutching their duffel bags. With the flimsy excuse they suddenly had to get back to their jobs, they deserted us like rats from a sinking ship, scurrying up the dock with nary a backward glance.

After a short walk around the harbor, I realized my limited options for escape and reluctantly returned to the boat, where I found my father and Gayle, dazed, and sitting in the cockpit. My father didn't mention my temporary mutiny; he was too tired to care about anything other than the cigarette he was smoking. Gayle, exhausted from puking her brains out, hadn't bothered to remove her life vest.

# 3

# The Great Tide Pool

*Monterey, California*

**DECEMBER 8–29, 1969**

Prepared to camp out at my grandparents' house until *Heritage*'s arrival in San Diego, my mother received news to return immediately to Monterey. Why she didn't return in our car remained a mystery; instead, my grandfather chauffeured them back in his. Perhaps, in a moment of generosity and thinking my mother was tired from the drive down, he'd lifted the sanctions he and my grandmother had placed on my mother for her failure to control their son. As far as they were concerned, my mother's complicity in our sailing adventure made her not only an accomplice, but an even bigger reprobate than my father. My grandmother believed it was a wife's duty to make her husband toe the line, especially if, like her son, he bucked convention. She'd been that way with my grandfather, hog-tying him into submission with her pork roasts and religion. In their eyes, my mother was weak and impressionable and lacked the backbone required to constrain their son. What they didn't know was years earlier, my mother *had* reined him in.

Saddled with a poor-paying job, a wife and three children, and nearing thirty, my father found himself in the throes of an existential crisis. Questioning his life and no longer certain he wanted to remain married, he'd asked my mother for a trial separation. Crushed, but also unwilling to continue in a loveless marriage, she'd agreed. Neither of them bothered to tell me or my sisters of their arrangement. One day, he simply disappeared. I was four, old enough to suffer, but young enough to adapt; I missed my father, but never thought to question my mother when our family routine resumed without him.

One night, weeks later, my father walked through the front door and collapsed. He was dirty, disheveled, and gravely ill. Wherever he'd been, he contracted hepatitis. While we remained in quarantine for two weeks, he spent the next nine in the hospital.

Bedridden and attached to IVs, with nothing better to do but stare at the ceiling all day, he'd concluded that perhaps life was better with us than without us. My mother, still in love with him, let him come home to convalesce. Contrite and trying his best, he assured us he was happy to be home. But watching him stare for hours out the living room window, I wasn't so sure; it was as if he was searching for something he'd lost but knew he'd never find.

After he recovered, my father asked for three things: a sportscar, a chance to look for a better-paying job, and what I feared most, that my grandmother move out. My mother agreed to honor his request with the caveat there would be no second chances. While Grandma settled into a shabby efficiency at the incongruously named Palace Motel, my father, zipping around in his new cherry-red MG, appeared happier than he'd ever been.

* * *

Awakening from a dead sleep by the sound of loud knocking and voices, I swung out of my berth, careful not to disturb Gayle, who was passed out below me, and made my way to the nearest porthole where I spied my grandfather, looking ill-tempered and my mother, Pam and Nancy standing meekly behind him.

I quickly rousted my father, who was asleep in the quarter berth.

By the time he and I made it to the cockpit, my mother, Pam, and Nancy brushed past us without a word and disappeared below. I glanced at my grandfather, who'd remained on the dock, disapproval visible in his steely gaze and the settled lines around his mouth.

"Good morning, Dad!" my father said, a little too enthusiastically. "Come aboard!"

"I'm fine right here," my grandfather said, his long legs spread wide to steady himself. "Looks like you had an accident." His eyes swept the midships, assessing the scarred side of the hull.

My father, attempting to make light of our disastrous entrance into the marina, replied, "It's nothing. Superficial. A little spackle and paint, and you'll never know it happened."

My grandfather snorted. "What's this about the Coast Guard bringing you in?"

"We had a little trouble with the steering."

"Where's those two fellas who were helping you?" Even though it was obvious from his challenging tone he'd already assumed Stan and Denny were gone, he looked around in case the two men suddenly materialized.

"They . . . uh . . . felt it would exceed their available free time, so they caught the bus back to Oakland last night."

"Sounds like they're the only ones with some sense around here," my grandfather said. With his arms folded and a look of satisfaction spreading across his face, his pronouncement rent the air and stifled the piercing cries of the gulls circling overhead. I waited for my father to say something, but he just stood there silently. I thought my grandfather was being a dick, and I couldn't understand why my father didn't defend himself.

"Well . . . what do you want to do?" my grandfather asked, barely suppressing his irritation.

"Looks like we're gonna be holed up here for at least a couple of weeks . . . guess the best thing would be for Lorraine and the girls to return with you and drive the Pontiac back up. I need to order a few parts, and I'll need the car to get around."

"Fine."

"How about some breakfast, Dad? My treat," my father said, as if a free meal would sway the old man to stay. "There's a great diner right up the road servin' the best eggs and bacon."

"I'd rather get going," my grandfather said. "Got a lot of things to do at the house and Mother is expecting me for dinner."

As soon as they left, my father turned to Gayle and me. "Clean up the goddamn mess below." Then he jumped onto the dock, chisel in hand, and with unabated vengeance attacked the damage to the hull.

Gayle and I lifted the waterlogged floorboards and set to work soaking up oily, black seawater that slithered like a dark sea creature between the bilge's ribs. As we emptied pail after pail of the noxious, viscous water, the sound of my father's chisel scraping back and forth along the splintered hull resonated inside the cabin. Its unrelenting fury overwhelmed the silence and was as powerful in its message as my grandfather's sharp and angry reproof.

By evening, Gayle and I had scrubbed away all traces of fuel oil in the bilge, washed and replaced the floorboards, and straightened up all the bunks. My father, exhausted from repairing the hull, came below to survey our work.

I looked down at my hands and fingernails, stained black and smelling of diesel and lube oil, and wondered if I'd ever get them clean again. In all the years working on the boat, it had never occurred to me to safeguard against tasks dangerous enough to warrant protective gear or, at the very least, a pair of thick rubber gloves and safety glasses. Instead, I rationalized it was a step up from handling lead. And better yet, I still had all my fingers.

\* \* \*

October 1960. The Barn. Livermore, California. On a Saturday morning, a few weeks after cleaning the barn, we pulled into the dirt drive, where a towering pile of ball bearings had been dumped to the left of the barn's doors.

"Great. They arrived just in time," my father said as he surveyed the pile.

While my father wheelbarrowed load after load into the barn, our job was to pick up and carry the lead ball bearings over to an open drum filled with toxic, liquid resin. As a cost-cutting measure, my father planned on using the balls for the keel's ballast, and my sisters and me, for labor.

Under the watchful eyes of Mickey, who stood quietly in his stall munching on oats and flicking away horseflies with his tail, Pam, Gayle, and I toiled. By evening, exhausted and covered in dust after hours of picking up thousands of balls with our lead-blackened fingers, I dropped the last ball into the drum's resin mixture. Mickey gave a snort of approval.

With the keel poured and hardened, the next step was to measure and cut the boat's oak ribs and mahogany planking. Wood scraps piled up and needed to be cut, bundled, and stacked, so my father gave Pam and me a cursory lesson in operating the bandsaw.

Before flicking the switch, he shared a cautionary tale with us about his friend Bob, a professional boat builder. "One day," my father said, "Bob's attention wandered and just like *THAT*,"—snapping his fingers for emphasis—"he cut off all his fingers!" He folded his hand at the knuckles and shoved it close to our faces. "Four digits lost in the sawdust." He eyed us and squinted, as if determining our odds, before pointing his finger and warning, "If you girls don't want that to happen, *keep the task at hand.*"

I looked down at my hands, trying to imagine stumps where my fingers were. I was only eight, and if a grown man could make that mistake, I thought, I'd have to be extra careful. Without fingers, I'd never be able to climb those tiny ladders or hold a spyglass.

* * *

Too tired to wait for Gayle and me to cook dinner, my father offered to take us to the diner. Without stopping to consider what kind of mood he was in, Gayle and I grabbed our float coats, grateful if not for the company, at least for the chance to avoid cooking in the cramped galley.

That night, stuffed with a hamburger, fries, and a chocolate shake, I lay down in my narrow bunk and thought about why no one in our family ever seemed happy. Witnessing my grandfather's disdain and my father's rage, I wondered what was in store for me. Had my father suffered my grandfather's contempt only to become just like him? Would I become just like my father? It reminded me of the phrase I'd learned in catechism: "The sins of the fathers are visited upon the children." How was I going to stop feeling angry when that was all that surrounded me? I wished I could retrieve one of my joints. When I was stoned, I didn't give a shit.

I pulled the covers over my head and tried to ignore that, for now, this was going to be my life.

At noon the next day, my mother arrived in our car. Using the flimsy excuse he had to replace one of his drill bits, my father immediately appropriated the Pontiac and roared away.

With our grouchy captain driving around Monterey, we huddled below, warming ourselves around the kerosene heater, and enjoyed lunch. Even my mother allowed herself to relax and laugh. I wished she'd be like this in my father's presence, but like us, she transformed from wife and mother to mere deckhand when he was around.

I tried to remember the last time she'd seemed carefree. Besides their brief separation, it had been when my father accepted an eighteen-month overseas government contract in Enewetak, a tiny atoll in the middle of the Pacific Ocean.

The minute my father's plane took off for Enewetak, Grandma, who'd been living at the Palace Motel, moved back in with us, happy to take up residence on the living room couch in our new, smaller, two-bedroom apartment. On her own for the next year-and-a-half, my mother side-lined the station wagon and took to driving around town in my father's MG.

While my father was away, the arrangement between my mother and grandmother worked to everyone's advantage. I'm sure my mother was lonely and missed him, but she kept her feelings well hidden. Unaware of her longing, my sisters and I lived happily under a roof full of feminine energy, where bonhomie and freedom ruled. For us, it was a life without routines and restrictions. Like the stray cats that sidled up to our back door looking for a nightly handout, we played outside long after sunset, returning only when our stomachs rumbled. It was an easy, carefree existence.

\* \* \*

With the cabin scrubbed from bow to stern, the fittings polished, and the equipment stowed, my father couldn't object to our spending the afternoons relaxing and reading in our bunks. Putting aside my dog-eared copy of Salinger's *Catcher in the Rye*, I traded in Holden Caulfield for Steinbeck's Doc and the rest of the gang in *Cannery Row*. As I lay in my bunk and read, the slow chugging of fishing boats leaving the harbor and the tangy smell of seaweed drifting through the porthole transported me back to Steinbeck's Monterey. I collected marine samples alongside Doc and enjoyed a glass of Eddie's special punch at the Palace Flophouse and Grill with Mack and the boys while Dora and her girls paraded by. And with its boilers at full throttle, the Hediondo Cannery vibrated with activity as workers cleaned and packed silver rivers of sardines.

Page after page, Doc, Mack and the boys, Eddie, Lee Chong, and Dora and her girls sprang forth, fully formed and alive, making my life a little more tolerable and the world a little brighter.

During days when my father co-opted the car and my mother and sisters preferred the warmth of the cabin's kerosene heater, I bundled up in long underwear, jeans, a turtleneck, and a couple of sweaters under my rain slicker, and headed above deck. Even when the fickle December weather won out, bringing with it thick, gray sheets of rain from the Pacific storms that pounded the coast, I longed to be outside, happy to be walking on solid ground.

"Just be back before your father gets home," my mother warned.

"Don't worry." Jumping off the boat, I raced up the dock. Right before I reached the marina gate, I noticed a boy about my age working on the deck of *Tasco III*, a large, double-ended motorsailer. He glanced up and smiled. Curious why he wasn't in school, I stopped and asked if the boat belonged to his family.

"Nah," he said, motioning me aboard.

I climbed on deck and followed him down the hatchway to a spacious, wood-paneled salon.

"You gotta see this," he said, making his way toward the fo'c'sle. Normally reserved for bunks, the space was now a darkroom.

"He's a famous photographer . . . he's going to the Galapagos with his four sons. I'm gonna sail with them as far as Panama."

I looked at the stack of trays and bottles of developing solution and imagined the photographer's sons working side by side with their father, joking and laughing, as images of giant tortoises, Komodo dragons, and blue-footed boobies emerged in the developing trays. Why was it so easy to imagine strangers happy and not my family? And why did I think just because the cabin's dark wood and plush interior exuded a feeling of warmth and tranquility that this photographer didn't yell at his kids the way my father did?

"Pretty cool, right?"

"Uh, yeah . . . cool."

Maybe my problem was I couldn't stand the thought of anyone else's happiness if I didn't have it myself. I have to get out of here before I get any more depressed, I thought. "I'm going for a walk on the beach," I said. Heading toward the companionway, I added, "You can come, if you'd like."

As we walked along the beach, he told me he'd hired on as deckhand and, like us, it was his job to get the boat in order and ready to sail. The owner and his sons wouldn't arrive until the end of the week when they were scheduled to depart.

"How'd your parents let you get out of school?"

"How old do you think I am?" he snorted. "I graduated last year."

Embarrassed, I mumbled an apology. Why did such stupid things come out of my mouth? I just didn't know how to talk to boys, and worse yet, they were just as quick to remind me. I was about ready to bolt when he turned to me and asked, "So, when are you guys leaving?"

"We're waiting for an engine part . . ."

"We're supposed to spend New Year's in Panama," he said. "Should take us about two weeks."

We reached a small expanse of beach, lined with rocks. He bent down and picked up a large, smooth, black pebble. With an expert flick of his wrist, he threw the stone into the water. I watched it skip along the surface before it disappeared into the foamy depths.

"You're not gonna stop along the way?" I asked, incredulous anyone could sail for such a long distance without touching land. I had lasted all of two days, and it was like I had died and gone to hell.

"Nope. Just straight down to Panama."

The wind shifted and smoke from a beach fire reached us. We took off down the beach, running as fast as we could, and when we stopped, we were both out of breath and sweating. Standing side by side at the water's edge, I glanced over at him and wondered what it would be like to kiss him. I had kissed only one other boy, my friend's brother, who lived down the street from me. Recalling that disastrous wet-fish encounter, I wondered if all kisses were as wet and gross. Maybe there were ones nicer, softer, and drier.

I wondered if he thought I was pretty. He returned my glance, as if he had read my thoughts, and I felt a flush rise past my neckline and race toward the top of my head.

Suddenly, the image of my father materialized.

"I gotta get back," I said.

When we reached the dock, I was grateful *Tasco III*'s berth was at the head of the marina, because farther down I could see my father stationed in the cockpit, waiting for me. Without looking back or saying goodbye, I raced down the dock.

"Where the hell were you?" my father said. The tip of his cigarette glowed as he took a deep drag. He sat on the edge of the seat and leaned forward, like a rattlesnake ready to strike.

"I went for a walk on the beach," I said, keeping a safe distance between us.

"Who were you with?" he asked accusingly.

Even though my fish-kiss-date had not reached first base with me, my father believed there were many more who'd already raced around and scored a home run. I knew the real reason my reputation had been unfairly maligned was my association with Anne Cowell, the bad girl who lived down the block, and every father's nightmare. It was true she'd introduced me to the joys of marijuana, rock music, and skipping school, but I was too intimidated to show up when her posse of teenage admirers came around. I lacked the courage to flirt, much less talk to boys like Anne did; navigating my home life was complicated enough.

"No one," I lied. Somehow, I knew it was safer than telling the truth. "I was alone," I added for emphasis.

"You've got no business walking alone in the dark. D'you know what kind of individuals are out there?"

I wanted to shout, yes, maybe a nice boy! But I said, "I'm sorry."

"You should be sorry. You left your sisters with your chores. Get down below and help before it's too late."

I slid down the stairs, only to be met by my mother's silence and my sisters' accusing stares.

As I peeled potatoes, I pondered the significance of a kiss. Why did my father think that was so terrible? Characters in my books did it, famous actors in movies did it, even ordinary people on the street did it. "A kiss always leads to other things, bad things," my father would say. Since I couldn't even imagine a kiss, except for the one sloppy, wet one, from my neighbor's brother, how could I expect to imagine what the "other things" were? It *was* true that I longed for attention. I *had* wanted to kiss that boy and feel the softness of his lips. Maybe "bad things," I worried, *were* in my future.

I didn't venture past *Tasco III* for the next two days and then on Saturday morning, as I was sitting in the cockpit polishing the port winch, I heard laughter and shouting. The sharp blast from an air horn sounded, and *Tasco III* glided by. On board were the famous photographer, his four sons, and the deckhand. They all waved as they passed me.

I watched as they headed through the surging narrow entrance and beyond to the outer harbor, where they raised sail and disappeared. Running over to the ratlines, I climbed up for a better view. With my arms tightly wrapped around the topmast and my feet firmly planted on either side of the spreaders, I could see *Tasco III* in full sail, heeling over and riding the swells. I stayed there until she was no longer visible, wishing I could fly away and follow her, leaving behind the turmoil below.

Respite from my father's outbursts arrived with the auspicious appearance of Mr. Soule, who owned *Firefly*, a small sloop located a few slips from us. When my father casually mentioned his frustration over our delayed engine part, Mr. Soule, who was a mechanical engineer, generously offered to make the part in his machine shop.

Lanky and a little shorter than my father, Mr. Soule had kind gray eyes and possessed the magical ability to calm even the most difficult of men. We couldn't figure out what Mr. Soule saw in our father, but we didn't care. A devout Christian Scientist, Mr. Soule would have befriended any soul in need, so it was more to his good and generous spirit than my father's that they became chums.

Whenever we heard Mr. Soule's cheery morning salutations, it meant the start of a good day. An ardent and genuine admirer of *Heritage*, he showered my father with compliments. "What a beauty she is," he'd say, and then give a long, low whistle, as if *Heritage* were a sexy swimsuit model. "Jim, you did one heck of a job with her," he'd enthuse. He always said "heck" and "darn." We figured Christian Scientists weren't allowed to swear. Too bad Catholics didn't abide by that rule.

When Mr. Soule showed up, my father transformed into a relaxed and friendly guy. The only other person besides Mr. Soule who had that effect on my father was our family friend and fellow sailor, Joe Eklund.

A towering six-foot-seven Norwegian Viking, with massive hands and sporting a full white beard, Joe had spent every day for an entire year with us, helping my father build our house in the Oakland hills. Joe was always right there, offering words of encouragement to my sisters and me or calming my father after one of his outbursts. When one of us would torque a length of wood, causing the table saw blade to jam and my father to scream, "Stop binding the goddamn board!" Joe would drop whatever he was doing and stride over. With a wink and a smile, he'd press down on the board with his thumb and help guide it through.

He'd been our Kris Kringle, and his presence, like Mr. Soule's, brought joy and goodwill. But Joe also had his own dreams of sailing away. Two years after completing our house, he departed for Mexico in his home-built sloop. It had been more than a year since receiving his last note, postmarked from a small port along the Gulf of California, so we were grateful when Mr. Soule showed up.

Two days before Christmas, Mr. Soule, his wife, and six kids stopped by and invited us to celebrate the holiday at their home. After surprising my sisters and me with homemade presents and Mrs. Soule's delicious turkey dinner, Mr. Soule coaxed my father into giving us a day off to enjoy an afternoon sail on *Firefly*.

The next day, Mr. Soule and his son, David, stopped by *Heritage* to pick us up. Even though the invitation offered a chance to escape chores for a few hours, it wasn't as if we were dying to go as it was perfect sea-sick weather—cold, windy, and choppy. But considering we'd just shared Christmas with them, how could we refuse?

After *Firefly* backed out of the slip and before we left the inner harbor, Gayle and I spotted the sleek, dark head of a sea otter, and I wondered if it was the same one that I'd seen swimming around our dock. Leaning over the side, Gayle and I let our fingers trail in the water as the otter swam up to us.

"I see you've met Freddie, the harbor mascot," Mr. Soule said. "He might think your fingers are snack food, so I'd think about keeping them out of reach." We quickly yanked our hands out of the water. "Here, take this," he said, handing us fish bait he'd retrieved from the ice chest.

Gayle and I leaned over the side. Freddie raised his head and looked at us with his dark, liquid eyes and gently pulled the fish from our fingers with his paws. Floating on his back, he gulped down his meal.

"You're lookin' at the good life, right there," Mr. Soule said. "His full name is Fat Freddie 'cause all the boat owners feed him so much. He's so darn lovable, though, it's hard to resist him, especially when he rolls over and looks at you with those puppy eyes."

"Now you girls just sit back and relax and have a good time. David and I will do all the work. When y'all are hungry, just let us know. David packed a great lunch."

It didn't take long for the three of us to hang over the rail. Pam, Gayle, and I shook our heads when David offered us a sandwich.

"Here," Mr. Soule said, handing us some soda crackers. "Best thing for a queasy stomach."

"We're really sorry," Pam said, speaking for all of us as we wiped the bile and saliva off our life vests.

"I'll teach y'all the car game, and then at least you'll laugh when you barf," David said.

"Car game?" I asked.

He laughed and said, "Dad and I brought a client of mine out for a sail one day. He started in on a big bag of greasy potato chips as soon as we got underway, and Dad and I suggested he might want to take it easy. 'I never get sick,' he said. So, we start talking cars since he owned a car dealership, and suddenly he's over the side feeding that entire bag of chips to the fish. I kept asking him questions like, 'What's the fastest selling car you have?' and he'd answer, 'Fooorrrddd!' or 'What's the best mileage car?' and he'd answer, 'Chevvvey!' and finally, I asked him, 'What's the best priced vehicle?' and he'd spewed, 'Buuuuuick!'"

We got the chance to play the game before reaching the marina, and although it didn't make us feel any better, it proved highly entertaining for David and Mr. Soule.

With the steering fixed, it was time to think of leaving the comfort and routine of dock life and the generosity of the Soules, and head south to San Diego. One evening after dinner, my father informed us he'd placed a notice on the yacht club bulletin board to see if he could find a seasoned sailor to help us down the coast. This time around, he announced, he was going to make sure that whomever he hired would stay on board until *Heritage* reached San Diego.

The next morning, a short but compact and powerfully built man with a head of pure white hair marched down the dock and introduced himself. "Name's Thompson, and I saw your notice for crew on the yacht club bulletin board. Since I've got a weakness for gaff-riggers, I just couldn't turn this one down."

My father appeared leery of Mr. Thompson's age, which we figured must be close to seventy, but Mr. Thompson possessed more than enough credentials, having skippered the Scripps Institute *Te Vega* for years. But it was when he zipped up the ratlines with the agility of a teenager and balanced himself on the spreaders holding on with only one hand that my father welcomed him aboard.

With Mr. Thompson hired on as crew, my father casually suggested I switch places with Pam, who was eager to replace me. I felt conflicted over relinquishing my coveted spot onboard and the respite I'd have from seasickness if I did. More than that, though, was the nagging sense that my father preferred Pam's company over mine, so I reluctantly agreed.

The seas, which had surged through the harbor, had finally calmed and the sun, hidden behind storm clouds, broke through and warmed the air. I sat at the end of the dock and looked around at my home for the past month. Alive with the sounds and smells of sea life, I hoped I'd remember every detail before driving away with my mother and Nancy the next day.

I glanced over at Fat Freddie floating lazily on his back. Using a large rock, he pounded on a clamshell he'd placed on his furry chest. Cracking the shell open, he brought it up to his whiskered lips and ripped the soft flesh out with his sharp teeth. Then he gulped his meal down with a satisfied smack.

I sat on the end of the dock and watched him, wishing my life could be as carefree as his.

He looked over at me, acknowledging my presence by nodding his sleek head. His whiskers dipped into the green water, as if he agreed he did indeed have a life to be envied. If it's possible for an otter to smile, then Freddie grinned from ear to ear and, in doing so, gave me hope that happiness was possible, even for a screw-up like me.

4

# Exchanging Places

## *Monterey to San Diego*

**DECEMBER 29, 1969–JANUARY 5, 1970**

On the morning of December 29, *Heritage* motored past Monterey's narrow breakwater with my father, Pam, Gayle, and veteran seaman Mr. Thompson on board. My mother, Nancy, and I stayed on the dock until the boat was out of sight, then piled into the Pontiac and headed south along a stretch of coastal highway known as The Seventeen Mile Drive.

Upon reaching the first scenic outlook, we stopped and parked, hoping to catch a glimpse of *Heritage* sailing off the coast. Although the sky was clear, the fierce winds and heavy seas made me wonder how my sisters were faring and if they'd lost their breakfast yet.

I scanned the horizon, relieved to be on solid ground, yet disappointed I'd failed to gain my sea legs. I wondered if I lacked the intestinal fortitude Gayle seemed to have. My father had offered her the same option, but she'd declined. I couldn't understand why she wanted to make this leg of the trip. She'd been the sickest of all of us on the way to Monterey. While Pam was unaware of what awaited her, Gayle was willing to accept the inevitable. My younger sister always did the opposite of what I expected her to do. Though I'd shared a bedroom with her, she was a stranger. She never confided in anyone, especially me, preferring to share her emotional intimacy with a pen and paper, scribbling entries in a tattered notebook she carried everywhere. Either Gayle was a glutton for

43

punishment, or she sensed that Mr. Thompson's presence on board might make all the difference.

Maybe with his enthusiasm, expertise, and love of gaff-riggers, Mr. Thompson would be everything that Stan and Denny weren't. Was it possible that I'd given up a chance to experience a good time and great sail? Had I, for the umpteenth time in my sixteen years, made the wrong decision? I hated my indecisiveness and wished life's choices were as easy as opening up a map that showed, in plain view, a road to take to get you to where you wanted to go.

"There she is!" I said.

Excited, Nancy jumped up and down. "Where, where?"

I lifted her up and balanced her on my hip. "Right there," I said, pointing to the spot on the horizon, where I could see *Heritage* in full sail.

Nancy shook her head.

"Look at the white dot, straight ahead, where the sky meets the ocean. That's *Heritage*."

"Now I see it!" She waved and said, "Hi, Daddy!"

As I watched *Heritage* sail past from my secure spot on land, I realized I was no closer to calling myself a sailor than my four-year-old sister.

My mother put her arm around me and said, "It's going to be okay." I felt Nancy's warm breath on my neck and tightened my grip on her, hoping my mother was right.

Deep within me, though, lay the nagging doubt it wasn't. Underneath the indecision, regret, and envy lay the actual truth: the fear I'd never measure up.

For the rest of the afternoon, we drove down the Pacific Coast Highway, stopping for a late lunch in San Luis Obispo, before spending the night in the tiny town of Solvang.

Late the next morning, we drove through the Santa Ynez Valley. "It reminds me of Livermore and the barn," I said to my mother, as we passed the rolling hills, live oaks, and cow pastures interspersed with rows of newly planted grapevines. I lowered the window, stuck my head out, and inhaled. The air smelled rich and earthy, like the fields surrounding the barn.

I thought about those rare Sunday afternoons when my father allowed us a few free hours from chores to explore. After we'd finished sawing, bundling, and stacking; sanding, painting, and varnishing; and vacuuming hundreds of black widow spiders from the rafters, we'd cram our sandwiches in the pockets of our sawdust-covered overalls and bolt out the barn doors.

Sliding under the barbed wire fence, we'd traipse across poppy-strewn, cow-pied fields to the arroyo beyond. As meadowlarks flitted along the low-lying shrubs, we built makeshift forts or sat barefoot on the arroyo's sandy banks, eating peanut butter and jelly sandwiches, and watching schools of black tadpoles swim downstream.

One afternoon while Pam and Gayle picked poppies, I climbed up to a rocky outcrop I'd discovered near the arroyo. With a new pickax my father had given me for my eighth birthday, I chipped away at the glittering, mica-encrusted boulders and stuffed the pockets of my overalls with shiny rocks. I couldn't wait to show my father what I'd found. Pam shrugged her shoulders when I shared my find with her, asking what I was so excited about. "They're just some stupid rocks."

"How do you know?" I said. "Wait till I show Dad. He'll tell you how valuable they are."

Pam laughed. "He'll tell you they're worth as much as . . ." She turned, and spying a fresh, steaming mound said, "that stinky ol' cow-pie."

Weighed down by my find, I watched my sisters as they ran ahead, hand in hand, giggling. When I returned to the barn, I proudly showed my father my treasure. "Back to work," he said, and then, pointing to my bulging pockets and the glittering rock I held in my hand, added, "and get rid of that crap."

"What did you say, dear?" my mother said.

"The hills and vineyards . . ." I repeated, as I gazed out the window. As we sped along, we passed horses grazing in the distance and I thought of Mickey, who'd disappeared long before we finished *Heritage*. One day we'd arrived, ready to feed him the carrots and sugar cubes Mr. Sessler always set out for us, only to find Mickey's stall empty. Crestfallen, we hounded my father about Mickey's disappearance. "He's gone on to greener pastures," was all he said. I'd thought that meant Mickey, free from his dark enclosure, was happily romping through grassy fields and wildflowers. But as I stared at the horses, I knew that if Mickey was romping anywhere, it was with Grandma.

"Yes?"

". . . they remind me of the barn."

"Hmm," she said.

I knew my mother wasn't listening. If she had, she'd have understood I wanted to remember everything that had consumed my childhood— the good, the bad, and even the "crap" in between.

I'd held onto that shining piece of mica. Instead of getting rid of it, I'd added it to my rock collection I'd kept in a box under my bed. For years afterward, I'd take it out and look at it, admiring its iridescence and delicate beauty, and marveling at the deep satisfaction it gave me. Safe in its box under the bed, it was proof that no matter what I'd face in the world, there were things that could make me happy.

Early that evening, we pulled into my grandparents' driveway. As I surveyed the side yard, I noted the lemon tree, now twice as tall, still produced fruit the size of small beach balls. The cactus garden had expanded with every variety of cacti jammed into colorful ceramic pots and bowls.

The back door was open, so we walked in and found my grandparents in the kitchen.

"Took you long enough," my grandfather said, by way of a greeting.

My grandmother smiled, wiping her hands on her apron. From the smell of roast pork filling the kitchen, I knew we'd be sitting down to an early dinner. "Let's all wash up," she said. "You can bring your bags in after we eat." She turned to my grandfather, who was sitting at the table, and said, "You, too, Carly."

"Yes, Mother," he said, softly, conveying a tenderness and warmth he'd never shared with us.

As I dried my hands in the bathroom, I wondered if my grandmother had made my favorite childhood dish of noodles and gravy. It was the only thing that made visiting them every summer tolerable and convinced me that even though she found fault in everything my sisters and I did, somewhere in that bean-sized heart of hers was a tiny space where she felt love for us.

\* \* \*

Summer 1962. Burbank, California. "Hurry, Carly," my grandmother gently chided my grandfather. "I don't want my food getting cold. Wash your hands and let's sit down."

"Yes, Mother," my grandfather said, as he disappeared down the hall. Gayle whispered, "Why does Grandpa call Grandma his mommy?"

"Shhh! I don't know," I said.

When my grandfather entered the kitchen, he'd not only washed his hands, but his face and hair as well.

Gayle looked up at his towering presence, her eyes growing larger at the drops of water sliding down into his collar. "Your hair is all wet, Grandpa," she said.

"I like to come as clean as I can to God's table," he said, as he eased his bony frame into the plastic chair. "Speaking of that, it's inspection time." Thrusting our hands in front of him, my grandfather gave a grunt of approval. As my grandmother recited the dinner prayer, we bowed our heads. We never prayed at home, so we mumbled and ended with a loud "amen."

"You girls are going to memorize this prayer!" my grandmother scolded. "I don't know why your mother doesn't teach you these things."

Stuffing my face with noodles and gravy, I nodded to appease her, glancing over at my sisters, who did the same.

After dinner, my grandfather retired to the living room while my grandmother grilled us, as she washed the dishes and we dried, about our spotty church attendance. "You're headed straight to Limbo," she said, clicking her tongue.

Yelling above the upbeat Lawrence Welk Orchestra, my grandfather threw in his two cents from the living room. "Purgatory! That's where they're going . . . the lot of them!"

Pam and I gulped. Limbo was a step away from heaven and a step up from Purgatory, but Purgatory was a step away from hell. We exchanged glances and Gayle, always observant, took her cue from our silence and kept quiet.

\* \* \*

The plan was to wait at my grandparents' house until my father called us on the ship-to-shore radio once *Heritage* passed Los Angeles. But the next few days passed with no word from him. Confident that Mr. Thompson was helping my father sail the boat, my mother wasn't worried. But my grandparents' concerns were mounting.

"It's one thing to build something, keep a man's hands busy, but this trip your father's planning to take . . . to just up and leave his job and responsibilities . . ." my grandfather spat, not bothering to conceal his disgust.

On the fourth day, with no word from *Heritage*, my grandmother pulled out all the stops. Wrapping a string of rosary beads around her plump wrist, she handed two spare ones to my mother and me and made us kneel with her in the living room.

"O Heavenly Father, grant me this prayer. Please find my son Jimmy and bring him home safe to us," she said.

She left out my sisters and Mr. Thompson, so she must have been hedging her bets, hoping that if God could only save one soul, it had better be her son's.

That evening, my grandfather called the Coast Guard and informed them of a missing vessel. This began an all-out search for *Heritage*.

Meanwhile, after the ship-to-shore radio batteries died and the engine quit off of Santa Barbara, my father and the crew were taking it easy in becalmed waters as they patiently waited for the wind to push them southward.

During the early hours of the fifth day, the Coast Guard called my grandfather, informing him that one of the search planes had spotted *Heritage* forty miles north of San Diego. The plane could not make radio contact, but when they buzzed the ship, the crew aboard waved, and everything appeared normal.

After hearing the news, my grandfather turned to my mother and me. "Why are you doing this to us?" he said accusingly. Never good at a fast comeback, my mother averted her eyes and shrugged her shoulders. I stood there, wishing she'd say something to break the silence. Why, I thought, were we all so afraid of offending him when all he ever seemed to do was criticize and insult us?

My father called the next day unaware of the turmoil *Heritage*'s delay had caused as he enthusiastically recounted their wonderful time, relaxing and whale watching, while waiting for the winds to pick up. He suggested we leave as soon as possible for the three-hour drive to San Diego and hung up. Within fifteen minutes, we had packed and were ready to depart.

"Foolishness, pure foolishness," my grandfather muttered, as we piled into our car. We backed out of their driveway and waved goodbye.

# 5

# April Fools' Day

## San Diego, California

### JANUARY 5, 1969–APRIL 1, 1970

San Diego. Our jumping off point for Mexico. The last chance to purchase what were considered luxury items south of the border—more cigarettes for my father and two things the rest of us knew we couldn't live without, soft toilet paper and tampons. We learned from women on northern-bound boats that although the *mercados* were well stocked with bulky packages of Kotex, there was nary a tampon in sight. All I could imagine was a sea of Latin girls waddling around with pads as thick as baguettes between their legs.

"Maybe we should, you know, when in Rome," Pam said.

"No fucking way," I said. "Need I remind you we'll be in bathing suits most of the time? You'll look swell in a bikini with one of those stuffed in there."

As we watched my father stockpile cartons of Salems and cans of his favorite ham, we learned the meaning of "every man for himself." The race to fill the bins with our booty was on!

Along with boxes of tampons, we packed away rolls of "squeezably soft" Charmin, avoiding the Mexican version purported to be as abrasive as sandpaper and as hard as cardboard.

With the sides and bottoms of the forward bins packed with our necessities, and the teak racks above our bunks lined with cassette tapes showcasing an eclectic assortment of music—Peggy Lee, The Beatles, Janis Joplin, Glen Campbell, Creedence Clearwater Revival, Donovan, Buffalo Springfield, Joni Mitchell, Crosby, Stills & Nash—we crammed cans of creamed corn, Spam, peaches, pineapple, soup, coffee, baked beans, and corned beef hash into every available nook and cranny. We even used the bilge, the shallow space under the floorboards, to store cartons of eggs individually and painstakingly dipped in mineral oil to avoid spoilage.

We'd received more courses from the University of California Extension Program, so on top of sanding, painting, and varnishing every day, we had schoolwork to do at night, at least Pam and Gayle did. Preferring to practice my guitar, I jammed my books in the back of my drawer and drove everyone crazy strumming the chords to "Leaving on a Jet Plane."

For me, my guitar represented the cool in my uncool life. After failed attempts to master the ukulele, accordion, and banjo—instruments that, respectively, conjured up visions of the hula, polka, and square dancing—the guitar, with its free-wheeling folk sound, suggested a life I'd desired but didn't have. It was a life belonging to Anne Cowell. One of the most popular and feared girls in school and resident rebel, she did what she pleased, when she pleased, and where she pleased. At Anne's house, there were no rules or restrictions. Her mother, a divorcee and full-time teacher, was too harried to care or more liberal than most and allowed the daily carloads of long-haired boys to hang out at their house.

Anne was a triple threat—she sang her own songs, jammed with the boys, and danced with abandon. My only talents amounted to sanding and varnishing, sewing homemade clothes, and practicing my accordion, undeniably the most uncool instrument on the planet.

While I knew I'd never be Anne, my hope was I'd learn to play guitar and make a few friends along the way. And if that failed, I could switch to the harmonica, a farewell present from Anne, which was safely tucked away in the back of my drawer, along with my silver coins and plastic baggie of weed.

As our departure date to Mexico loomed, my father became crankier and more anxious. It was one thing to sail from San Francisco to San Diego, but it was another thing to head into foreign waters. To make matters worse, everyone he knew had turned into armchair critics, offering unsolicited advice on everything from *Heritage*'s sea-worthiness to questioning his sanity. It was enough that we were harboring our own personal doubts and fears.

Early one afternoon, my father flew down the cabin stairs. "Have any of you girls seen my socket-wrench kit?" he said. Busy with our studies, Pam and I shook our heads. He rummaged around, muttering to himself, until he finally turned and barked, "Lower the table so I can look for those goddamn tools!" We stacked our books and gathered our papers. "Get a move on! I don't have all day!" We hurriedly dropped the table leaf and stood to one side. "Jesus Christ, don't just stand there with your fingers up your butts . . . help me look for it!"

I glanced over at Pam. I knew she hated when he used that expression. If she were grinding her teeth any harder, she'd crack them; for me, it was another excuse to despise him.

"Goddamn son of a bitch!" He flung aside salon cushions, rifled through every drawer, and dumped the contents of the storage bins. He pushed past us and stormed back up the companionway. We could hear him swearing all the way down the dock.

"Why does he talk that way? It's disgusting," Pam said. "Think we oughta clean up?"

"Nah," I said. "He'll only come back and tear it up again. Let's just wait and see if he borrows another kit."

Pam nodded and lifted the table leaf back in place. We spread out our books and papers and went back to our homework.

Suddenly, from outside on the dock, we heard a voice calling out, "Hello? Uncle Jim?"

"Shit," I said, slamming my book closed. "That sounds like Susan!"

"Did you know they were coming?" Pam asked.

"Nope."

"Do you think Dad knows?"

"I think it's a surprise visit. He's not gonna be happy," I said.

"Oh Gawd, do you think the whole family is here?" Pam asked. We crept over to the porthole and saw my uncle, aunt, and two cousins peering into the cockpit.

"What are we going to do? Look at this mess!" Pam said.

"I'll go search for Dad and you keep them in the cockpit until I get back, okay? Mom should be back any minute with Gayle and Nancy, so try to keep them occupied until then."

We scrambled up the companionway and, as Pam helped them board, I jumped off and hightailed it down the dock.

I found my father, and on our way back to the boat, I gathered the courage to tell him the cabin was still a mess.

"We're dying to take a tour of the boat, but Pam wanted us to wait for you," my aunt June said to my father as we climbed back on board. "Now that you're here, the wait is over!"

"Well, ah, June, you kind of caught us in the middle of everything, so the cabin's not quite ship-shape," my father said, laughing a little too loudly, as he glared at Pam and me.

Ignoring him, my aunt disappeared down the companionway. With a hostile jerk of his thumb, my father made it clear he wanted us to follow her. As I descended the stairs I thought, how is this our fault? He's the one who wrecked the cabin.

"Well, my, my," my aunt said, surveying the mess. My cousins Susan and Teri had also descended, squeezing the five of us into the crowded cabin. Pam and I stood with our arms hanging by our sides, pressed up against the galley.

"It looks a lot better when everything's cleaned up," I said.

"Oh no, dear, it's lovely," she replied. What was she talking about? The cabin looked as if it had been ransacked by pirates. My aunt surveyed the mess and said, "I meant . . . it's . . . I'm just used to living in a house." I knew she meant she was happy as hell she didn't have to call these cramped barracks home.

After Pam and I herded my aunt and cousins back up the companionway to the cockpit, my father, clearly distressed, jumped up and suggested a stroll along the main dock, where the club's finer yachts were berthed. Not the smartest move to make, I thought, if you were trying to impress the crowd and avoid comparisons.

We sauntered along with my father performing a running commentary until we reached the end of the dock, where a large steel ketch was side tied. Even though it exceeded *Heritage* by only ten or twelve feet, its wide beam and high freeboard made it look massive. Like our boat, it was outfitted with seafaring equipment, and I assumed it was preparing to head north up the coast or south to Mexico.

A woman who appeared to be in her early forties stood on the cabin top, observing us. "Well . . . hello there! I see you're admiring my boat!" Tall, lean, and very tan, sporting a high, tight ponytail and dressed in white shorts and a bright yellow T-shirt, she displayed the agility of a teenager as she leapt from the cabin top and onto the deck. She unhooked the lifeline and motioned with her hand. "Well, come on, don't be shy!"

As my aunt stepped on board, the boat's owner glanced at her kitten heels and said, "Park those cute shoes right here. First rule of sailing! No heels on deck!" The alacrity with which my aunt removed the offending footwear caused the woman to throw back her head and snort. I couldn't tell if she was laughing at us or just pleased with herself.

My father, who was the last in line, held back.

With her hands on her hips, the owner chided, "Don't just stand there! There's plenty of room for everybody!" He reluctantly boarded and followed her to the large center cockpit and down the wide companionway.

Before even reaching the bottom of the stairs, I could hear my aunt oohing and aahing over the accommodations.

"Make yourself comfortable while I grab my husband," the owner said. "I'm Laddie, by the way. He's putting our kids down for a nap in our room." My father tried to put on a pleasant face, but I could tell he was kicking himself over his brilliant suggestion.

"This is my husband, Tony," she said in a loud whisper as they reemerged. "I'd introduce you to my little ones, but my husband would *kill* me as he just got them to sleep." Tony simply smiled and extended his hand to my father and uncle.

When Tony discovered my father was a fellow yachter, he told him they'd purchased the boat—the *Tolaki*—and sailed from British Columbia and were headed to Mexico and the Sea of Cortez.

After a few more minutes spent discussing itineraries, my father thanked them, and we all piled off their boat. All the way down the dock, my aunt gushed over Tony and Laddie's "marvelous yacht." My father, tight-lipped and scowling, walked behind.

Back at *Heritage*, my father spent the rest of the visit warding off questions from his brother regarding our safety, sanity, and preparedness. While my uncle's intentions may have been innocent, I could tell my father felt judged. For him, my uncle's questioning echoed my grandfather's, and implied a sense of moral superiority that they, and not my father, knew best. Frustrated by their lack of enthusiasm and support, my father comforted himself knowing that while he hadn't the financial security so valued by them, he possessed an inherent sense of aesthetics and taste, which he fervently believed trumped wealth.

Unlike my uncle Chuck, who'd started his own tool and die business in California just as my grandfather had in Illinois, my father chafed over the thought of spending his life making machine parts. Striking out on his own, with dreams of a different life, he'd become a master carpenter, gifted painter, and more than able draftsman. But without a degree, less talented, college-educated individuals rose in rank as he was passed over repeatedly for promotion. Even after spending a year and a half in Enewetak where he earned three times his yearly salary, with a wife and three young daughters, it was not enough to get ahead. It was only by trusting his artistic abilities he felt he could compete. While my uncle and aunt proudly displayed what my father considered were cheap, tasteless, black-velvet paintings in their living room, the walls of our small apartment were covered with beautiful watercolors he'd painted and framed. And while their house was unquestionably big with a pool, he'd remark that, unlike our Swiss-chalet A-frame he and Joe Eklund built, theirs looked like every other house in their cookie-cutter neighborhood. Most important, he believed by sailing the world aboard *Heritage*, he'd finally be on equal footing.

What my father failed to consider was that as long as he remained, in their eyes, a fiscally unsound dilettante who'd skipped from job to job, he'd never earn the approval he was seeking.

After my uncle's visit, my father's moods were increasingly unpredictable, so when he suggested my sisters and I take the day off and spend it at the San Diego Zoo, we weren't sure whether this wasn't some sort of test. If we go, will he make us pay later? If we remain, will he reward us? My mother stepped in and decided. "The zoo sounds like a great idea," she said.

In her rush to get back to the boat, my mother dropped us off at the zoo's entrance and sped away, leaving us with barely enough money to cover the price of our tickets. "I can't believe she did that," Pam said, counting the handful of remaining change.

Why did people like my parents even bother to have kids? I thought. Take my father, for instance. We seemed to be a constant source of irritation for him, like those plantar warts he was always getting on the bottom of his feet. As for my mother, it appeared we were a surprising afterthought, springing from her loins, fully grown, without requiring further guidance.

"Well, there's not enough here to take the guided tour trolley, so why don't we just walk the route?" Pam suggested. Since it was still cool, we all agreed and set off toward our first stop, the reptile house.

"You think Mexico has any snakes?" Gayle asked, her brow furrowed with worry as she studied the constrictor's thick trunk coiled around the branch inside the glass terrarium.

"We're going to be on the coast, not deep in the jungle," Pam said, dismissing her concern.

"I'd worry more about cockroaches if I were you. They're supposed to have flying ones the size of pterodactyls in Acapulco." My sisters shivered. I said it to get a rise out of them. Ever since Pam and Gayle had made the sail together from Monterey, I couldn't shake the feeling they'd excluded me from their club. Since arriving in San Diego, the two of them had talked about nothing but their trip with Mr. Thompson. They even had their own shorthand.

"Remember . . . the whale . . . ?"

"And then Dad . . ."

"When Mr. Thompson . . ."

"His joke . . ."

". . . the porpoise."

"And the sailor . . ."

Although it sounded like gibberish, it sent my two sisters into spasms of laughter.

Around each bend, we passed tapirs, hippos, kangaroos, tigers, lions, giraffes, and elephants. We went through the cold caves to watch polar bears and penguins swimming until finally we reached the monkey house. By this time, the sun was high in the sky, and we were as hot and irritable as the gorillas that pushed and shoved one another for the one shady spot under their enclosure's only tree.

As we moved on to the chimpanzees, a group of males sat holding court, vigorously massaging their private parts. Nancy pointed to them and said in a loud voice, "Look, they're all smiling and touching their pee pees." The surrounding crowd guffawed. We should have laughed along with them but, ill-equipped to give lessons on the sexual proclivities of male monkeys, much less *any* male, we made a hasty retreat to the exit.

With two more hours to kill before my mother picked us up, we arrived back at the zoo's entrance. "I'm too hot and too tired to move," I said. "Let's just sit here and people watch."

"I want to go on *that*," Nancy said, pointing to the miniature train. Gayle nodded in agreement. Pam counted out our remaining change and announced we had just enough for two train fares and two cans of soda. Gayle and Nancy hopped on board, while Pam and I sat under an umbrella and shared a Coke.

"Think Dad's gonna be all hot and bothered when we get home?" I asked.

"I'm too hot and bothered to care."

"It doesn't seem to matter what we do; Dad just gets pissed off over every little thing," I said. "He probably thinks he gave us a vacation and will make us work twice as hard tomorrow."

"I know *you'll* be working twice as hard. He's got it out for you!" Pam said.

"I know I piss him off. What did I do?" I asked, thinking about how my mere presence seemed to set him off.

"I dunno. There's something about you he just doesn't like."

"I hate him," I said.

"Sometimes I wish I could run away to Europe," Pam said. Even though I knew that was not a possibility, my sister had dreams of going away to college. While we'd never been buddies, I still considered her an ally. If she left, life onboard would be all the harder.

After our free, two-week stay at both San Diego Yacht Club and Southwestern Yacht Club, we moved to the Silver Gate Yacht Club. Away from the posh environment of SDYC and the "be here now" vibes of SYC, my father discovered people who were open, friendly, and enthusiastic about our plans.

Two such people were Larry and Babe Baldwin, a crusty couple in their sixties and the unofficial mayors of SGYC. After over thirty years of sailing, they'd retired and lived aboard their beamy ketch *Faith*, where they published a bound newsletter, *The Seven Seas Cruising Association*. Filled with valuable tidbits, it was a treasure trove of information for traveling yachtsmen, especially those heading into Mexico. My father bought a six-month backlog, hoping to find information on Joe Eklund's whereabouts. As we pored over letters, we discovered one by a northern-bound boat that told of meeting Joe in Cabo San Lucas. After he'd spent a year sailing in the Gulf of California, he'd sailed to Cabo to do some minor repairs before heading to Costa Rica. If he took his time sailing down the coast, my father said to us, we might catch up with him. My sisters and I couldn't wait to see Joe's big green parrot that he'd told us he was going to buy when he reached the tropics.

Following one last haul-out at Kettenburg's Boat Works to apply a fresh coat of copper anti-fouling paint on the keel and a new stripe for the boot-top, which had to be raised from all the extra equipment my father had purchased after reading Babe's newsletters, we topped off the water and fuel tanks. Then the whole family drove up to Burbank to face the stern, unsmiling faces of our grandparents. I think my father made the trip hoping that they would finally give their blessing, but all my grandmother said as we pulled out of their driveway was, "We sure hope you know what you're doing."

We drove back to San Diego in silence.

Two days later, in his desire to widen the distance between Burbank and *Heritage*, my father sold our car to the first buyer for a lot less than it was worth.

On our last night, my father raised his wineglass and made a toast. "Lorraine . . . girls . . ." He lifted his glass to each of us. "Tomorrow is the start to a new life." I recalled he'd made the same promise the night we sailed under the Golden Gate. His determined look and quiet confidence, though, struck me. Should I chalk up the first promise to bad luck and a false start?

Tomorrow we'd see.

In the predawn of April 1, 1970, *Heritage* motored out of Shelter Island. This was finally it. San Francisco to San Diego had been a trial run, the shakedown. Leaving American waters was the real deal. After almost three months, we were finally on our way to the adventure of a lifetime and the glorious life my father had promised. From here on out, it would be azure skies, golden beaches, and realizing my mother's bedtime stories of "water so blue you can't tell where the ocean ends, and the sky begins. . . ." An endless summer of fun. No more arguing, yelling, or backbreaking work.

With a reefed mainsail and the engine running, we were now a few hours and ten miles out from Point Loma. Another hour and dawn would rise behind us over San Diego. Without warning, the engine revved. My father leaned over and adjusted the throttle, but the sound continued to escalate until it rose to a deafening whine. Suddenly, the cockpit rocked beneath our feet. With a shudder and ominous death rattle, the engine exhaled and quit.

"Feet up off the floor!" my father said. He pulled the engine hatch up as the rest of us crouched on the cockpit seats, pressing ourselves to the far end near the companionway. A thick cloud of diesel smoke and burning oil billowed up, forcing my sisters and me over the rail.

"Shit, shit, shit," my father cursed.

While we dry-heaved over the side, my father shined a flashlight to assess the damage. He leaned down and pulled out a long piece of metal dripping in oil.

He held it up as if it were a piece of evidence at a crime scene. "It's the goddamn rod!"

He slammed the hatch and announced, "We've no choice but to turn back." Until he could pull the boat up on the ways and check the shaft, he explained, he wouldn't know the extent of damage. To soften our disappointment, he said, "With any luck, we'll be off and running by the end of the week."

I wanted to cry, but when I heard my father's voice crack, I caught myself, as did my mother and sisters. Somehow, we knew our disappointment was nothing compared to his.

I looked up at the stars and wondered how the universe, with its ordered cosmos, could also create chaos and disaster.

With our shamed Buda engine succumbing to an act of seppuku, we could do nothing but wait, leaving *Heritage* to bob in the darkness until dawn.

# 6

# Return to Port

## San Diego, California

**APRIL 1–MAY 5, 1970**

My father wrote of that miserable predawn disaster:

> *There was nothing to do except sail back and claim our leaving was just an April Fools' joke (on us!). We sailed into a side-tie and the next day, were towed back to Kettenburg's.*

When dawn broke and the sky lightened to a pale gray, my father ordered us to raise the sails. Under full canvas, with only a whisper of wind, *Heritage* crept at a snail's pace until rounding Point Loma, where the breeze increased considerably. Barreling toward the harbor entrance, my father realized too late there was no time to turn *Heritage* into the wind and reduce sail. As we reached the harbor and tore through the narrow opening, outgoing boats careened out of our way and more than one windsurfer jumped off his board.

"Get up there and grab the bowline!" my father yelled. I raced forward, grabbed the line, and stood there shaking. Unsure of what to do next, I braced my legs against the lifelines as I watched the channel narrow and the number of boats multiply.

"See the dock right off your starboard?" my father screamed over the wild flapping of the sails. "We're gonna side-tie to that. When I come in, jump off and cleat that bow line!"

By now, I noticed that, instead of running toward the dock to help, the crowd stood slack-jawed by the impending disaster unfolding before their eyes. I tried not to think of them witnessing what might be *Heritage*'s swan song.

"I'll loosen the sheets!" my father said and then yelled at Pam and Gayle. "You two drop the main and the jib!"

I glanced at my sisters and their terrified faces said it all.

The sails flapped wildly against the rigging as they fell in a jumbled mess on the cabin top and deck. I climbed over the lifeline and, like a gymnast on a balance beam, teetered on the rail, poised and ready to execute my leap toward the dock.

"Goddammit, we're coming in too fast. We're gonna overshoot it!"

The boat veered. It was now or never. With coiled line in hand, I leapt and prayed that I'd make it to the dock without getting flattened. Miraculously, as I flew through the air, the line payed out like silk cord behind me, and I landed feet first, hitting the dock in a sort of fast skip, the way a frigate bird lands after a long time at sea, stopping just short of the prized cleat.

Like the seasoned sailors I'd read about in books, I lassoed the line around the cleat and held my breath as *Heritage* came to a groaning stop just a few inches short of the piling.

My father stood at the wheel with his mouth agape and his glasses off. Not until the crowd roared with approval did he offer a stingy grin.

By this time, with *Heritage* secured, onlookers ventured down to the end of the dock. One of them, a seasoned, seaworthy-looking man, thrust his tattooed forearm at me, and grasping my hand, pumped my arm up and down. "You must'a cleared fifteen feet, young lady. You looked like you had wings or sumpthin'. I wasn't sure you'd make it, but you touched down like one of them pelicans."

When he released his grip, I stepped back and glanced over at my father. He'd turned his back to the crowd and was busy coiling the stern lines.

During dinner that night, my father acknowledged me with a terse "job well done," sufficient praise, I concluded, after the silent reception I'd received from my sisters and mother.

The next morning, Kettenburg's hauled *Heritage* out of the water so my father could examine her damage. While my father sent my mother, Gayle, and Nancy on an errand and out of harm's way, he ordered Pam and me to stay.

From a safe distance on deck, Pam and I watched the crane operator maneuver and lower the steel arm, so my father could attach and shackle two heavy-duty belts around the engine. With one mighty thrust, the steel arm jerked up, and the Buda rose, spilling filthy, black oil all over the engine bed and deck.

"You girls start the cleanup," my father said, suddenly looking ill. "I . . . I gotta check on something." He headed for the ladder and descended before we could object.

Pam and I looked at each other and then down at the gaping hole in the cockpit.

Blackened oil filled the bilge. Pam sighed and said, "I'll sponge, if you pump." We crouched in the hold, straddling our feet against the boat's ribs, and got to work.

My father stayed away the rest of the day.

Using my mother's small inheritance from Grandma, my father ordered a new Starrett diesel engine from Wilmington, California. While he waited for its delivery, he removed the propeller and shaft and started work on a new engine bed, unaware of an impending teamster strike.

While we waited for the union to settle, our new engine lay nestled in a crate in a warehouse. With the propeller and shaft removed, we couldn't go back in the water, but we couldn't stay on the ways, either. Aware of our dilemma, Kettenburg's moved us off the ways to a permanent cradle on the far side of the yard. Meanwhile, my father hounded the Starrett company daily, cursing the teamsters and fervently wishing a few scabs would cross the picket line so they could deliver our engine.

During this wait, my father disappeared for long stretches in a borrowed car with my mother and Nancy. Pam, Gayle, and I passed the time sitting on deck reading, studying, or watching the busy yard below us.

One day there was a surge of activity as we watched the boatyard haul out a seventy-five-foot wooden schooner and deposit her in a cradle alongside *Heritage*. Fresh from a two-and-a-half-month sail from Florida, the *Mayan* had sailed into the harbor heading toward the San Diego Yacht Club, when an eight-meter plowed into her and ripped off her fourteen-foot bowsprit.

The elegant and roomy Alden-designed schooner dwarfed *Heritage*. I longed to climb aboard and have a look down below, but the owner was never there. Instead, we watched a crew of workers arrive and begin work repairing the damaged bowsprit.

Shortly after the repair, Bud, the yard foreman, hustled over with two of his workers. Barking out orders, his men quickly set about hosing down *Mayan*'s teak decks, scrubbing her sail-covers, and polishing all her brass and chrome fittings. I leaned over our railing and asked Bud if he knew who the owner was.

"Yeah."

"Who is he?" I asked.

"You'll find out soon enough. They'll be here 'round noon," he said with a wink, as he walked away.

A few hours later, Pam peered down into the cabin, where Gayle and I were sprawled in our bunks, reading. "Hey, you guys, I'm not sure, but I think the owner of the *Mayan* is the guy from Crosby, Stills, and Nash!"

We scrambled out of our bunks, practically knocking heads, as we raced up the companionway to the cockpit and peeked out. Three men who looked to be in their late twenties or early thirties, old by our standards, with scruffy beards, shoulder-length hair, wearing tie-dyed T-shirts and faded bell-bottoms, stood in *Mayan*'s cockpit as one of them fiddled with the lock on the cabin's hatch.

"Goddamn lock. It's frozen. I need some WD-40." His hair obscured his face, so I couldn't tell if Pam was right. With a friendly wave, he smiled and called over to us. "Wouldn't have some WD-40 on you, would you, girls?"

I couldn't believe it! Just last night, I'd listened to "Marrakesh Express" and now here I was, a stone's throw away from real live rock stars!

I flew down the companionway and rifled through my father's toolbox. Racing back up the stairs, I stood on the deck facing them and hoisted the can triumphantly above my head.

"You can throw it over. Or you can come on board if you'd like," he said. That was all we needed to hear. We scrambled down the ladder and up theirs.

After introductions, I learned Crosby was *Mayan*'s owner.

"Just the three of you girls, no brothers?" Nash asked.

"Actually, there are four of us, but the youngest is just a *baby*," I said, hoping they noted the distinction, as Crosby took the can and sprayed it into the frozen padlock. In no time, the lock opened, and Crosby invited us below.

As we descended, the spicy scent of patchouli filled the air and wafted throughout *Mayan*'s opulent interior. Several guitars were propped against the settee's cushions. And as we passed one stateroom, I glimpsed a double bunk covered with a paisley-patterned velvet bedspread.

"We shouldn't be down here with these guys," Pam whispered behind me. "Dad will be really mad if he finds out."

"What do you think these guys are gonna do? They're famous. It's not like we're in any danger. I'm not going anywhere," I announced, as I moved through the main salon and poked around the fo'c'sle.

"Ahoy!" a voice shouted from outside. Pam, Gayle, and I froze. It was my father, who'd returned early from his outing with my mother and Nancy.

"Now what are you gonna do, Smarty Pants?" Pam hissed.

"We haven't done anything wrong," I said, straining to hear the conversation taking place between my father and the rock stars. Was he aware of who they were? As far as I knew, my father barely listened to any kind of music, much less rock music. Maybe he just thought they were hippies, albeit wealthy ones. More than likely, he'd heard about them from all the frenzy in the yard. Just looking at the *Mayan* was enough to know the owners were not ordinary folks.

When my father saw us pop our heads out of the companionway, he growled, "What are you girls doing up there?"

"Oh, they're no bother," said Crosby, cheerfully. "In fact, they were nice enough to find some WD-40 for us . . . had a frozen lock. Come on up and have a look if you'd like."

Once on board, my father eyed us. "You girls have plenty of work to do."

Our cue to leave. Embarrassed and resentful that he'd treated me like a baby, I silently descended the ladder, and along with my sisters, climbed back up to our cockpit.

As we sanded and polished on *Heritage*, and my mother read to Nancy down below, my father was thoroughly enjoying himself, sharing a beer and relaxing in *Mayan*'s cockpit. Listening to them laugh as they clinked their bottles infuriated me. He was sucking up to *my* rock stars. Back in Oakland, he'd forever railed against "long-haired hippies," and their relaxed be-here-now vibe, so I wondered what had changed his mind? Maybe Crosby owning a boat twice as big as ours, or fame and its magnetic pull, challenged my father's convictions?

His contradictory behavior provided fertile ground for my discontent. While he demanded complete fealty and respect from us, he didn't seem to give much in return. His mantra of "Do as I say, not as I do," rang hollow when it appeared it was way more fun to do as he did. The adult world seemed to be littered with varying shades of gray and shifting standards, where rules were muddy and mercurial and as changeable as the weather. For me, the world was black and white. There was only right or wrong, truth or lies, good or evil.

I thought about the conflicts and the challenges I faced. To take the confident leap toward adulthood, I needed to know there would be something solid to land on, even if it meant skipping like a frigate bird to the very end of the dock. But almost every adult I'd met said one thing and did the other. Like the coiled line that had payed out like silk cord behind me, words and their actions had to flow, bridging the gap, so when the time came to leave adolescence, I'd land safely, if not a little gracelessly, on the other side.

Over the next week, we watched the *Mayan* prepare for her trip up the coast to San Francisco. During the evenings, I listened to their music and laughter, which drifted in through the open porthole above my narrow bunk. If only they knew who I really was, they would have invited me over, I thought. I imagined sitting cross-legged on that paisley bedspread, smoking a joint and listening to them as they sang and played their guitars. Never mind the fact, my father would have never allowed it, or, for all the flowing alcohol, drugs, and free love, these rockers were not stupid; at sixteen, I was jailbait. That didn't stop me, though, from imagining their attentions were serious, when Stills called out one morning, "How'd you like to sail up the coast with us?"

Unlike the fantasies I harbored, Pam rolled her eyes.

"Ask your dad," Stills said, grinning as he disappeared down the hatchway.

"Fat chance," Pam said, laughing at me.

I stuck my tongue out at her.

"What's the big deal?" she retorted. "I think they look old and grubby. Yuck."

"What would you know, Miss Strait Laced?"

"More than you, moron."

"Creep."

"Idiot."

Disinterested, Gayle sauntered away, whispering something in French.

When my mother heard that Stills had invited us to crew up the coast, she told us, "I have half a mind to tell those young men off, even if they are famous!"

"Oh, for crying out loud. Just forget it," I said.

It made any further discussion moot when, later that day, workers prepared to move *Mayan* out of her cradle and back into the water. The boatyard, which a few moments before had been a flurry of activity, was now unusually quiet. We, including my father, looked up just in time to see Graham Nash walk through the yard, followed by two of the most beautiful women any of us had ever seen. They were both dressed like Jane Fonda in *Barbarella*—in thigh-high boots, micro-mini skirts, and sheer peasant blouses open to their navels that revealed, compared to our flat chests, two pairs of the biggest breasts my sisters and I had ever seen. From his expression, my father seemed to agree.

Normally, the most reticent of men, my father preoccupied himself by performing a tiny task that appeared to demand his full attention on the foredeck. Pam and I exchanged glances, each of us noting the other's embarrassment over the realization that our father, standing transfixed at the bow, could not stop staring, as the two beauties strode toward *Mayan* and shimmied up the ladder, exposing what little they were covering. So intent were we watching him watch them, we didn't hear my mother come up the hatchway.

She glanced over just as the women bent over the top of the ladder and exposed the bottom of their butt cheeks. "If you can pull yourself away from work for a minute, Jim, lunch is ready," she said dryly. She looked back at us, rolled her eyes, and then disappeared below. Following her, Pam turned around and mouthed, "Gross," to which I laughed and nodded in agreement.

With the *Mayan*'s departure, along with her rock stars and glamorous girlfriends, we returned to the drudgery of finishing up *Heritage* for her return to the water.

Finally, the Starrett dealer, either taking pity on our plight or just plain tired of my father's incessant phone calls, sold us their floor model. Packed and sent the same day, the crane lowered the new sea-foam-green painted diesel engine into its new bed on May 1, 1970.

The next morning, the crane moved *Heritage* from her cradle to the ways. Once she was in the water, my father motored over to the far side of Shelter Island to wash the accumulated shipyard dirt from her decks.

While topping off our fuel and water tanks, we discovered that the *Mamusah*, a luxurious, fifty-two-foot ketch, would soon depart for Mexico. Little did we know, her owners would become our traveling companions for the next thousand miles.

# II
# FOREIGN WATERS

7

# *Mañana* Fever

### Ensenada to Isla San Martín, Mexico

**MAY 5–10, 1970**

Four months to the day of our arrival, we departed San Diego with only the port and starboard lights and the glowing end of my father's cigarette to guide us out of the dark harbor and into the bay. Bundled in our float coats, we huddled in the cockpit and tried to ward off the brisk, biting wind. I couldn't believe summer was just around the corner.

Our four-month respite on terra firma was over, and the familiar toxic mix of cigarette smoke and diesel fumes had returned. Before long, Pam, Gayle, and I were heaving over the side, while the youngest crew member and cook appeared nonplussed and in possession of iron stomachs.

"Looks like Nancy has found her sea legs, but I took something before we left this morning . . . and I'm perfectly fine," my mother said. We knew what she meant. A few days before we left, she'd purchased anti-nausea suppositories and urged us to use them before departing. But the thought of its targeted destination was way more repugnant than emptying our guts.

Around mid-morning, we passed to the lee of Islas Desiertas, better known as the Coronados. The four desolate and barren islands that comprised the archipelago boasted a long-standing reputation for their uncanny resemblance to corpses in repose. My father believed superstitions were reserved for fools, but nonetheless, he steered well clear of them.

By late afternoon, we reached Ensenada, our first foreign port. As we motored past the breakwater and into the harbor, we spied *Mamusah*. My father swung *Heritage* close to *Mamusah*'s stern and shouted out a loud, "Ahoy!" When no one appeared, he veered off and idled while I went below to retrieve Babe's binder. I flipped through the letters and found one that included a small map of the harbor, marked with several X's showing desirable anchorages. Taking note, my father found one, anchored, and had us pay out plenty of chain.

Early the next morning, dressed in our best to meet the port captain and register *Heritage* and crew to the Republic of Mexico, my father christened me "dinghy-boatswain." I was proud he trusted me enough to deliver everyone to shore but resented the fact he considered the job below his station. And I couldn't shake a nagging sense this was a half-empty commission.

Harboring an expectation my first south-of-the-border town would be a colorful mélange of pastel painted houses, crystal-clear waters, and white sandy shores, Ensenada was a disappointing study in dull mono-chromatic browns. As I rowed my father and Pam through the brackish water and past a collection of drab buildings, I noticed even the morning sky was awash in a brownish haze.

After a second trip ferrying my mother, Gayle, and Nancy, I secured the dinghy to a piling and joined my family on the walk to the port captain's office. Halfway there, my father suddenly stopped, adjusted his wool beret, and performed a little jig in the middle of the cobblestone-lined square. This was so completely out of character I wondered if he had lost it. Mortified, I looked around to see if anyone other than our family had witnessed this embarrassing display. Unlike my reaction, Nancy was delighted by his uninhibited prancing. As he bobbed up and down, she laughed and raced over to his outstretched arms.

With a big, wide grin plastered across his face, he scooped her up and strode away, like the Pied Piper, bouncing my youngest sister on his shoulders while the rest of us scurried like lemmings behind him.

When we reached the port captain's office, we were told to report to immigration, which we had passed at the beginning of our walk. My father grumbled under his breath, turned us around, and started the nine-block trek back. His good mood rapidly disintegrated.

Upon entering the grungy immigration office, my father positioned himself near the door, while Pam, relying on two years of high school Spanish, stumbled through the officer's questions. The rest of us stood to the side, watching the verbal volley like spectators at a tennis match. Back and forth they went, Pam quickly losing points each time she stammered or faltered and her mustachioed, feral-faced opponent successfully gaining points by responding in rapid-fire Spanish.

"What's the problem now?" my father asked.

"I don't know. It's something about going back to the port captain."

"Tell him we just came from there!"

"*Por favor, señor . . . acabamos . . . de llegar del . . . capitán del puerto,*" my sister said haltingly.

"*Lo siento, pero, es necesaria una firma del capitán del puerto,*" the officer replied.

"What? What?" my father asked.

"*Un momento, por favor,*" Pam said to the officer.

She turned to my father and explained. "He said we have to get the port captain's signature first."

"Christ."

"*Qué?*" The officer cocked his head and narrowed his eyes at my father.

"*Nada, nada,*" my sister said hurriedly to the officer. "*Gracias,*" she added.

"*De nada,*" he said dismissively. Ignoring us, he returned to his paperwork.

We spent the next two hours walking back and forth between the two offices, racking up more and more signatures until, finally, both officers stamped our papers.

*Heritage* had officially entered foreign waters.

By this time, my father's patience had evaporated. He tapped out the last cigarette in his pack and groused, "Goddamn inefficient, if you ask me." We stumbled behind him and headed back to the boat; all I wanted was to be in my bunk reading my paperback. Nearing the harbor, my father noticed the wind had shifted and ordered us "to pick up the pace." When we reached the pier, we could see the wind had swung *Heritage* around. She'd tripped her anchor and was now a quarter-mile closer to shore and hard aground. With at least a foot of bottom paint showing, she wobbled back and forth on her narrow keel like a drunk in high heels. Her bow faced the beach and the anchor chain scraped against her side.

"You two, get in the dinghy with me," my father said. As he rowed Pam and me back to the boat, an old fisherman, who'd been motoring around in the harbor in his twenty-foot *panga*, offered to help, so my father, using hand signals, directed him toward the bow.

Stationed on the foredeck, Pam and I helped my father pull up two hundred feet of chain from the anchor locker and pile it onto the deck. After attaching our spare plow anchor to the chain, my father, without looking, heaved it over the side into the old man's *panga*. Ducking just in time to avoid a good skull cracking, the grizzled fisherman flashed a toothless grin and took off, paying out the length of chain.

After the fisherman reached his destination and dropped anchor, my father then turned his attention toward the chain scraping against the boat's starboard side. With the help of the incoming tide, he winched, link by link, until *Heritage* inched her way back into deeper water. He turned the engine on and backed out far enough to turn her around. While he winched in the remaining chain, he had me steer toward the spot where the old fisherman had dropped the plow.

Right as my father hauled in the last bit of chain, a large fishing boat departed, freeing up a mooring. *Heritage* was now secure. After thanking the old man, we watched him motor off in his *panga*, clutching a carton of Salems from my father's coveted stash.

My mother, Gayle, and Nancy, all but forgotten in the excitement, waved to us from the pier. I jumped into the dinghy to retrieve them while Pam retired to her bunk. My father sat in the cockpit and sucked on a beer, thoroughly spent from hauling in over four hundred feet of chain.

The next morning, my father announced he needed to replace a hose clamp and promptly took off in the dinghy. I suspected he wanted time alone, but I wondered how he was going to get by without Pam translating.

When he returned with his purchase, I discovered the answer to my question; he'd bumped into *Mamusah*'s owner, Max Fraser, who was fluent in Spanish. After helping my father locate a clamp and sharing a meal in town, Max extended an invitation for cocktails aboard his yacht.

Although we'd heard about the Frasers in San Diego, my sisters and I were excited and curious to meet them, especially their daughter, Sara, who was my age.

"Well, ahoy there!" Max's wife said, as our dinghy bumped against their boat's midships. Mrs. Fraser looked down at me and smiled as Max lent a hand to my father, mother, and Nancy. "I have a nice treat for you and your sisters when you return."

I quickly rowed back to the boat and picked up Pam and Gayle.

When we were all onboard, Mrs. Fraser said, "Why don't you girls come down below and help me with the drinks and hors d'oeuvres?"

My sisters and I followed her down the companionway and into the main cabin. To the right was a large settee, curved in a U-shape and decorated with navy blue cushions. To the left was the galley, equipped with a big sink, a full-size stovetop, and half-refrigerator. On the counter sat a potted mint plant, four pewter cups, and five tall glasses.

"Sara!" Mrs. Fraser shouted. She rolled eyes and then nodded her head toward the fo'c'sle. "She's been in a bad mood all day." Turning back to us, she smiled and in her husky voice, asked, "Who'd like to help me with the iced tea?" Pam raised her hand.

"What can I do, Mrs. Fraser?" I asked.

"Well, for one thing, you can call me Mubs!" She laughed and then yelled, "Sara! Get out here, now!" Then, without taking a beat, she suggested, "Why don't you empty the ice trays into this bucket? . . . and you, sweetie," she said, addressing Gayle, "can pick the mint."

While we filled the tall glasses with tea, Mubs lined up the pewter cups and added a couple of ice cubes, simple syrup, and a generous shot of whiskey to each one. And with a dramatic flourish, brandished each cup

77

with a couple of mint leaves. "This is called a mint julep, girls." Taking a healthy sip, she added, "You'll love this when you're old enough to drink." We were just happy to have ice cubes.

"Well, look who's emerged from her lair!" Standing behind Mubs was a teenage girl with a round face just like her mother's. "Girls, this is my daughter, Sara."

Sara rubbed her eyes and yawned.

"If your majesty would care to join us . . ."

Sara stared at her mother, expressionless.

Pam, Gayle, and I stood there listening to their tête-à-tête, unsure where the conversation was heading, when Sara threw back her head and laughed.

"Hey guys, want me to show you around?"

"I need everyone's help first. Then you're free to give the girls a tour." Mubs handed Pam and me each a tray of drinks while she retrieved a plate of foie gras and caviar and another with several kinds of cheese and crackers for Sara and Gayle to carry up to the cockpit.

As soon as we deposited the food and drinks, we followed Sara down the companionway. Opening the door to her stateroom, which was the size of our main cabin, I noticed there was a spacious double bunk, two bookshelves, and even a small desk. The forward hatch was open, sending a pleasant breeze through the room. "When we get farther south, of course, we'll put on air conditioning," Sara said. My sisters and I looked at each other in disbelief.

As we moved back toward the main cabin, Sara showed us her head, which had an automatic toilet, full-sized sink, and shower.

Passing by a closed door on the way to her parents' stateroom, she rolled her eyes. "That's our deckhand Mike's room. . . ."

"Where is he?" I asked.

"It's his day off."

After checking out Mubs's and Max's room, we made our way back to the cockpit. Mubs raised her glass and said, "Here's to meeting four lovely girls."

"Be careful with the compliments," my father warned. "After all, we don't want them getting big heads." Fat chance, I thought.

"The Frasers are from Tiburon," my father emphasized. Tiburon was in Marin, the wealthiest county across the Bay from San Francisco, where rock stars and celebrities lived, our cue that any future comparison would be pointless.

Mr. Fraser, we learned, had retired after selling his furniture business. Cashing in on a lifelong dream to sail to South America and on to the South Pacific, he'd sold their home and purchased *Mamusah*, a gleaming, beamy, fifty-two-foot, double-ended ketch equipped with two powerful, top-of-the-line, Westerbeke engines and the latest in luxuries. *Heritage* would have the pleasure of *Mamusah*'s company before her departure across the Pacific. I looked forward to spending time with someone other than my sisters as our families traveled down the coast.

Things were looking up.

At dawn on May 8th, armed with a walkie-talkie Max had generously supplied, *Heritage* set sail with *Mamusah* toward Isla de San Martín, eighty miles south. With the engine at full throttle and genoa raised, we kept up with *Mamusah*'s double engines, hugging her stern like a pilot fish.

Unlike the rocky Coronados, San Martín spread out in front of us looking like, as Pam observed, "a flat pancake topped with a dollop of whipped cream." I told her it looked more like "a saggy, old-lady breast," with its nippled, solitary mound rising from the barren landscape.

"What is wrong with you?" she said.

I just laughed and shrugged.

Determined not to lose sight of them in the fading light, my father steered as close as he could to *Mamusah*, but just as darkness descended, her stern light went out. Panicking, he grabbed the walkie-talkie. "*Mamusah, Mamusah*, this is *Heritage*! Do you read me? Your stern light's gone! We're crawling up your back!"

"Cut the engine!" he ordered.

I reached over to the binnacle stand and turned the key.

With the engine off, my father ordered me forward to listen for the sound of *Mamusah*'s engines. But Max had heard my father's frantic call and calmly jerry-rigged a flashlight to his stern. In my father's letter to

a friend back in California, he presented himself as a quick-thinking
seaman:

> *While holding course, I made immediate radio contact with Mamusah
> to alert them. A flashlight lashed to their stern pulpit made me breathe
> easier, and shortly thereafter, I dropped the hook in the island's lee.*

Relieved to have *Mamusah* back in our sights, we followed them to
Hassler Cove, a small hook-shaped anchorage on the eastern side of Isla
San Martín. Still jumpy from losing *Mamusah* earlier, my father assigned
each of us to a night watch.

Nothing more than an open roadstead, the cove offered little protection as we pitched and rolled all night. In the morning, having barely
slept, my father brought the boat a little closer to shore, hoping to ease
the rolling. *Mamusah*, with her shallower and more stable draft, remained
at the gravel bar as her crew slept soundly.

Once we reanchored in calmer waters, Pam and Gayle asked permission to take the dinghy and go ashore. My father reluctantly consented
and helped them unlash the dinghy from the cabin top and lower it into
the water.

"You can come with us," Pam said, unenthusiastically.

"Not interested," I said, feigning indifference, to cover my anger
over her disinterest. With only a hundred miles under our belts, we were
already sick of one other.

With Gayle positioned in the stern, my father handed down the oars
while Pam held onto the rail to steady the dinghy. "Remember, turn the
boat stern-to before you get into the surf line and row straight into the
beach. If you get turned sideways, you'll broach the dinghy, and you'll end
up in the water." Pam nodded and pushed off.

For half an hour, they ran along the beach, bending down and gathering items, and then depositing them into the dinghy. Watching from
the boat, I regretted not joining them. What if they were finding beautiful shells or sand dollars or sea glass?

Deciding that half an hour was too long to have a good time, my
father blasted the air horn. Pam waved, pushed the dinghy into the water,

and held it as Gayle attempted to climb in. The next thing we knew, Gayle was rowing toward the boat, leaving Pam stranded and jumping up and down on the shore.

"Goddammit," my father muttered. "I leave you kids on your own for one second and look what happens." I stared at him, resentful his comment included me.

As Gayle approached, my father said, "Why the hell did you leave your sister on shore?"

She looked at him with a tear-stained face. I could see she was soaking wet. "The . . . the wave just came, and . . . and Pam didn't get in. I was afraid to go back."

"Get out," my father said. She gathered up the abalone shells she and Pam had found and climbed aboard.

With a cigarette clamped between his lips, he set off in the dinghy toward Pam, who hadn't stopped waving her arms as she ran back and forth on the beach. I watched him as he surfed into shore where she was still hopping like a mad toad. She's probably afraid we're going to leave her, I thought. Serves her right. But then, when I imagined what she must have felt watching Gayle row away, I figured I'd be hopping mad, too.

I could hear my father swear and shout at her as she stood wavering, knee deep in the waves. Finally, she hopped into the stern. By the time they returned, they were both soaked.

"That's the end of your dinghy landings for a while," my father announced, as water cascaded out of his khaki trousers and onto the deck. "Let's get going or *Mamusah* will leave without us."

"Can I at least get into something dry?" Pam complained, pulling at her soggy clothes.

"After we're underway." He turned on the engine and brought the bow forward while Pam and I took turns at the windlass.

"I'm freezing," Pam said, as she helped me guide the dripping chain into the anchor locker.

"Yeah. But look how wet we got," I said. "It would've been for nothing if you'd changed before this. God, I wish we had an electric windlass like *Mamusah*." We'd learned earlier everything on the Fraser's yacht was electric. No manual bilge pumps or windlasses for them, no siree!

"I bet Sara just sits in her cozy cabin," Pam said.

None of us could believe Sara had the forward half all to herself and only had to share the head with Mike. On *Heritage*, six of us shared one tiny head. Since we'd always used the bathroom facilities the California marinas provided, it wasn't until we headed south of the border that we discovered the limitations to our onboard facilities. With barely enough room to perch on the toilet without ramming our knees into the door, and the possibility of asphyxiation from the doll-sized, stainless-steel sink dispensing foul-smelling water and the sulfurous cloud enveloping us every time we pumped the toilet, we avoided the head as much as possible. Using it only when dire bodily functions demanded, we'd resorted to a sturdy canvas bucket emptied over the stern and cleaned with seawater.

"Mike does all the work anyway," I said, wishing my father had hired a deckhand for our trip. Unlike the spacious *Mamusah*, there wasn't space for another body in our boat's cramped cabin. What had been enough room when we first built *Heritage* was now less than adequate for two adults, three teenagers, and a preschooler. I had to accept the fact that we were the only deckhands *Heritage* would ever have.

Leaning over with the boat hook, I pulled up the anchor and laid it on the deck. With the anchor secured and *Mamusah* in sight, we made our way back to the cockpit.

"Did you see all the abalone shells we picked up?" Pam said.

"They're beautiful," I said, and then, suddenly overcome with jealousy, asked, "Are you guys keeping all of them to yourselves?"

"Don't be stupid. Of course, you can have one."

Back in the cockpit, Pam and I discovered two abalone shells propped against the coaming. She looked around and asked, "Where are the rest?"

Gayle, feeling queasy, remained an uninterested party, but five-year-old Nancy looked up and innocently commented.

"They're gone."

"What do you mean, gone?"

"I gave them to the fishies."

"Oh, Gawd, no! You little squirt. Mom!"

My mother's head popped out from the cabin. "I'm sorry, dear," she said. "I turned my back for one second and by the time I turned around, she'd thrown most of them overboard."

Pam grabbed the last two shells. "I got wet for nothing!" She stomped down the stairs and vanished into the cabin.

I called out after her.

"I guess this means I don't get to keep one?"

8

# A Wild and Hellish Ride

## *Cedros Island to Turtle Bay*

MAY 10–15, 1970

In a letter to his brother, my father described our leg to Turtle Bay:

> *We set a course for Cedros Island, seaward of Sacramento Reef, where the one hundred sixty-foot schooner Goodwill met her fate a year ago. By late afternoon, the wind picked up and continued throughout the night, with a following sea, making it difficult to steer.*

We followed *Mamusah* all morning. Toward late afternoon, Max radioed my father, suggesting they set a course close to shore and just east of the reef. But the idea of relying on *Mamusah*'s radar and the risk of losing contact during the night convinced my father we might end up on the rocks like the *Goodwill*, so he politely declined. Max sounded his air horn and waved, and *Mamusah* receded into the distance until she was a tiny dot on our stern.

As we headed west, I worried whether we'd made the right decision. Without radar, *Heritage* would have to rely on my father's skimpy navigational skills. Never having had the patience to complete the celestial navigation course he'd signed up for before the trip, our captain compiled a makeshift assemblage of old charts, compass readings, log line checking, and the occasional wild stab at guessing the current's speed. A slight miscalculation could easily veer us off course and cause us to sail past Cedros.

All afternoon we motored with the main, foresail, and staysail up. The shoreline had disappeared, leaving us alone with only the ocean for company. As the shadows lengthened and dusk approached, the wind shifted, and seas rose. By night, the wind whistled through the rigging as *Heritage* slammed into the waves. With only our dimly lit spreaders and starboard and port lights guiding us, I wondered if my father had second thoughts. I know I did. Sitting in the cockpit with my mother and sisters, *Heritage* pounded through a sea so vast and under a sky so starless, it was as if we were sailing the cosmos toward a yawning black hole.

Ordering me to take over the helm, my father descended into the cabin to use the head. But halfway down, he slipped and landed on the cabin floor.

Howling like a wounded animal, he shot back up the companionway. "There's goddamn water all over the place!"

The pounding seas had forced their way through the planking, filling the bilge until the floorboards lifted and separated. He'd landed on one of the rib's sharp edges and sliced his ankle.

We all sat there, unsure of what to do. My mother, Nancy, and Gayle (who was busy vomiting into a bucket cradled between her knees), made themselves as small as possible, huddling together on one side of the cockpit while Pam and I sat on the other side, directly in the line of fire.

"Goddammit, don't just sit there!" he said to Pam. "Get that hand pump out from underneath the quarter berth." Then, glaring at me, snapped, "Get the canvas bucket from the cockpit locker!" Shining the flashlight on his ankle, he cursed as we stared at the blood pouring from his wound. He looked up and roared, "Get a goddamn move on!" Stumbling over each other like blind mice, we scrambled to find the required equipment.

His moods, as unpredictable as the shape-shifting waves crashing around us, kept us on hyper-alert. We scurried into position. Wedged between the stairs, Pam crouched over the bilge and hand pumped into the canvas bucket. Once filled, she passed it brigade-style first to my mother, then to me to dump over the side. Hour after hour, with the engine at full throttle in mounting seas, we bailed.

Without warning, a loud pop, like a gunshot, reverberated from somewhere near the foremast.

"Christ, now what?" My father grabbed the flashlight, snapped himself to the lifeline, and hobbled as far as midships. Seconds later, he returned. "The forestay travel block snapped. Somebody, go up and pull that goddamn sail down before it gets dragged into the water!"

I knew he meant the "somebody" was me, so I hooked my harness onto the lifeline, and worked my way up the deck, gripping the rigging as the boat dropped in and out of the troughs. When I reached the bow, the sail was whipping back and forth, as useless as a bird's broken wing. I shouted to my father to release the sheet and then yanked hard on the halyard. The sail slid to a jumbled heap on the deck. With water cresting over the bow, it was too risky to open the hatch and stuff the sail down into the forepeak, so I lashed it to the stanchions. As I fought my way back to the cockpit, I wondered if every captain was as excitable as ours.

My father's palpable anxiety made it all but impossible to separate his role as father and captain, so early on we'd arrived at a reluctant but tacit agreement; while on board, he was not our father but the captain, and we were not family, but crew. Although I believed he had the better deal, I knew he alone was responsible for making the right decisions and for keeping us safe. Most important, it was up to him to reassure us everything was under control, even when it wasn't. So long as he lived up to his part of the bargain as captain, I could stand doing all the dirty work as crew. What I found inexcusable was when my father, buckling under pressure, revealed his own uncertainty and fear. I wanted to shout over the wind and waves what he said to us every time we were afraid, "Buck up! Look alive! And get a goddamn move on!"

Thoroughly soaked and shivering, I resumed my place in the bucket brigade until Pam stumbled up the stairs and pushed past my mother, yelling, "Fire!"

As smoke billowed through the quarter berth from the engine compartment, my father immediately reduced the engine's RPM.

"Out of the way!" he said as he pulled up the engine hatch. We crouched on the seats, averting our heads as the smell of burning oil and rubber hit our nostrils. "Take the helm," he said. He dropped and straddled the engine. A shower of sparks burst around him. Ripping off his prized beret, my father used it to beat them down. "Cut the engine!"

I lunged forward and turned the key.

With the engine off and a reefed mainsail, *Heritage* pitched and rolled in total darkness. My father was rapidly losing his struggle between repairing the damage and retching and was in no mood for conversation. "Get me the flashlight!" he said, sending all of us scrambling. My mother located it and pointed the beam directly in his face. "Not on me, fer Chrissake! Shine it over there!"

After he spliced and re-taped the damaged wires and restarted the engine, my father resumed his place at the helm. By this time, we'd sailed far enough west to clear the Sacramento Reef, so my father set a fresh course, heading southeast, and back toward shore. Now in following seas, *Heritage* stopped taking on water, and our bucket brigade ended. With the cabin floor still wet and slick from seawater and oil, we hunkered down in the cockpit and waited for the morning light.

Like a spectral ghost, dawn hovered on the dark horizon. The sun rose higher, and the golden outline of Cedros appeared. Jutting up some thousand feet from the ocean, the island peered down on us like a sentinel as we passed, leeward, under its shadow. Transfixed by its sheer size, we stared in wonderment, unaware of what was approaching from the stern.

Too late to do anything other than to point over my father's shoulder and croak, "What's that?" I stared at the approaching wall of water. Perplexed, my father turned around.

"Christ!" he yelled. "A pooping wave!" He revved the engine and spun the wheel hard to starboard, but it was too late. "Hold on!" he commanded. The wave crested, bore down, and flooded the stern, momentarily lifting us off our seats.

With the stern weighed down with water and the prow pointing upward, I wondered if this was it. Is this our *Goodwill* moment? Are we going down without a trace? Will my tombstone read "death by pooping wave"?

Then, like a drowning victim clawing to the surface and gasping for air, *Heritage* righted herself, pushing hundreds of gallons of seawater through her scuppers and over her rails.

With only a few inches of water remaining in the cockpit, we stopped bailing and lay exhausted on the cabin top, splayed side by side, warming ourselves in the morning sun, while my father, equally spent, manned the helm.

At the end of his letter to my uncle, my father made light of our hellish night:

> *After a wild ride all night, the crew grabbed forty winks while I took her down the thirty odd miles of protected water into Turtle Bay.*

As *Heritage* motored along, the steep cliffs eventually gave way to low-lying hills and a light, steady breeze blew. My father cut the engine, ordering us off our comfortable cabin-top spot to raise the sails. He brought the boat into the wind as we readied ourselves. For only the second time, we were relying solely on sail power.

"Let's get that foresail up. Now unreef the mainsail. Pull, damn it! There you go. Now, cleat her off. Okay, now it's the jib and staysail!" he sang, as we three raced bow-to-stern, pulling halyards, raising canvas, and cleating sheets. What my father liked more than having the sails up, I decided, was barking out orders. "Let's get that tops'l up, too!" he shouted heartily, as if we were sailors on a nineteenth-century whaling ship.

Over canvassed, *Heritage* heeled so far to one side, her lee deck was awash. To avoid sliding overboard, Pam and I clung to the mainmast. Drunk on the sheer thrill of captaining his boat and free from seasickness, my father was oblivious to our distress until he heard our screams.

Safely back in the cockpit, I observed my father's unabashed pleasure as *Heritage* raced toward Turtle Bay. As he leaned back at the helm, propping up his now cleaned and bandaged ankle and enjoying a long drag on his cigarette, it occurred to me he was living his dream. It was as if he'd finally found what he'd been looking for all those years ago when I had watched him staring out the living room window.

Leaving my father at the helm and my sisters and mother in the cockpit, I made my way forward to the bow. Peeling off my float coat and turtleneck, I looked down at my long underwear, gray from use, with the assurance that as we traveled farther south, it too would be shed. I leaned back against the forward hatch and basked in the warm breeze, inhaling the pungent smell of baked earth. I loved the fact I could smell the land better from the ocean than from shore. The rich smell of earth and salty sea air made me feel a part of the world and, for a moment, my loneliness disappeared.

Connected to the sea, earth, and sky, years of suffering at the hands of elementary and junior high school bullies faded with each exhale. And with each inhale, the anger lessened toward my parents. Sorely lacking in parental skills, they'd simply passed the poor advice they'd received from their parents on to me.

"Fight back!" my father said.

"Run?" my mother suggested.

Neither suggestion seemed worthy of implementing. Instead, I'd resigned myself to the fact I'd never fit in. While I could have avoided some of the torture in junior high by replacing my Soviet-style jumpers for pretty A-line dresses and my waist-length, Pippi Longstocking braids for a cute bob, my stubbornness cost me; I spent seventh, eighth, and ninth grade friendless and alone.

I ran my fingers through my now short, fashionable shag. My long-haired years had ended abruptly after salt spray, wind, and seasickness turned my tresses into a rat's nest. After my mother failed to untangle the knots, she brought me to a salon, where the stylist cut it all off and gave me "the latest look." I remembered leaving the salon and wondering how one hairstyle, like my shag, could elicit such approval, while another, like the braids I wore in junior high, elicit such hatred.

As we rounded Point Eugenia and sailed into Turtle Bay, I reached into my back pocket for the harmonica Anne had given me. As I cupped my hands around it and blew, searching for the same notes I'd strummed on my much-maligned guitar rendition of "Leaving on a Jet Plane," a chorus of chattering voices joined me. I leaned over the railing to see six dolphins, with their sleek gray bodies and glistening backs, surfing the bow wake. I pressed the harmonica to my lips again and blew. Instantly, my companions lifted their pointed bills, clicking and whistling.

By now, my mother and sisters made their way up the deck. Just when they reached the bow, all six dolphins leaped out of the water. "Keep playing!" Pam and Gayle said. I cupped my hands and blew. Vindication was mine.

Turtle Bay, a mere three hundred miles south of Ensenada, was distinctly different. Gone were the cacti and sagebrush, replaced by a barren, sienna-colored still life of hardened, cracked earth and air that was crisp and dry. Yet, for all its brittleness, the landscape was bustling with vitality. Like Monterey, Turtle Bay was a cannery town. But instead of sardines, abalones reigned here, evidenced by the smashed shells piled high along the beach. Near the water's edge, hundreds of black seals barked and jockeyed for space on the crowded shore. Circling above them, thousands of birds—seagulls, pelicans, and cormorants, along with many others with names I didn't know—squawked and cried.

*Mamusah* had arrived hours earlier, and by the time we'd finished topping off our tanks at Gordo's floating gas station, Max had already scouted out the town and made friends with the entire population. My father and Max couldn't have been more different in personality and temperament.

Looking every inch the gentleman yachtsman in his white shorts, white polo shirt, white boating shoes, topped off by a black captain's hat, Max's manner complemented his clothes. He was as calm as my father was excitable, as cheerful as my father was somber. Just as Joe Eklund, Mr. Soule, and Mr. Thompson had, Max brought levity to our lives.

After completing our regular in-port chores—scrubbing the decks, pumping the bilge, airing the bedding, assisting my father—my sisters and I spent as much time as possible on shore near the Frasers, especially Max, who seemed to draw people and adventure to him as naturally as breathing.

Ashore, with his portable stool and watercolors, Max would find a spot, sit down, and sketch a scene, as a crowd of admirers gathered around him. While he painted, he tried out his Spanish, and, unlike my father, was not afraid to make mistakes, sometimes causing the village children to clutch their sides in laughter. Max often joined in, laughing the loudest, which made me appreciate him even more; humorous self-deprecation was a rare commodity in our family.

After handing out his paintings to his young fans one afternoon, Max, along with Sara, invited us for lunch at one of the local restaurants. When we finished, Max called to the waiter. Smiling and gesturing toward his empty plate, he said, "*Mi complementos para el cochino.*"

The waiter stood, staring. Oblivious to the waiter's shocked reaction, Max turned to us and explained with a satisfied wink, "I just complimented the chef on this delicious lunch."

"*Cochino es . . .*" The waiter made squealing sounds.

Max looked confused. The waiter continued to squeal, which made us erupt in laughter. He then pointed toward the kitchen. "*Cocinero!*"

"Uh oh," Max said. He'd thanked the *pig* for making our lunch. Everyone laughed, including the chef. Max stood up, cap in hand, and with a sweeping bow said, "*Lo siento, señor, complementos para el cocinero!*"

It was here at Turtle Bay, when onboard and alone one afternoon, I spied Pam's letter to her high school friend, Cindy, lying on the table not yet sealed. Even though I knew I shouldn't read it, I carefully removed it from its envelope. Reading it, I realized how lonely she was; with only a two-year age difference, we should have been close, but my presence offered no solace.

I wondered if she resented the wake of disasters I'd left behind. My antics and delinquencies at high school had embarrassed her. When I entered Skyline as a sophomore, she was a senior, an honor student, a member of Spartan Club, and a volunteer in the school office answering phones. I thought about the day she received a call from the local precinct about two delinquent students detained in a holding cell.

Anne and I had spent the morning getting high and walking around the neighborhood when a patrol car surprised us. When Anne responded to the officer with a four-letter word and I compared him to a mud-loving farmyard animal, it resulted in a free paddy-wagon ride and a long afternoon locked in a holding cell.

While Anne had relaxed on the cell's hard metal bench waiting for her mother to bail her out, I'd wrung my hands, thinking about my father's reaction. I'm not sure Anne was ever punished, but I'd been slapped with a strict curfew, more boat work, and all of my sisters' chores. Added to that, my father decided my fashion aesthetic, like my attitude, needed an adjustment.

I'd worked all summer before entering high school sewing a Carnaby Street–worthy wardrobe, shedding my Julie Andrews's *Sound of Music* dirndls in favor of Jean Shrimpton and Twiggy peasant blouses and mini-skirts. This time, I didn't want to be different; I wanted to fit in. But when I descended in my favorite pinstriped miniskirt, white peasant blouse, navy tights, and clogs, my father ordered me right back upstairs.

"No more looking like a streetwalker," he said.

Wearing an ugly below-the-knee houndstooth wool skirt of my mother's, I sat hunched in the backseat, next to Pam, as my father sped to the bus stop and dropped us off. As soon as he was out of sight, I sprinted home and changed. I stuffed my mother's skirt in my book bag and walked to school. All day I thought about how miserable my life was and how I hated my father.

Somewhere between the bus ride home from school and turning onto our street, I decided that any life was better than the one I had. After the bus pulled away, I started walking north, making my way toward Berkeley. Three hours and seven miles later, I stood in front of Anne's older brother's college house.

At twenty-one, Niles seemed closer to my parents' age, and I worried he'd send me home, but feeling desperate, I mustered the courage and knocked on his door. Surprised to see me, he listened to what I'd done, then laughed and invited me in.

The next day, while he attended class, I filled the hours with the only thing I knew how to do: scrubbing and cleaning. When he returned home in the evening, I made myself scarce, killing time by wandering Telegraph Avenue. Slipping back in the house, I'd lay awake on the hard, living-room floor in a borrowed, stale-smelling sleeping bag. Lying there in the dark, I'd wonder if my parents and sisters missed me.

When Niles learned my parents filed a missing person report, he announced I had to leave. That afternoon, I trudged the seven miles back home. Walking through the back door, Pam glanced up and said, "Boy, are you going to get it!" And Gayle, who I noted was wearing my brand-new suede skirt and pumpkin-colored silk blouse, welcomed me back with, "Now I have to share the bedroom again."

"What do you want?" my father asked when he and my mother returned home from work that evening. He looked tired as he ran his hands through his hair.

"Just a couple of free hours," I said.

"What do you mean, free?"

"Not working on the boat."

"Anne's off limits," he said.

After spending ten days wandering aimlessly around Berkeley during the day and sleeping on Niles's hard floor at night, and cleaning up after three filthy college students, life on the lam had lost its appeal. For a few hours of freedom, I could give up Anne.

Unable to stem my unhappiness, I ran away again less than a month later, this time staying with another set of renegades close to where we lived. After five days of being dirty, tired, and lonely, though, all I wanted to do was go home, take a bath, sleep in my bed, and have my family talk to me again.

My desperate measures, however, yielded only negative results. I returned to a less forgiving household and a stricter school environment. Not only would I receive all Fs during my truancy, but for the entire semester. Informing me of this decision was my high school guidance counselor, Mr. Bianchi, a mean-spirited, diminutive man with tiny hands and a high-pitched giggle. "I suggest you sign up for typing class, young lady. You'll need it as a *secretary*. College material, you're not."

I hated that one more adult had decreed my future. I promised myself that by the end of the year, I'd exact revenge. My chance showed up sooner than expected when I discovered that Skyline was the last high school in the district to end the "no jeans for girls" policy. The next day, I promptly showed up to class wearing bell-bottom jeans. Just as quickly, my teacher sent me to the vice principal, who passed me on to Mr. Bianchi, who gleefully announced my suspension.

"Fine," I said. "But, for your information, it's not an ordinance or state law. I checked. So, if you suspend me, I'm going to sue the school for discrimination."

The next day, twenty girls arrived at school wearing jeans, and forty the next. Soon after, the school rescinded the "no jeans" policy for girls.

Mr. Bianchi, who shot me dirty looks as I passed him in the hallway, hated me more than ever. I was certain he was biding his time until he could, once again, prove my worthlessness. Meanwhile, as I celebrated my role as rebel and troublemaker, Pam suffered the embarrassment of being my sister.

I carefully folded Pam's letter and slipped it back in the envelope. I hated being a fuck-up, but I didn't know how to stop. No matter how hard I tried, I was always messing up. Even onboard, I couldn't resist creating a scene to prove my point. And then, when it backfired, I was angry and spiteful. Why couldn't I take the high road? Instead, I took the lowest of the low and pissed everyone off.

# 9

# The Fog Comes on Little Cat Feet

*Asunción Bay*

## MAY 15–18, 1970

We left Turtle Bay on a beautiful cloudless morning. Accompanied by a symphony of barking sea lions and the cries of a thousand gulls, and our steady surfing companions, we headed for our next port, Asunción Bay, fifty miles down the coast. My father was smiling and looked happy. Max's calm demeanor must have been rubbing off on him. My father hadn't dropped his bastardly ways, but we hoped that with his continuous exposure to Max, his anger, like our layers of clothing, would shed the farther south we traveled.

By noon, a bank of fog cut us off from *Mamusah*. Visibility was less than a foot as we sat together in the cockpit, barely able to see one another. With the engine at low throttle and gliding through a blanket of whiteness on a glassy sea, it created a dizzying sense of vertigo, making it difficult to discern if we were moving forward, backward, or sideways.

"One of you girls needs to get up to the bow," my father said. None of us moved. "One of you, get going!" he repeated. We all sat motionless, barely breathing, until Pam finally got up and slowly made her way up the deck.

No way was I going to risk falling in. I had no confidence that my father could find me in this pea-soup fog. I leaned over to my mother. "Just what does he think Pam is going to see?"

"If she falls in, Jim, I'll never forgive you," my mother said, in a jittery tone, obviously upset by what I'd said.

"Are you hooked on to the lifeline?" he called out to Pam. It was stupid for him to send her up there. I bet he couldn't even see the glow from the end of his cigarette.

"It's just that I hear something," my father said, as if to justify placing his eldest in harm's way. He throttled back to a bare idle.

"I don't hear anything," my mother said.

"Shhh. There it is, again," he said. We were now enveloped not only in whiteness but in an eerie silence as we all strained to hear something beyond the sound of the engine. "If only this goddamn fog would lift." He called out again to Pam, "You see anything?"

"I'm not sure, but it looks like there's a bright line of white ahead." Her disembodied voice made it all the stranger.

"Wait, there's another flash!"

I felt my father's hand grip my shoulder.

"Take the helm, while I go forward," he said.

I ran my hand along the coaming and thrust my arm out in front of me until I felt the wheel.

"I don't see anything," my father said to Pam.

"See that white line right ahead?"

"Where?"

"There!"

"Jesus Christ! Hard to starboard! Hard to starboard!"

I spun the wheel hard, jibing the mainsail. The boom swung to starboard, barely missing my father's head as he leapt back into the cockpit.

"Jim, what's that crashing noise?" my mother asked, gripping Nancy tightly.

Looking to our port, we could see what Pam saw. The flash was from cresting breakers and the noise my mother heard was the sound of heavy surf. For every twenty miles covered, the current had pushed us five miles closer to shore. A minute later, and we would have driven the boat right up onto the beach.

Within seconds of us veering away and getting back on course, *Mamusah* slipped up on our stern. The Frasers had set out a few hours after us, but when they tracked us on their radar, they ran their engines at full throttle to warn us.

Admitting to us that *Heritage* was ill-equipped for certain weather and his relief over *Mamusah*'s presence, my father used a less reverential tone, describing it to one of his boating friends:

> *We tagged along behind her like an obedient puppy, taking care not to get out of visual range. Nothing could be worse than having two boats in proximity charging about in dense fog and only one of them knowing where to go.*

Setting a course, which would take us safely inland of some offshore islands, we hugged *Mamusah*'s stern, worried we might lose her again. By afternoon, just as the fog lifted, we approached Asunción Bay. With the sun breaking through and the fog burning off, we found ourselves anchored near a cannery town like Turtle Bay, but less inviting. Near us, the only activity was from a small coastal freighter discharging its cargo into an amphibious craft, which trundled ashore like a fat duck to the gray, narrow strip of beach.

After we rowed ashore and purchased fresh bread from the village bakery, we were eager to move on, but the weather decided otherwise. The next morning, fog once again surrounded the boat like a funeral shroud and, unwilling to chance losing each other again, both my father and Max decided to wait until the weather improved.

For three days we hunkered down, waiting for the fog to lift. Pushed by thirty-five knot winds, the fog rolled down the hills like a silent avalanche and dumped its whiteness into the harbor. Once again, we donned heavy sweaters and float coats over our long underwear and turtlenecks to keep out the chilling cold that found its way through our clothing and down into our bones.

On the fourth day, my parents rowed ashore, leaving us four girls on board. Their justification was that as the town offered little in the way of attractions, it would be a quick trip to pick up a few supplies. Left to our own devices and alone for much longer than our parents had promised, we bickered, exchanging a few solid punches until we were all crying.

Finally, tired of pummeling one another, we called a truce and retreated to our separate bunks.

For a town that held so little appeal, my father seemed to have a good deal to write about:

*Lorraine and I and Mr. Fraser from* Mamusah *(traveling companion boat) went ashore this morning before the wind came up. As typical, the church is the social center for the town and occupies a prominent site. The priest, who is the only English-speaking person here, has been very helpful to us, directing us to the local bakery and telling us a bit about Asuncion.*

*As with Turtle Bay, the primary industry we were told is the government-controlled fish cannery, which the fishermen work as a cooperative rather than individually. While Turtle Bay's principal crop was abalone, Asuncion has not only that, but spiny lobster. The only other notable building is a government building for social health. They have contact with Ensenada by plane about twice a week. We are anchored next to a small freighter unloading foodstuffs and empty cans to be filled with abalone from the cannery.*

It was during this time of waiting that my father also wrote back to my grandfather's younger brother, my great-uncle Clarence. We'd received a letter from him and my great-aunt, Mae, when we reached Turtle Bay informing us of their Mexican vacation plans. They had deduced from my father's letters to my grandparents that *Heritage* would arrive in Mazatlán while they were there and wanted to confirm the dates. Whether my father felt meeting up with them might create another opportunity for criticism, or, even worse, the fear that in a moment of uncertainty he might reveal his own misgivings, he was elusive concerning our itinerary.

*Weather permitting, we depart tomorrow at dawn with two short hops to Magdalena Bay and then a two-day trip to Cabo San Lucas. Beyond that point, we have divided interests. On one hand, we would like to push south as fast as possible to get beyond the hurricane area (below Acapulco) by June 15th. The other choice is to go up to La Paz and fool around there until October, with relative protection from the high winds. In any case, we have to live each day for what it's worth. We are not experienced enough at this cruising thing to say we will be at such-and-such place by such-and-such time. If we can get together, we will attempt to do so.*

We all knew that he would do everything he could to avoid this rendez-vous, choosing to wait it out in some unknown cove or head north into the Sea of Cortez or even bypass Mazatlán altogether. He seemed to know that an encounter with his relatives, even my genial Uncle Clare, might shake his convictions. For my father, there was no turning back.

## 10

# Dancing in the Moonlight

### *Bahía Santa Maria and Magdalena Bay*

**MAY 19–23, 1970**

After four days in Asunción, the fog lifted, and *Heritage* headed for Abreojos Point. We had our walkie-talkies, plus *Mamusah*'s radar to keep us safe and on course. For the first few hours we traveled within sight of each other, but when the fog returned Max radioed, suggesting we change course for Magdalena Bay.

Reduced visibility slowed our progress and by early evening, with twenty miles to Magdalena Bay and ten more beyond that to the closest anchorage, both captains agreed to head to Bahía Santa Maria.

Arriving as the light was fading, none of us felt like lifting the dinghy off the cabin top and rowing to shore just to stand on solid ground for a few minutes. But as soon as *Mamusah* anchored, Max was in his Boston Whaler and heading for shore.

As we prepared to dine that night on yet another meal of canned ham and beans, Max called out to us from his Whaler. My father slid out from the settee and climbed up the companionway. We leaned forward in our seats straining to catch their conversation but could only hear my father's exclamations of "What a surprise! They're huge. Thanks again!" and then the sound of the Whaler pulling away.

"Girls! Look what Max brought us."

We scrambled up the stairs and found my father grinning and holding up a bucket filled with *langosta*. Max had traded a seventy-five-cent box of gun shells to a local fisherman, who in return had plucked twelve of the biggest ones from his day's catch. Max generously gave us six.

"Tell your mother to put away the beans and ham and look for a big pot," my father ordered, and then changing his mind said, "Never mind, I'll tell her myself." While he was below with my mother, we four sat next to the lively crustaceans.

Although it was Pam who took the lobsters out and placed them on deck, I made the mistake of laughing at Nancy, who shrieked and scrambled along on all fours while they scuttled after her. My father popped up just in time to catch me and assumed I was the culprit. Some twisted code of ethics I'd made up and adhered to since elementary school prevented me from ratting out Pam even though I wanted to. So, I stood there and said nothing as my father threatened to send me to my bunk without dinner. It was only when the cook requested the spiny runaways that my father shifted his attention away from me and toward his stomach.

A little before noon the next day, we weighed anchor and motored out of Bahía Santa Maria. Hoping to glimpse any stray California gray whales who had not yet migrated north, I made my way to the bow with the binoculars and wedged myself between the cabin and forward hatch. We'd missed the chance to see them after bypassing Scammon's Lagoon, their calving grounds. And even though most of the massive cetaceans arrived by January and departed by April, there were sightings from traveling yachts as late as May. I was envious Pam and Gayle had witnessed whales breach close to *Heritage* on their leg to San Diego, and I wanted my chance.

All afternoon I searched for them, but none appeared. To temper my disappointment, my favorite marine friends showed up. This time, instead of surfing the bow as they had in Turtle Bay, they played leapfrog at our midships. Shooting out of the water in ten-foot-high arcs, they cartwheeled, spun, and somersaulted over one another.

We were now 615 miles south of San Diego and over two-thirds of the way down Baja's coast. The wind was on our quarter as we sailed wing and wing toward Magdalena Bay. Things were looking up—blue skies, steady winds, and smooth sailing.

In a surprising move, considering my mother had spent most of the trip consigned to galley duty, she boldly assumed the helm. Unlike me, who had my father's height and build, my mother was petite and slight. With her feet dangling six inches above the cockpit floor and her small hands gripping the wheel, she looked like a little kid as she steered *Heritage* past Punta Entrada and into the Magdalena Bay.

Unfortunately, my mother's successful captaining would not last. Within minutes of entering the Bay, she accidentally jibed, and the boom snapped all the way from port to starboard, nearly splitting my father's head open like a ripe cantaloupe.

"Goddammit, Lorraine! You almost killed me!"

"I . . . I . . . I didn't mean to, dear," my mother said. Flustered, she took her hands off the wheel and froze.

"Don't let go of the damn wheel, fer Chrissake!"

"I don't know what to do! Someone, please take the wheel," my mother said, looking as if she wished she'd never mustered the courage to sit there in the first place. Like one of those sea turtles I was on the lookout for, I could see her sink into her shell and retreat to safety.

"Jesus, can't you feel when the wind is on your back, and when it shifts?" my father asked. Silence. My mother had completely retreated. "One of you girls take over," he said.

Gayle, who had glued herself over the stern rail even though the waters had calmed to a ripple, was, by default, exempt. And I guess Pam figured I could out-stare her, because she sighed, threw her leg over the seat, and grabbed the wheel. Free of helm duty, I skipped up to the bow to avoid possible injury the next time the boom snapped.

Too late to take on fuel at the naval dock in Puerto Cortez, where there were no viable anchorages to spend the night, we dropped hook off of Puerto Alcatraz, a tiny fishing village located a few miles north of Cortez.

With my father and Max onshore, the crew on *Heritage* relaxed, and with drinks in hand enjoyed the approaching sunset. It was rare to be in proximity to each other without sniping or taking one another to task over some imagined infraction, and rarer still, to enjoy a few moments free from the tyranny of tension.

"Look, I bet they're going out to chase drug runners," I said, as three Mexican Navy cutters steamed past on their way out to the Pacific. "Check out the size of those guns on the foredeck. That'd blow one hell of a hole in the side of a boat."

"Well, didya ever think that maybe those druggies might deserve it?" Pam said. "They are breaking the law, after all."

"Yeah, but they think every *gringo* on a boat is suspect. That includes us," I said.

"As if they're going to go after a boat like ours. . . ."

"Exactly," I replied. Surprised by my shift in sentiment, Pam eyed me suspiciously. I sat back and smiled, confident my joint-filled bag hidden among my underpants would remain safe from the Mexican Navy's prying eyes.

Flanked on each side, the lead cutter powered ahead, in V formation, against a sky streaked with pinks, oranges, and purples. As their bows cut through the bay, disturbing the smooth, reflected surface with their wakes, a kaleidoscope of colors rippled out toward us. Transfixed, we didn't hear the ruckus taking place on shore until Pam said, "Oh, Gawd."

"What?" I said.

"It's Dad."

We all looked over and watched as two figures on the beach turned over a dinghy filled with water.

"Bet he didn't see the waves coming in from the cutters, and he broached the boat." I stifled a laugh, imagining his surprise when the wave slammed him from the back and drenched him. "I wonder if Max got wet, or just Dad."

"That means he'll be in a bad mood when he gets back to the boat," Gayle said.

"No shit, Sherlock."

"Shut up."

"Fuck off."

"Mom!"

"All right, girls, that's enough." My mother narrowed her eyes at me. "I get enough swearing from your father."

I'd been "swearing like a sailor" since middle school and wasn't about to stop now. If my father expected me to shoulder a man's job, then I could damn well swear like one. She should thank her lucky stars that none of us smoked, I thought. The way my father lit one cigarette after another, it was amazing we didn't suffer from respiratory failure. They didn't call them coffin nails for nothing.

If my mother thought that my father was going to be the only one getting away with bad behavior, she was in for a surprise. Fuck him and his cigarettes, fuck my mother and her indignation, fuck Gayle and Pam for not liking me, and fuck Nancy for being a happy-go-lucky five-year-old.

After dropping Max off, my father rowed over to *Heritage*. "Why didn't you warn me about those goddamn ships going past?" he said. He was soaked from head to toe.

"Sorry," we all said in unison. Like he would have heard us all the way from the boat, I thought. Who was he kidding?

"Sorry doesn't cut it."

As he heaved himself aboard, he threw the painter at us. My sisters and I lunged for the line, falling over one another, and knocking heads like the Three Stooges, as we grabbed it and pulled the dinghy toward the stern to tie off. Worried what he'd say next, we remained rooted near the stern. He turned to my mother and asked brightly, "What's for dinner?"

"It'll be ready in a jiffy!" my mother said, lying. "How about you girls come below to help me put it on the table?" Taking the hint, we tumbled down the companionway, glad for once to help the cook and leave the captain alone to smoke and ruminate.

After dinner, in dry clothes, with a full belly and an after-dinner smoke, my father relaxed in the cockpit. Enjoying the night air, he told us he and Max had walked to the cannery, where they let him use their phone to call the Naval Base on Puerto Cortez. Both boats would leave the next morning to take on fuel and go ashore for supplies.

The next morning, after leaving Alcatraz and fueling in Cortez, *Heritage* followed *Mamusah* to Magdalena Bay's entrance. Just before passing

Punta Entrada, the fuel line broke on the ever-crappy Starrett, forcing our return. Radioing Max, my father told him to continue without us, confident that with a forecast of good weather, *Heritage* could handle the leg by herself.

After my father spent a few hours installing a new fuel line, we weighed anchor and motored out for the second time. With the sun directly overhead, the bay flashed silver as teeming schools of mackerel broke its surface. Alongside our midships, a pod of dolphins accompanied us out of the bay, the same ones I wanted to believe, that had welcomed us on our arrival.

We soon headed into the Pacific swells for our last Baja leg. Another 180 miles and we'd be in Cabo San Lucas, where my father promised we'd be shedding our long underwear once and for all.

That night I drew the short straw for the dreaded midnight-to-two watch. The wind always seemed to kick up at that hour, requiring the individual on watch to constantly adjust the sails. It was difficult to rack up quality sleep in the hours before midnight, so whoever drew that watch started out tired. On this night, however, with the help of a full moon, the Milky Way, and a light breeze, I sat behind the wheel with minimum effort and just enjoyed the expanse of ocean and beautiful starlit night.

Avoiding the shoal that extended from Cabo Tosco to Punta Lobos, ninety miles south, I steered *Heritage* well to seaward. It was the first time the outlines of the distant hills and the sharp peaks of the Sierra de la Laguna were no longer visible.

The night's tranquility ended, however, when squadrons of flying fish shot out of the waves and soared over the cockpit before diving, one after another kamikaze style, back in on the other side. The solitude I'd reveled in moments before was no longer important. I now had the best seat in town and no one to share it with.

As if my father was listening from below, he popped up from his quarter berth near the cabin stairs. "Couldn't sleep," he said, brusquely. "Thought I'd join you. It's a nice night."

I was so glad to have company I didn't comment when he reached into his shirt pocket, shook a cigarette out of the pack, and lit it. Under ordinary circumstances, I'd have made a smart-ass remark about the fact he even slept with them, but I clamped my mouth shut. It was nice that he was sitting with me, sharing the night.

"Look at that sky, will you?" he said, stabbing his finger skyward. We both looked up, transfixed by the Milky Way when a single fish, whirring like some extraterrestrial insect, failed to clear the deck and instead, landed with a thud on my father's foot.

Spooked, he leapt off the seat. "What the hell?"

"Flying fish," I said, trying not to laugh. "They've been doing it all night. Only this one is a loser."

He picked up the fish by its tiny dragon-like wings and cradled it in his palm, before leaning over and gently dropping it in the water.

I looked at my father as he settled back on the cockpit seat and, for a moment, wondered why I couldn't be more like that stupid fish, so he'd handle me as gently and as tenderly. Did I have to sprout wings before that happened?

"Sometimes the sea looks more alive at night. Don't you think, Sport?" He took a long drag on his cigarette.

My father hadn't called me by my nickname since leaving San Francisco. I felt a lump form in my throat. Afraid I might start bawling, I grunted in agreement.

I'd never learned how to engage in an actual conversation with him, even when he initiated it. If I didn't pick up the ball right away, he got self-conscious and clammed up. The result was like what always happened to the Starrett—with the key turned, the engine would roar to life, only to sputter and die in less than a minute.

I thought about how it had always been that way, or at least as far back as the day he returned from Enewetak.

\* \* \*

1960. Travis Air Force Base. Dressed in our Sunday best, my sisters and I watched the transport plane carrying my father land and taxi to a stop. He'd been gone for eighteen months. I was now seven and finishing first grade.

"Where's Daddy?" my younger sister Gayle said. She was only four and the baby in the family.

I looked at my mother, who was looking at the men getting off the plane. She kept smoothing her dress with her hands. Up and down they fluttered like two little birds.

"Daddy! Daddy! Daddy!" Gayle jumped up and down.

"Hush," my mother snapped. Gayle started bawling. Pam and I grew quiet. We weren't used to her losing her temper.

My mother lifted Gayle up and wiped my sister's tear-stained face with her handkerchief. Then she gave her a kiss and said, "Let's see if we can find Daddy!" She looked down at me and my older sister, Pam, and mouthed, "Sorry, girls." Her smile reassured both of us that everything was okay.

"There he is!" Pam said.

"Where?" My mother scanned the line of men. All of them were carrying big, green duffel bags as they walked toward the terminal doors.

"With the flowered shirt," Pam replied.

"That's not him," I said.

"It's Dad!" Pam insisted.

"No, it wasn't." I was excited to see my father but anxious about the change his return would bring. We'd gotten used to him being gone. Before he left, he and my mother argued. Would everything be okay, or would he leave us again? If he stayed, what was going to happen? Already things were different: Grandma had moved back to the Palace Motel, my mother had yelled at us, and my sisters and I had fought all the way to the base.

"Excuse me, ma'am?" A sandy-haired man in uniform walked up to my mother. "Your husband on the Enewetak list?"

"Yes, he is."

"His debriefing's gonna take a while. How'd you and your girls like to wait inside, seeing it's mighty warm out here?"

After devouring handfuls of sour balls and candy corn and watching the minutes tick by on the wall clock, Pam poked me and pointed to a man wearing a short-sleeved flowered shirt and greenish-brown shorts. In a few quick strides, he was towering over us, and returning our stares with an awkward grin. He wore clear-framed glasses and had hair blonder than Gayle's. His skin was the color of my penny collection.

"Jim?"

"None other," the giant said, in a voice deep and unfamiliar. His face was rugged, with two sharp lines running along each side of his mouth that made him look mean, even when he smiled as he was doing now.

My mother disappeared into his embrace. When they separated, my father looked down, shifting his gaze among the three of us, as if trying to remember who we were. Gayle climbed off the chair, toddled over to him, and grabbed onto his leg. He bent down and picked her up, swinging her high in the air. Pam walked over and stood next to him. I slipped behind my mother.

"Go on, honey, give your father a hug." She pulled me out from behind her and pushed me toward him.

"No," I said.

My father looked at me, his eyes masked by the reflection on his glasses. "Aren't you glad to see me?"

"I guess so." I didn't want to tell him he looked different, a stranger.

"I don't know what's wrong with her. She was excited on the way here."

"She just needs to get used to me. Right, Sport?" he said, placing his large hand on my head. I squirmed out from underneath his grasp.

When we reached our family's weathered blue-and-white station wagon, my mother slid into the passenger seat and my father got in the driver's side and adjusted the seat, sliding it all the way back. He turned the engine on and stepped on the gas but stopped before exiting the parking lot. "I almost forgot," he said. He got out and walked around to the back of the wagon, where he had thrown his bag. When he returned, he was carrying three presents, which he handed to us before starting the car and heading out of the lot.

As we sped along, on our way home, Pam unwrapped hers first. It was a beautiful, black-lacquered music box inlaid with mother-of-pearl. When she opened the lid, a strange and lilting melody filled the air. Then Gayle tore at her wrapping, pulling out a straw monkey with black button eyes and bright red lips, and cradled it in her arms.

"Open yours!" they both said.

I stared at my present, trying to guess what my father had picked out for me. It had to be even better than a music box or a monkey. I opened it, and as I pulled back the tissue paper, I blinked back tears.

"What did you get?" Pam asked, leaning over Gayle to catch a glimpse. I lifted my present out of the box and held it in my hands. "Ooohh, a tiny guitar," she said.

"It's called a ukulele," my father said.

I looked down at my gift. "I don't know how to play this."

"It's easy. Run your fingers across the strings where the hole is."

I brushed my fingers over the strings. Pam made a face and clapped her hands over her ears. Gayle copied her.

My mother turned around and smiled at me. "Don't worry, dear. With the strings tuned and a little bit of practice, I'm sure it'll sound great."

I hated them. But most of all, I hated him. Why did he choose this for me? While Pam hummed along to music and Gayle bounced the red-lipped monkey on her knee, I stared at a present that required work. Unlike my sisters' gifts, its enjoyment would have to be earned.

* * *

Whether by design or happenstance, the universe, bearing witness to our discomfort, bridged the silence between my father and me by offering communion in the form of a magnificent fish. Like a Shakespearean actor commanding center stage, it rose out of the phosphorescence, not more than twenty feet from the port stern. The full moon, functioning as the perfect key light, shone on the evening's star performer, who shocked his audience of two by skipping backward over the top of the waves on his splendid, regal tail before plunging back into the black water.

Resurfacing, with its great silvery fin spreading wide and undulating, the fish danced full circle in the moonlight before descending again into the pulsating foam. As if only stopping to catch a watery breath, it rose out of the waves a third time and shot straight into the air, twirling twice before diving and disappearing.

My father and I looked at each other without speaking. There was nothing to say. We had shared the unimaginable. We sat in silence for what seemed like an eternity, before he said, "Think I'll go back down and catch forty winks." With that, he disappeared down below.

Alone again, I thought about the marlin. Not tonight's magnificent fish, but one I'd witnessed when I was thirteen. My father had taken me, along with my grandfather and great uncle, on a sportfishing trip to the Sea of Cortez. Meant as a birthday celebration for my grandfather, bad weather and an aborted plane landing threatened a premature departure. But on the last day the weather cleared, and we headed out in the gulf. All day long, the boat trolled in choppy waters as my father, grandfather, and great uncle set and reset their rods. After a long, hot, unsuccessful day, the boat was heading back to shore when my father's line caught and began to run. As the captain throttled down, careful not to lose tension on the line, my father worked his rod against the pull of the great fish. The tighter the line, the more valiantly the fish fought. Time and again, I witnessed the marlin rise out of the water and plunge back in as my father played the line, first reeling in, then releasing, then reeling in, until, at last, the great fish must have realized that with each leap, it was being pulled closer to its death.

Back on shore, I snapped a photo of my father standing proudly beside the lifeless marlin. Although he was smiling, he also looked self-conscious, as if he'd realized that what had brought him joy, he'd destroyed.

I wondered if tonight's performance had touched my father's soul as it had mine. Had he recognized the universe's divine spark not only in the fish but in himself? Whether or not he believed in God was up for debate, but what I was sure of was he didn't think much of religion. I'd heard stories how in high school, he stopped going to church after a Benedictine brother beat the crap out of him and justified it as a divine directive.

For me, religion carried its own burdens. I'd watched how my grandparents had treated my father. With their brittle love and harsh judgment, there was no room for grace and acceptance. If being devout meant being like them, I wanted no part of it.

What I'd experienced on this night, though, seemed as far from their world as anything I'd ever felt. In all the summers spent at their house, I'd never witnessed the joyous celebration of life displayed by this princely fish. If *this* was God talking, then I wanted to believe. I longed to feel that joy. I wanted to dance on my tail in the moonlight.

# 11

# A Bump in the Night

## *Cabo San Lucas*

**MAY 24–31, 1970**

In the predawn hours, *Heritage* set an easterly course back toward shore. By standing off to sea, we'd avoided the dangerous shoals south of Punta Coneja, but now had to head inland to steer clear of the San Jaime and Golden Gate banks.

With the main and foresail raised and engine running, we reached the coast in time to witness dawn breaking over the Laguna Sierra range, flooding its eastern peaks in a cascade of rich, velvety purples, before spilling over the coastal bluffs in a pastel wash of lavender and rose. Then the blazing first rays of sun pierced the sky, gilding the sea and *Heritage's* sails in shimmering gold.

In her royal raiment, *Heritage* turned south, once again hugging the coastline. We'd crossed the Tropic of Cancer and were now officially in the tropics. In a little over fifty nautical miles, we'd reach our next port, Cabo San Lucas.

After fifteen hundred miles traveling down the coast, *Heritage* altered her southerly course to the east as she rounded Cabo Falso. The rocky fifty-foot-high bluff and southernmost point of the Baja California Peninsula marked a new transition. It was *hot*.

Raiding our drawers for shorts and T-shirts, the three of us relaxed on the foredeck, dangling our legs over the side, as *Heritage* edged closer to our destination.

In the distance, Cabo's quintessential picture-postcard formation of rocky islets, The Friars, jutted up from the sea. Slightly west, and built into the cliff, was the brand-new luxury hotel, La Finisterra, the latest hot spot for A-list celebrities. I looked up at the hotel and imagined I was one of its famous guests, like my favorite actors, Robert Redford and Faye Dunaway.

Acting was something I thought I might be good at, even though I could only lay claim to a single, sixth-grade performance playing Clara Barton's granny and a year of tenth-grade drama, where my teacher, Mr. Farnsworth, suggested I "look carefully at another career." What did he know? All he ever talked about were his glory days on the New York stage. If he was so great, why was he teaching high school drama in Oakland, California, three thousand miles away from Broadway? As far as I was concerned, he was just another in a long line of adults who'd made it their mission to remind me of my limitations.

Lost in plotting my Hollywood future, I barely noticed La Vigia, the triangular five-hundred-foot peak, which rose between La Finisterra's beach on the west side and the quickly approaching Friars.

"Look, there's the giant hole!" Gayle said. Near high tide, the Pacific swells crested over and through the bird-lined arch.

Rounding the islets, we sailed into Bahía San Lucas. Laid out in a perfect white crescent, with the northern end tucked behind The Friars and the southern end, open and wide, its crystal-clear bay and beautiful beach looked exactly how I'd imagined. My mother's bedtime stories were no longer stories; they were real.

If only Grandma could have seen this, I thought. Even though I'd outgrown my childhood desire for fighting pirates, I longed for my grandmother's comforting and steady gaze. With her, I'd always been good enough just the way I was. I never had to earn her love; it had been given freely, with no strings attached. I'd forced myself not to think or even talk about her since her death. But sometimes I wondered if I'd ever be able to make it on my own with no one to love me as she had. I had to believe that somewhere out there, she was still with me.

At least thirty boats were anchored close to shore, all flying flags from different countries. My father maneuvered around them, as I stood on the foredeck holding the sounding lead.

"Okay, what's your reading?" my father asked.

I threw the lead overboard. The line hung straight down. "I just payed out forty feet." As he moved forward, I pulled up the line, hand over hand, as fast as I could to ready myself for another reading. The water was so clear you could see schools of brightly colored fish and the sandy bottom, which appeared nearer than it actually was.

I threw the line over again. This time it hit the bottom just short of the thirty-foot mark. "Thirty feet!" I called out.

"Let me get a little closer!" he said.

"Y'all better anchor on the eastern side," a sunburned man drawled, as we passed close to his stern. "Too crowded here." Grumbling all the way, my father steered *Heritage* over to the less desirable eastern side, where the shelf precipitously dropped to a hundred fathoms. By following the man's friendly but assertive directive, we found ourselves about as far from the dock as you could get.

"I'll have to bring her in closer to shore before we drop anchor." He ordered Pam forward to check the surf line.

"What's your reading?" he said, as he inched *Heritage* toward shore. "And give it to me in fathoms, dammit."

Again and again, I swung the lead over. *Zip, zip, zip. Plunk.* "Five fathoms!" *Zip, zip, zip. Plunk.* "Four fathoms!" *Zip, zip, zip. Plunk.* "Three fathoms!"

My arms ached from hauling up the line. Pam yelled we were too close to the beach. I could feel the swells underneath *Heritage* and out of nowhere, that bongo surfing tune, "Wipe Out," popped into my head.

"Twelve feet . . . I mean, two fathoms!" I said, correcting myself.

"Drop anchor!" he said. Gayle heaved the anchor overboard, and I watched as it hit the sand and scattered a school of small, striped yellow-and-blue fish. For a moment I worried the anchor might trip and push us onto the beach, but my father reversed in time, and the anchor held.

To the outside world, my father was far more philosophical:

*We closed in, searching for a place to anchor. With some boats being here for weeks, it was only natural we got the less desirable area.*

No sooner had he turned off the engine, than two very tanned people rowed over. "Welcome to Cabo," the man said as he handed up a couple bottles of beer to my father. "Nice job anchoring."

My father, practically blushing, grinned like a kid and said, "Gee, thanks." And then, as an afterthought, added, "Guess I've got a good crew." How was it, I wondered, that it took a *stranger* to elicit a compliment from my father about us?

After the couple rowed away, my father sat back and sipped on his welcome gift and thought of his next move: instructing us on how to erect the cockpit awning. In his mind, I think he believed that by ordering, he was participating.

*Sail covers were put on to protect the Dacron from the tropical sun, and we rigged awnings for personal comfort, especially in the cockpit.*

In his letters, he always used the royal "we," rather than acknowledging who was actually performing the work—Pam, Gayle, and me. So, my sisters and I dug into the forward locker and hauled out the now mildewed sail covers and canvas awning that we'd spent many a night cutting, stitching, and sewing back on the living room floor in Oakland.

Drenched in sweat after unfurling it over the boom, snapping it into place, and securing it to the stanchions, we were told we were free to change into our swimsuits.

Ready to jump off the side, the three of us blanched when we looked into the clear water and watched as gigantic shadows glided underneath the keel. They weren't sharks, but they were a heck of a lot bigger than the tiny yellow-and-blue fish that darted around the anchor. Choosing safety over chance, we doused ourselves on deck using our canvas bucket.

In his letters, my father continued to present an idyllic, happy-go-lucky family life.

*Tomorrow morning, after clearing with the port captain and immigration, we are going to explore the little town here in Cabo. Afterwards, I promised Nancy we would have a picnic on the beach.*

Nancy got her picnic, but with the surf too rough, the sand too hot, and the sun too strong, they quickly returned, resorting as we had to dousing and cooling off with the trusty bucket.

Officially cleared, my father allowed us a few days off. We were now free to explore Cabo San Lucas and its beach, or read, or even study. Gayle and Pam dutifully cracked open their schoolbooks, Gayle burying herself in French and Pam working on her Spanish. As for me, I'd sent an S.O.S. to Sara, who, just as delinquent, promptly sped over in *Mamusah*'s Boston Whaler.

"Look what I brought," she whispered, a wide snaggle-toothed grin spreading across her freckled face. "Mike bought it off some French guy whose boat is on the other side of us," she said, as she showed me the joint. "He gave me some, so I wouldn't rat him out to my parents."

"Where're we gonna smoke that without getting caught?" I whispered back.

"Mom and Pop are busy entertaining, so they told me I could take the Whaler to shore."

Zipping around the flotilla of boats, Sara and I headed to a small strip of sparkling-white sand close to The Friars. Near low tide, with little surf, we easily landed the Whaler and dragged it out of the water, where we positioned it between the shore and ourselves, shielding our activity from prying eyes.

Sara fished around in her light-blue bag for her trusty neon-pink Bic lighter. After lighting the joint and taking a deep drag, she passed it to me.

"Good shit," I said after exhaling. We looked at each other, nodded solemnly, and then burst out laughing.

We sat there passing the joint back and forth while we shared a diatribe of teenage angst—constant boredom, forced schoolwork, the stupidity of grownups, and finally how good it felt to pull one over on everyone. Here we were, as high as kites, not more than a hundred yards from our families, and no one the wiser.

"Why are your eyes red?" Nancy asked, as I climbed aboard and plopped myself down in the cockpit seat beside her.

Her intense gaze made me scramble to come up with an answer. "Sara and I swam in the ocean and, uh . . . I got saltwater in my eyes." Sucking her thumb and clutching her Raggedy Ann doll, Nancy continued to stare. Suddenly paranoid, I blurted, "Think I'll go down and study for a while."

The next day my father and Pam left early to go into town to look for a new oil filter for the engine and investigate the Japanese truck garden all the yachters had been raving about. I had wanted to go but Pam had managed, not only as the eldest but as the family's interpreter, to leverage her position. The way my father viewed it, he wasn't going to piss off the only link between him and the locals. He was smart enough to realize he didn't have the patience to learn another language, and if his daughter could provide that amenity, he could afford to extend himself.

What should have been a reward for her language acumen, though, turned out otherwise. Upon their return, we learned it was "a walk-through-hell." After loading themselves down with two sacks filled with fruits, vegetables, and two huge watermelons, they trekked back, struggling in the wet, loose sand until deciding to search for solid ground. Hiking up to a ridge, they discovered a narrow animal path covered by thorny cacti that finally led them back to the dinghy.

When they climbed back on board, they were tired, bloody, and sunburned.

As my mother, Gayle, Nancy, and I finished one watermelon, we all agreed my father's and sister's suffering was worth every bite.

Around midnight, I suddenly jerked awake, banging my head on the bunk's ceiling. "Shit!"

"What the hell is going on?" my father said from the quarter berth.

"I guess I was dreaming," I said, rubbing my nose and forehead.

"Thanks for sharing," Pam said sarcastically.

"Yeah," Gayle chimed in.

"Get back to sleep, everyone," my father ordered.

I lay back down, feeling unsettled. "Something's wrong," I said. Rolling out of my bunk, I scrambled past my father and up the companionway to the cockpit.

Standing in the moonlight, I stared at the scene before me. "Dad!"

"What?"

"We've dragged anchor!"

He emerged just in time to hear cursing on our port. Standing on the deck of a massive luxury motor cruiser was a man wielding a boat hook. "Get your fuckin' engine running! You're gonna hit us!"

"We'll get her moving in a second," my father hollered back.

"You'd better," the man said, gouging our freeboard with the tip of his hook. "Do you know whose boat this is?"

"Does it matter?" my father asked, as he fended off *Heritage*.

"Damn right it does!"

"Whose boat is it?" I asked, unable to contain my curiosity.

"Jerry Lewis, that's who!" he crowed, as if my father and I were supposed to cower in fear of "The Nutty Professor."

"Well, since he's a comedian, tell'm, the joke's on him," I said.

"Look, you little asshole," he said.

"Call my daughter that again, and I'll take that boathook and ram it up your ass!" my father said. I shot him a grateful look before he turned to me and ordered, "Get forward, dammit, and raise that anchor!"

As I stumbled forward in the darkness, I could hear him yelling at Pam, Gayle, and my mother, "Up and at 'em!"

My father started the engine to keep *Heritage* from making further contact with Lewis's yacht. Pam joined me taking turns working the windlass until the chain and anchor lay heaped on the foredeck. *Heritage* slipped away, leaving The Son of Flubber's boat without a scratch. This time, my father motored west over to the more desirable anchorage, where the sandy shelf ran farther out, confident our anchor would hold.

As I crawled back into my bunk, I closed my eyes and drifted off, hoping there'd be no more bumps in the night.

After almost eight days in Cabo San Lucas, my father had a decision to make—we could head north toward La Paz and explore the Sea of Cortez during June, July, and August, waiting out the hurricane season when the *chubascos* roared up the Mexican coast. Or we could travel over to Mazatlán and then south to Acapulco to beat the weather. My mother, sisters, and I wanted to venture into calmer waters in the Sea of Cortez, but the captain, confident we'd sail in and out of Mazatlán before Uncle Clare and Aunt Mae showed up, decided to push on.

The next morning, we weighed anchor and motored over to the cannery to take on fuel and water. Looking down into the water from the fuel dock, I saw more fish than I'd ever seen in my life—teeming masses of swirling, silvery columns, flashing back and forth.

"*Muchos pescados,*" the fuel operator said. "Dey come for how you say *sangre y tripa de pescado?*"

"Blood and guts of fish," Pam said, helpfully.

"Si, blood and guts of dey feesh," he said, jerking his thumb back in the cannery's direction.

"I wish I knew what all these were. Look at that one," I said pointing to a foot-and-a-half-long, yellow-striped fish with two long whiskers sprouting from its chin.

"*En espanol, la cabra, en ingles . . .*" He then made a high-pitched bleating sound and with two fingers pointed like horns, butted up against me. Backing away, I wondered if he was flirting with me.

"Oh, I get it," Gayle said, excitedly, as if we were playing a game of charades. "It's a goatfish." Deciding it was her turn, she pointed to a two-foot-long fish with extremely high dorsal fins.

Strutting in a small circle and flapping his arms, the operator let out a loud, "Cock-a-doodle-doo!"

"Rooster fish!" Gayle yelled out. "This is fun. Now it's your turn, Pam."

Pam peered into the water. She pointed at a school of fish with gigantic eyes.

"*En espanol, ojotones,*" he said, his wide-eyed ingenue expression a dead giveaway.

"Big Eyes," Pam said.

All four of us, including the fuel operator, were now gazing intently into the water. Concentrating on our game, we almost fell in when my father barked, "Girls! Let's get a move on! Time's a wasting."

He grabbed the fuel pump from the operator and said to me, "Hold that funnel steady." I kneeled on the deck, steadying the plastic funnel over the open hole of our starboard fuel tank. He then gave the operator a thumbs-up. The fuel came gushing out of the two-inch diameter hose, quickly overfilling the funnel and spilling all over the deck.

"Goddamnit! Stop! Stop!" Dad held up his hand to the operator. "Pam, tell him to slow down fer-Chrissake."

"*Despacio, por favor!*" Pam said. The operator nodded and pulled up on the lever.

Fuel had spilled from the scuppers and into the water, creating pools of iridescence as colorful as the fish swimming below its oily surface.

Although the rate of fuel flowing from the hose had slowed, a noticeable leak ran from where the hand valve joined the hose. My father now had diesel all over his hands, shoes, and the front of his shorts. Considering his stomach's intolerance to fumes and waves, this did not bode well for our upcoming stretch to Bahía Los Frailes.

With both fuel tanks topped off, the operator handed us a freshwater hose and watched while we ran around spraying the decks and scrubbing oil off with Joy dish soap. Then, after filling our water tanks, we sprayed each other, knowing this would be the last freshwater shower until we reached Mazatlán.

As *Heritage* motored away, my sisters and I waved goodbye to the fuel operator, who returned our farewell by tucking his hands under his armpits and cock-a-doodle-dooing. Passing *Mamusah*, we waved goodbye to Max, Mubs, Sara, and Mike, who were staying a few extra days in Cabo before we'd see them again, in Mazatlán.

After a smooth motor up the coast, we passed La Palmilla. Named after the nearby point, the hotel rivaled the Finisterra, but attracted a more eclectic crowd with its private airstrip and remote location. As its red-tiled roofs and white Moorish arches disappeared from view, we continued northward until we reached the safe and quiet waters of Los Frailes, our last anchorage before crossing over to Mazatlán.

After a restful night's sleep, my father decided after breakfast that we all deserved another day to relax before crossing the Sea of Cortez. In a rare, good mood, he announced, "I'm gonna take it easy and read a book." Then he added, just to make himself clear, "Whatever you do, just don't bother me." Leaving him to enjoy his siesta in the stern, we readied ourselves for a dip in the warm gulf waters.

Unlike Bahía San Lucas in Cabo, where massive groupers patrolled the waters like Russian submarines, Los Frailes's crystal-clear waters were home to schools of small, brilliantly colored angel and damsel fish, purple sea urchins, and tangerine-colored starfish.

This would be our first swim in Baja waters. On the way down, the ocean had been too cold or too deep or too murky or too rough, but the warm, clear, and calm waters of Los Frailes beckoned us in. With their new swim floats strapped around their waists, my sisters and I spent most of the day taking turns jumping off the bowsprit and dog-paddling around the boat.

Exhausted and ready to relax, we entered the cabin through the forward hatch so as not to disturb the captain. Hearing snores coming from the cockpit, I poked Pam and said, "Shouldn't we wake him? He's been in the sun all afternoon." My father had fallen asleep in the cockpit, unshielded from the sun except for the book lying across his bare chest.

Pam looked at me and shrugged. "Hey, he told us under no circumstances were we to bother him."

"Man, he's gonna fry," I said.

"Yeah, well, Captain's orders."

"Maybe we should tell Mom," I said, feeling slightly guilty.

"Be my guest," Pam said, "but if he finds out that you told Mom to wake him . . ."

"You're right," I said, thinking about how nice it was that the only noise we heard was the steady sound of snoring and not the sound of his voice, yelling. And I, for once, enjoyed breathing the air without the smell of cigarette smoke. We let him sleep.

When my father awoke, he discovered he had one doozy of a sunburn. Fried from his forehead to the bottoms of his feet, he could do nothing but sit motionless in the cockpit while my mother applied wet towels to his blistered skin. We braced ourselves for an explosion, but given his strict directive, he had no recourse but to remain silent. My sisters and I climbed back through the forward hatch, leaving my mother and Nancy to nurse him.

Sharing a seat with Pam and Gayle on the foredeck, I watched the sun sink below the horizon. Millions of stars, as dense as the teeming masses that swam near Cabo's fuel dock, emerged and twinkled against a velvety black backdrop. A trail of shooting stars streaked across the inky sky as we marveled over the thick gauzy strip that made up the Milky Way. A slight breeze ruffled the fine hairs on the backs of our arms and necks, enveloping us in a warm, tropical embrace.

"Look. There. Right at the horizon," Pam said. Gayle and I turned, recognizing the four bright stars, two of them twinkling horizontally and two vertically, directly above the line dividing the sea and sky.

Beckoning us with its brilliance, what better light was there to give us safe passage across the gulf than the Southern Cross.

# 12

# Love Fest

## *Sea of Cortez*

**MAY 31–JUNE 1, 1970**

We weighed anchor before dawn, setting out on the 180-mile stretch across the southern end of the Sea of Cortez to Mazatlán. The perfect weather and steady northwesterly kept us on course, a relief for us girls, since my father could hardly help. Saddled with a blistering sunburn that curtailed even the tiniest of movements, my father was useless; it was left to us, including my mother, to trim the sails and to straddle the helm.

Shaded by the awning we'd erected for him, my father sat in the cockpit, occasionally barking out orders, but mainly assuming the mantle of a pharaoh as we stood at attention. All that was missing were the toga outfits, palm fronds, and bunches of grapes.

We were finally sailing in bathing suits, and because of the light, steady breeze and calm seas we could move about without our harnesses. I sat on the forward hatch next to my mother and Nancy and watched a school of dolphins leap and twirl as they surfed alongside *Heritage*'s bow. Although I'd never ceased to be amazed by the dazzling display of Olympian gymnastics, it had become an everyday occurrence, so I was on the lookout for something more impressive.

I didn't have to wait long.

Off the port, close to *Heritage*'s midships, the dull thud of something solid banged against the boat's ribs. *Clunk. Clunk. Clunk.*

"Did we hit a log?" my father asked. He was paranoid about the boat sinking from the flotsam and jetsam that ran parallel to the coastline. He'd read too many stories about mariners who'd lost their yachts from water-logged timbers. Acting like pistons, these upended telephone-pole-sized logs would ram straight through a boat's hull and sink it quicker than it took to throw a life raft overboard.

My mother, Nancy, and I scrambled down the deck to find out what had hit us. Two giant sea turtles the size of small Volkswagen Beetles were playing bumper cars with *Heritage*'s hull. *Clunk. Clunk. Clunk.*

"Mommy, giant turtles!" Nancy said. Hopping from one foot to the other, with her Raggedy Ann bouncing by her side, she said, "Look, they're glued together!" Sea turtles were everywhere, in pairs, and strad-dling one another, *in flagrante delicto*, with their giant flippers languidly paddling in the warm, sapphire waters. It was a love fest. As far as the eye could see the blissful aquatic twosomes bobbed, all headed west, toward a honeymoon landing back on the shores of Baja.

I turned to my mother and said, "Can't wait to hear you explain this."

My mother pursed her lips. Clearing her throat, she turned to my youngest sister and said, "You're right, sweetie, the turtles are playing a fun game of . . ." She halted, searching for the word. I waited and wondered if she was preparing to explain the facts of life to my sister. Suddenly, a smile spread across her face, and she gushed, "piggyback . . . they're playing piggyback!"

"Oh, so that's what you and Dad call it," I said.

My mother shot me a nasty look and wagged her finger back and forth, her signal to cease and desist.

I thought back on my parents' failure to explain the birds and the bees to us. I had to learn about it the hard way, from books and my more informed friends. Nancy, at least, was learning about it through nature. Sooner or later, she was going to discover the answers to her questions, as it was all around us, in both the sea life and the free-wheeling cruising community.

Here was a chance for my mother to redeem herself, and with hun-dreds of copulating turtles it was a perfect educational moment.

"Does the one on the bottom get to play on top?" Nancy asked, watching the giant love machines float by.

"If they're nice to each other, they'll take turns," I said and laughed.

"Is the one on the bottom getting tired?"

"Wouldn't you, if some fat ol' turtle was on your back?" I asked.

She giggled and climbed on my back, wrapping her arms around my neck. "Which one is the girl turtle?"

"Dunno," I said.

"Can they get unstuck?"

"Well, yes, th-th-they can," my mother stuttered.

"Only when they're finished and ready for a cigarette," I said, under my breath but loud enough for my mother to hear.

"That is *not* amusing, young lady," she said.

"It should be," I replied. "That's the problem with this family. No one has a sense of humor."

"That's not true and you know it!"

"Name one time when we've all had a good laugh."

"There've been plenty."

"You didn't answer the question."

"Well, I can't think of one offhand, but . . ."

"I rest my case."

"You're impossible!" my mother said, throwing her hands up in exasperation. "You'd make a perfect lawyer!"

As I sat on the port side mulling over all the things I didn't want to do with my life, like being a lawyer, I missed being the first to sight the pod of orcas.

"What are those?" Pam asked, pointing off the starboard as half a dozen black fins broke the surface. I rushed to the other side, and we watched as the killer whales swam close to *Heritage*, circling around and underneath her like neighborhood bullies challenging and taunting the new kid on the block. Then they rolled, exposing their snow-white bellies, as if to say, "I'll show you mine, if you show me yours."

My father tracked the orcas as they continued to circle the boat. I could tell their sheer size and numbers made him nervous. We all knew orcas preferred seals to sailors, but I guess my father worried one of them might decide to get amorous with *Heritage*'s tender ribs and poke a hole in her hull.

"Here," he said, tossing all of us the moldy and sour-smelling orange life vests that had been stored in the aft locker since San Diego.

"These *stink!*" we all said in unison. My sisters and I reluctantly slipped on our vests.

Nancy's eyes widened as my mother cinched the vest's belt around my sister's tiny waist. "Are they gonna eat us?" she asked.

"No, honey," my father said. Reassuring her, he added, "just a little precaution."

"If they do, I hope it's fast," I said, trying not to think about my limbs getting torn bit by bit from my body. My youngest sister wailed.

"Oh, fer Chrissakes, look what you've done," my father said.

"I was just kidding." Once again, I'd made a joke at my sister's expense to cover my anxiety.

"I read somewhere they don't like noise," my father said. "I'm gonna start the engine, and we'll motor for a while." The engine roared to life and with the genoa still up, *Heritage* picked up speed. Whether we were outdistancing the orcas, or they grew bored, their distinct white and black forms receded and finally disappeared altogether.

When enough time had passed, my father told us we could remove our vests. We shrugged them off as fast as we could and stowed them, praying that would be the last time we would have to use them. I'd much rather sweat to death in my float coat, I thought, than to have to put one of those on again.

Because of the calm, flat sea, this was the first time we had crossed a large body of water, with none of us experiencing the standard trip over the rail. My father was especially happy. Even with his blistering sunburn, he reveled in having a quiet stomach. With the calm weather and smooth seas, he decided that after traveling over fifteen hundred miles without casting a single line it was time to have fresh fish for dinner.

Attaching a large feather fishing lure to a piece of heavy line, he flung it over the stern so that it trailed alongside the log line. Occasionally, he'd have one of us tug on it to see if there was any tension. It was Gayle's turn to pull when she said, "Dad, I think something's on the line!"

"You're right," he said and leaned over, pulling hand over hand on the line. As the line got shorter, we could see the fish making small leaps in the stern waves. Catching a fish was exciting, but watching it make a valiant but pointless struggle to free itself gave me reservations about eating it.

My father leaned down and pulled the fish up and over the railing, landing it on the deck with a thud. "What a beauty! Must be twenty pounds!"

I looked at the big silver fish, with its dark stripes glistening in the sunlight. Near its heaving gills were four round, black spots the size of its eyes and as dark as the fear I imagined emanating from them. It thrashed wildly, its wide mouth opening and closing as if it were desperately trying to catch its breath.

*Thwack. Thwack. Thwack.*

My father used the dinghy's tiller as a bat and clubbed the fish until it lay still, its obsidian-colored eyes turning a dull slate-gray. A thin trickle of blood ran from its head to the cockpit scupper. I watched as the brilliant stripes running along its body quickly faded. "Who wants to gut it?" he asked, looking a little off-color. No one moved or said anything. We'd all lost our appetite. It was one thing to be served a piece of cooked fish at home or in a restaurant; it was another to eat something we had just murdered.

"Here, Lorraine," my father said, nudging the fish with his foot toward her. "Why don't you take it down below and clean it?"

As the designated cook, my mother reluctantly complied. No one said what all of us were thinking: *You killed it, Dad, so you should clean it.*

After witnessing the brutal mauling on deck, Nancy regressed back to thumb-sucking and her nasty piece of blanket for comfort. The rest of us were left to contemplate the brevity of life.

# 13

# El Escorpión

## *Mazatlán, Mexico*

**JUNE 2–10, 1970**

The sun was up by the time we sailed past Pajaros, Venados, and Lobos, three islands on the northern end of Mazatlán's bay. Our destination lay south of the city, where a man-made channel ran all the way from the sea to a large inland lagoon to allow access and safe harbor for traveling yachts, sportfishing fleets, commercial ships, and the La Paz–Mazatlán Ferry.

A causeway from the mainland to the lighthouse formed one side of the harbor, while a long breakwater enclosed it from the sea. The ferry and commercial ships docked farther up the lagoon; we shared anchorage directly inside the breakwater with the fishing fleets.

As we motored past the entrance, the tangy bite of freshly caught fish pervaded the morning air. Several boats filled with tourist anglers and their fishing trophies had already returned from their predawn excursions.

All along the causeway, where sportfishing craft docked side by side, record-sized sailfish, sharks, and marlin swung from hooks. Posing next to their hapless victims, proud anglers smiled for a quick Polaroid. My sisters and I thought it was gross, especially when we realized we had to tie our dinghy next to the carnage—reminding us of our murdered bonito—each time we rowed ashore.

As usual, our first chore ashore was to enter the port by visiting both the port captain and immigration. Once cleared, we took the rest of the day to walk around the first city we'd seen since San Diego.

Marveling over the Spanish colonial architecture with its vibrant, brightly painted buildings, we explored every shop and cobblestone street and strolled along the *Malecón*, Mazatlán's famous seafront walkway. Located off the main plaza, the Central Mercado offered everything from the mundane to the exotic—carcasses of beef and plucked poultry hung alongside skinned iguanas, javelina, and snake; bananas and oranges competed with mangos, guavas, and guanabanas; and staples like tortillas and rice sat next to rich pastries and raw goat's milk.

There was even an ice-cream parlor, where we ordered huge chocolate and vanilla cones. Pam, Gayle, and I devoured ours before it all melted down our shirts, but Nancy was happy to spend the rest of the afternoon in her ice-cream-stained T-shirt, sporting a Zapata-sized chocolate mustache.

On our third day visiting town, my father took a different route back to the boat, convinced it was faster. Walking down a narrow street, we chanced upon a shoe shop selling *huaraches*. My father, suddenly feeling generous, asked if we all wanted a pair.

Ten minutes later, with tennis shoes in hand, we clomped down the street, wearing our new donkey-urine-cured leather and tire-soled sandals. What we didn't consider, as we traversed the streets in our open-toed shoes, were the cockroaches that skittered about in the fading light. Annoyed by our continuous squealing and hopping, my father yelled, "Knock it off! What are you, a bunch of scaredy cats? They're just bugs. They can't hurt you."

As we made our way down the cobblestoned street, the sun dropped like a brick, plunging us in darkness until we reached the dimly lit landing to the causeway. Without warning, Nancy raced over and crouched down under the light. "Look, look, Daddy, it's a little crab."

The creature was crawling sideways like a crab but had an unusual black tail, which curved into a perfectly shaped C. As it moved toward her, it raised its tail as if to strike.

"Don't move, honey," my father said, and in a few quick strides, scooped her up.

"That's no crab," Pam said. "It's a scorpion!"

Holding Nancy in his arms, my father led the sprint down the rest of the way, until we reached the well-lit causeway.

Rowing back in our dinghy, we noticed a double ender, like *Mamusah*, had arrived and was anchored between us and the Frasers. No lights were on, so we figured we'd have to wait until morning to meet them. But after we were aboard and below, we heard splashing and laughter. Surprised anyone would swim at this late hour, we scrambled up to the cockpit. Sure enough, reflected by the full moon, four heads bobbed in the water. Two more figures teetered on the newly arrived boat's railing, ready to leap.

"Hey, I wouldn't get in the water if I were you," I called out.

"Oh, yeah?" one of them said. It was a man's voice, slurred and whiskey thick.

"Unless, of course, you want to walk around like a pirate," I said.

The second voice, high-pitched and female, tittered, "What'd she mean, Roger?"

"Nothing to worry your little head about, my wee lass," her companion replied, in what he must have thought sounded like the perfect Sean Connery Scottish accent.

"Oh, Roger," she giggled, and jumped.

"What my daughter is trying to say is the harbor's not a place you want to swim in," my father said.

"Thanks, Captain. We'll take that into consideration." Ignoring my father's warning, the man called Roger sang out, "Ready or not, girls, here I come!" and belly flopped into the water to the delight of five squealing women.

"Let's go below, girls," my father said, pissed that his friendly warning had gone unheeded. As Pam and Gayle started down the companionway, I couldn't help but get in one last jab.

I leaned over the railing and said in a loud voice, "Hey, Dad, here come the sharks! I can see their fins in the moonlight." Smiling, I settled back in the cockpit as the screams of six swimmers filled the night air.

"Not funny, young lady," my father said, poking his head out of the companionway.

"What?" I asked. "I was telling the truth."

There were sharks in the harbor. I just didn't clarify they'd already been fed. After the anglers departed, the crews cut up and disposed of the day's catch. But instead of dumping the remains on the other side of the breakwater, they dumped them in the harbor. The bloody chum created a veritable feeding frenzy.

The next day, Roger, obviously not one to hold a grudge, invited all of us on board to show off his expensive toy. He introduced us to his all-female crew—Bonnie, Debbie, Shirley, Suzy, and Patsy—as if he were a farmer showing off his prize heifers. "Roger's girls," as we dubbed them later, stood placidly by, greeting us with open-eyed bovine stares and wide smiles.

In our estimation, all five would not have won blue ribbons at the fair. But they, along with Roger, seemed oblivious to any deficiency. This amazed us, since we were a family whose sole purpose was to point out even the most minuscule defects to one another. Roger was balding, with a forehead shaped like a dinosaur egg and an ego to match; Bonnie had acne; Debbie had miles of cellulite; Shirley had a nose shaped like an eagle's beak; Suzy had enormous, pendulous boobs; and Patsy looked like a man. Roger considered them great beauties; they worshipped him as if he were 007.

"I just sit back and relax and give the helm to Suzy," Roger said. "Did you know she graduated with top honors from the Coast Guard Academy in Texas?" he bragged to us. "Why, Suzy could captain one of those commercial ships that pass us and dock at the lagoon! Shirley's the best chef and can cook up any dish I request. Studied at one of the greatest culinary schools in Paris. Bonnie and Patsy take care of all the boat work. Debbie can speak fluent Spanish. Got the perfect crew, I do. That's for sure!"

"If they do all that, what do you do?" I asked. All the women looked at him and then at each other before they burst out laughing. Roger just smiled.

The next day, Roger and his girls weighed anchor, heading for the South Pacific where, my sisters and I assumed, he'd continue to keep his crew giggling and satisfied. Although it was probably the last we'd ever see of them, they'd left an indelible impression. We learned that somewhere in the world there's someone for everyone, and sometimes there's *more than one someone* for everyone. Even though Pam, Gayle, and I snickered over this and enjoyed the discomfort our parents displayed when pressed to explain Roger's unusual setup, it was a lesson that happiness could be found in the doing and not, like us, in the pursuing, where it always seemed to be just beyond our reach.

My father's definition of indulgence was enjoying life's luxuries through subterfuge. He and my mother had spent a romantic weekend at the upscale Las Playas Hotel years ago, on the only vacation I'd remembered them taking. When we reached Mazatlán, he decided we all needed to enjoy the hotel's amenities, but this time, for free.

Recalling the Las Playas's layout, he explained how to reach the pool without being noticed. "Walk through the lobby as if you own the place," he said. Traipsing behind my father in our urine-cured *huaraches* and clutching our beach towels, my sisters and I kept our heads down and scurried as fast as we could through the lobby and out the archway to the pool.

Once there, my father triumphantly pushed the chaise lounges together and ordered us to lay our towels across them. Happy he'd beat the system, he let us order fruit drinks and sandwiches from the bar.

For a few hours, my sisters and I enjoyed living like the other half as we sipped our umbrella-topped fruit drinks and splashed in the aqua-tiled, freshwater pool.

Even though *Mamusah* was anchored next to us, we spent little time with them. Whenever the Frasers were getting ready to go into town, we were returning, or vice versa. Sara, who had slacked off on her schoolwork since leaving San Diego, had holed up in her stateroom, trying to finish a semester's worth of study. When she called out to me to come over on our last day, I gladly accepted, happy to get away from my sisters and parents.

Sitting on her double bunk, she showed me what she'd been working on for school. She was taking five subjects to my three. It occurred to me that Sara, who I didn't consider the brightest bulb in the box, had applied herself. Instead of feeling a sense of kinship with her as I had in Cabo, it seemed she had more in common with my sisters. They were all studying and thinking about their future. Once again, I felt separate and alone. Everyone seemed to know where they were heading except me. All I could think about was getting off *Mamusah* and away from Sara before I burst into tears and embarrassed myself.

I mumbled some excuse about getting back and started to leave.

"Here," she said, handing me a couple of joints. "Mike scored some when he was in town yesterday. He says it's really strong stuff, so these two will last you a long time."

"Thanks," I said, tucking them in the back pocket of my shorts. I lowered myself into the dinghy and pushed off with my oar.

"See you in Zihuatanejo or Acapulco," she said and waved before disappearing back into her cabin.

Agitated over what had transpired, I took a quick row around the harbor. When I got to the far end where the lagoon started, I set the oars in the dinghy and sat looking back at the two boats. I didn't know what I was feeling. I wanted to cry and scream at the same time. I didn't want to be anywhere. Not in this dinghy and not back on *Heritage*. I brought my knees up to my chest and Sara's neon pink lighter fell out and landed on the seat beside me. I'd borrowed it in Cabo San Lucas and had forgotten to return it to her.

I looked at the lighter and fished around my back pocket for one of the joints. Lighting it, I took a deep draw. The smoke, strong and acrid, made me cough. The second and third time I inhaled more slowly.

Just as Sara had promised, it didn't take long to feel its effect. Suddenly, everything was okay and clear to me. I laughed when I saw my father signaling me to come back; I laughed when my oar slipped out of my hands and floated away; and I laughed when I floated toward the breakwater to the open sea beyond.

I laughed and didn't give a shit.

When Sara, who'd popped up on deck for a break, realized I was in trouble, she jumped in the Whaler, retrieved my oar, and towed me back to *Heritage*. "Pull yourself together," she said as she motored off.

"What the hell happened out there?" my father asked.

"Uh . . . I accidentally dropped the oar over the side, and the current pushed me out."

"Let's get the dinghy up. We're leaving as soon as we weigh anchor."

Making my way forward, I cranked the windlass and thought how strange it was to be stoned with my father only a few feet away. I could only hope I wouldn't do something stupid like stumble and fall overboard.

I pulled in the last of the chain and dumped it into the chain locker. The physical exertion, combined with the joint's powerful effect and the effort it took to appear normal, was exhausting. All I wanted was to crawl into my bunk. I reminded myself never to do this again.

As the harbor receded, I sat alone on the forward hatch and closed my eyes, listening to the sound of the wind and waves. Feeling the softness of the breeze running along my skin, I wept silently.

# 14

# Sea Snakes

## *Yelapa, Mexico*

"Daddy, look at the big snake in the water!" Nancy said.

Busy trying to guide *Heritage* through Banderas Bay, my father ignored her.

"Daddy! Daddy! Daddy!"

He took a long, slow drag on his cigarette. I watched as the steady stream of smoke exited his nostrils and trailed behind him. "It's probably some waterlogged branch," he said.

Wouldn't that serve him right if he was wrong, I thought, as I scooted down from my perch on the cabin top.

"Where?" I asked her.

With her stubby forefinger, she pointed to a spot on the water.

Except for our wake, nothing disturbed the glassy surface. "Are you sure?" I asked. The glare of the noonday sun and a cloudless sky made it impossible to detect even the smallest ripple. Maybe my father's right and it's just some piece of flotsam, I thought.

"Look, it's right there!" she said, pointing down, next to the hull.

It was a snake all right . . . about the length of a yardstick, swimming right alongside us, not even a foot away, corkscrewing in the water and alternately exposing its bright yellow underbelly and then its chocolate-brown top stripe.

My mother, who'd been sitting next to my father in the stern, made her way toward us. She peered over the side just as we passed another snake. "Oh, goodness," she murmured. Then, turning back to my father said, "Dear, I think Nancy's right."

"There's another one!" Nancy squealed.

Gayle and Pam emerged from the cabin and raced up the deck. Now we were all hanging over the side, peering into the cobalt waters, spotting them gliding alongside our hull every twenty or thirty feet as if we had come upon a watery lair. Over and over they rolled, ranging in length from two to three feet, with their oar-like tails propelling them along the surface.

With one hand on the helm, my father peered over the side and watched them roll in the stern wake.

"Remember when Mr. Thompson told us about them?" Gayle said, barely able to contain her excitement.

"When the snake . . ." Pam said.

". . . and its fangs," Gayle replied.

"With the facemask . . ."

"Yeah." Gayle didn't elaborate. She didn't have to. They were at it again with the verbal shorthand they'd used in San Diego.

As *Heritage* headed into the bay, the snakes were now swimming in twos and threes every few feet. Gayle stared at them and said, "They're creepy looking."

"I'm not getting off the boat," Pam announced.

I thought about my appointment as dinghy boatswain and weighed its merits now that I had to row through snake-infested waters. *What if the boat broaches and I fall in the water before making it to shore*, I wondered. Swimming among them seemed worse than being surrounded by sharks. You expected sharks in the ocean. But snakes in the sea, no.

"Let's see if they bite." I gave Gayle a slight nudge.

"That's not funny!" She swung her arm back and slugged me.

"Jeez, I was just joking." I knew I deserved the punch, but I couldn't help myself. Just a small payback for excluding me, I thought.

"I remember Mr. Thompson saying they can only open their jaws wide enough to bite your pinkie finger or baby toe," Pam said.

"Hmmm, something small," I said. I looked around and spied a coil of three-eighths line belayed to a shroud and grabbed it. Uncoiling a couple of feet, I dangled the end over the side and tried to bop the snake's head with it. *Bop. Bop. Bop.*

Bingo! With a lightning-fast jerk, it swiveled and struck. I pulled on the line and, unaware the snake had snagged one of its fangs on the end of the rope, lifted it half out of the water. Nancy screamed, and we all fell backward. Wriggling free, the snake swam off, glad to be rid of us.

Preoccupied with our black and yellow friend, we barely noticed our surroundings. While Baja had graced us with its stark monochromatic and arid landscapes, and Mazatlán with its Old-World charm, this was the first time the tropics burst upon us in an explosion of color. As we closed in on Yelapa, on the southernmost shore of Banderas Bay, bright green palm trees stretched all the way up the mountainside and gold thatch-roofed cabanas lined the steep sandy beach. A freshwater stream, which ran from the jungle and down to the beach, summoned us, like a Siren's call, to splash in it.

My father, eyeing the stream, thought otherwise. "Looks like you women will be busy washing laundry," he said.

Once we anchored, we forgot about our yellow-bellied friends, and only thought about getting off the boat. But rowing to shore, I discovered, was less like a dinghy landing and more like running a kayak through the rapids. Like Cabo, Yelapa's shelf dropped precipitously, creating breakers that heaved rather than rolled, but its rock breakwater, constructed at a sharp angle to the narrow beach, created waves that converged and churned from opposite directions like a river.

My father, of course, didn't take any of this into consideration. Preferring to leave the details up to me did not imply he had complete confidence in my abilities; it simply meant he didn't give a damn. So long as I deposited him onshore dry, he was a satisfied customer.

With a little practice, I was able to get everyone safely to shore during the first two days. But on the third, my luck ran out, much to the glee of the local men who watched me as they enjoyed their afternoon siesta under the palms. Aware of their stares, I wondered if they were taking bets on how long before I landed in the water. If they had, the payoff was worth it as I worked to keep the dinghy's stern toward shore. It turned and shifted and the next thing I knew, my father and I were in the water.

Terrified of a face-to-face encounter with one of the yellow and chocolate-striped fiends, I didn't look for the overturned dinghy or my father, but swam as fast as I could toward shore. Dragging myself up the steep beach, I checked for fang marks.

"Goddammit!" my father screamed behind me. He'd body-surfed onto the beach and crawled up to me. "What the hell happened?" The laughter to our right drowned out my feeble apology. The men were clutching their sides and howling, "*Ahh yai yai! Mira! Los gringos están en el mar!*"

"Go get the goddamned dinghy," my father said.

"But, Dad, there are *snakes* in the water."

"Get the goddamned dinghy!"

I wanted to shout back, "No fucking way!" But, as much as I hated him, I was afraid to defy him. Cursing under my breath, I waded back through the surf and swam as fast as I could to the overturned dinghy. Clutching the painter in one hand, I side-stroked toward shore, focusing on the sky and not on the flashes of yellow I imagined slithering by me.

After I dragged the boat out of the water, I found my father sitting on the sand. Trying his best to ignore the men's laughter, he busied himself by cleaning his glasses with his T-shirt.

"Let's get back to the boat," he said.

"Didn't you want to talk to the guy about dropping the stern anchor near the bar?" I asked. I'd rowed my father to the beach so he could secure a better anchorage. The bar owner, an American whose yachting life ended when his boat drifted and sank near the breakwater's rocky wall, also controlled Yelapa's best anchorage.

"I'll ask him tomorrow," he snapped.

Ignoring the good-natured shouts from the men on the beach, my father pushed me out and hopped in.

Around midnight, I awoke with a start. Just as I had in Cabo, I sat straight up and smashed my forehead and nose on the low ceiling.

"Shit!"

"Shhhhh!" my mother and sisters said in unison.

My father hissed from the quarter berth, "Go back to sleep!"

"I'm going up on deck," I announced. I swung out of my berth and scrambled up the stairs to the cockpit and looked around. The moon was full, and I could easily make out the other boats at anchor.

My father, who emerged behind me, checked the stern anchor and then the mooring line. "Looks like everything's okay," he said.

"Something isn't right. I can feel it in my bones."

"You sound like your grandmother," he said peevishly. Over the course of her life, Grandma had predicted many things, all of which had come true.

"I'm not going below until I find out what it is," I said. My father sighed, sat down, and lit a cigarette.

I closed my eyes, inhaling the night air, and cocked my head.

"What are you doing?" my father asked.

"I'm listening."

"For what?"

"I'm not sure."

"As soon as I finish this cigarette . . ."

"Wait," I said, realizing the telltale banging against the boat was absent. "The dinghy's gone." We both looked over the stern where the dinghy should have been.

I scanned the shore and spied a moonlit sliver of white. "There it is." The dinghy's white hull bobbed against the rocky breakwater.

"We can't wake any of the other boats to help, but . . .," my father hesitated before adding, "*we* could try to get it."

"How are *we* going to do that?" I said. I couldn't believe my father was suggesting I jump in and swim with the snakes again, and in the dark.

He sighed. "Guess we'll have to wait 'til morning and hope it doesn't drift or get too banged up."

I nodded and headed back down to the safety and security of my bunk.

The next morning, we discovered the dinghy tied securely to the stern. Later, when an Avon raft pulled up alongside us, our good Samaritans introduced themselves as the owners of *Faraway*, a thirty-eight-foot sloop, which had arrived before dawn. Before dropping anchor, they'd spotted the wayward dinghy, retrieved it, and tied it to the only boat without a beach craft.

John and his mother, Hilke, along with their two pets, a German shepherd named Schatzi, and a Siamese cat named Tinkerbell, were on their way down the coast before heading west across the Pacific, where they planned to run a mission in New Guinea.

Grateful, my father invited them for lunch at the beach-side cantina.

"Well, girls, with the dinghy back, that gives you plenty of time to wash laundry before lunch," my father said, after John and Hilke motored away. I hated him when he said things like that. Just because we were girls, why were we required to perform all the traditional female chores, like laundry, cooking, and cleaning, along with everything else? Since the trip had started, I'd never seen my father wash or cook anything. I grumbled, wishing for the millionth time I was a boy. I knew my father never would've made a son cook a meal or do laundry. If I ever got married, which I doubted, I'd make my future husband split the work with me or better yet, hire someone to do it.

Resigned to laundry duty, Pam, Gayle, and I piled into the dinghy. With the laundry bag and box of Ivory detergent sandwiched between Pam and me, I rowed us to the far side of shore. When we reached the stream, the local women were busy washing and beating their clothes against the rocks. They all smiled and laughed when they saw how much we had to wash.

"*Mucho trabajo*," one of them said, pointing to the pile.

"*Si, el capitán es muy sucio*," Pam said. The women all giggled.

"What did you say to them?" I asked, wishing I had studied my Spanish.

"I just told them Dad's very dirty," she said.

"Judging from their reaction, they must have the same problem," I said.

"Yeah, looks like it's universal."

As we crouched in the shallow stream beating our soapy clothes against the rocks, I said, "Hey, guys, if we hurry, maybe we can cool off at the waterfall everyone's been talking about." All the other boat owners, except us, had made the short hike up to the base of the waterfall to enjoy its freshwater pool. My father had continually found things for us to do on board, but if we finished the laundry, we could get our chance without having to ask permission. After all, we had the dinghy. We only had to make sure we got back in time to pick up my parents and Nancy for lunch with John and his mother.

With our clean, wet laundry packed into the beached dinghy, we headed into the jungle. Passing lush foliage and squawking parrots, Gayle asked, "Do sea snakes like fresh water?"

"I hope to hell not," I said, praying the pool would be free of even guppies. I just wanted to swim in a place where the only things moving were my fingers and toes.

After a fifteen-minute hike, the trail abruptly ended. Before us, a one-hundred-foot waterfall cascaded down a wall of smooth white rock and emptied into a crystal-clear freshwater pool. It was only waist-deep, so we sat on our butts, submerged to our necks. "Oooh, I could sit here forever," Gayle said.

Pam nodded and agreed. "It feels soooo good."

"I'm so sick of being sticky," I said. We were the only boat that didn't have a shower. It hadn't been that much of an issue sailing down Baja because it had been so cold. We hadn't bothered to change our clothes, much less wash more than our hands and faces, until we reached Cabo. Except for hosing ourselves down at the refueling station and our fresh-water plunge at the Las Playas Hotel in Mazatlán, we'd had to settle for salty seawater sloshes using the same sturdy canvas bucket that serviced our bladders. Anyone else might have balked over this arrangement, but we were veterans of roughing it.

"I'd like to float here forever," I said, feeling the coolness of the water below and the warmth of the sun above.

Pam waded over to the rocks near the edge of the pool where she had placed her watch and checked the time. "We gotta go," she said.

Gayle and I groaned. It was hard to abandon the silky water. Slipping on our *huaraches*, we trudged along the stream toward the beach. Just before the clearing, two men with machetes blocked our path, motioning us to walk around them.

"*La serpiente es muy peligrosa!*" they said, pointing to the enormous snake in the middle of the path. Its severed diamond-shaped head lay next to it. Now we knew we were neither safe on land nor at sea.

We ran all the way back to the dinghy.

# 15

# Arabian Nights

## *Manzanillo*

**JUNE 15–25, 1970**

Leaving Yelapa, we reached the southern end of Banderas Bay and rounded Point Corrientes, heading south. To our port, a one-hundred-foot waterfall cascaded down to the ocean. I couldn't imagine the trip getting better than this. Beauty was all around, and with *Mamusah* as our traveling companion again, the captain appeared relaxed and confident.

After motoring on tranquil seas all day and through the night, dawn arrived in a blast of heat. As the sun rose higher, the temperature climbed and by mid-morning the thermometer registered 96 degrees. Sweat poured down our arms and backs as we sat in our bathing suits in the cockpit under the awning. Not even the buckets of seawater we poured over each other eased the searing heat.

We were now nearing Santiago Peninsula, which jutted out into the middle of a broad, half-moon–shaped bay, dividing Santiago Bay to the north and Manzanillo Bay to the south. We continued motoring along Manzanillo Bay until we reached its southern end, where the docking facilities were located. Much to our disappointment, the closer we got to land, the more we could see it resembled arid Cabo, rather than lush Yelapa. A crowded, fuel-fouled harbor amidst a backdrop of olive-and-tan houses and dun-colored hills replaced the waterfalls, palm trees, and clear water.

Considered the largest port on Mexico's west coast, Manzanillo had fishing fleets, steamers, and commercial ships vying for space near the deep-water piers the Mexican Navy had built. Reputed to be a poor holding ground for smaller yachts, *Heritage* and *Mamusah* found a place to anchor directly off a strip of beach that fronted one of the hotels. The water was still foul and oily, but at least we felt safe knowing we wouldn't get rammed in the middle of the night.

Once both boats anchored, Max picked up my father in his Whaler and motored over to the pier to make the required trip into town, clearing our entry with the port captain. Meanwhile, we fanned ourselves under the canvas awning, frustrated we couldn't cool off over the side. Our only diversion was watching the fishermen on the beach wade out and cast their circular nets. Like cowboys lassoing cattle, they twirled the nets high above their heads and over the water. Returning to shore, they'd sit on their haunches and smoke a cigarette or two before wading back to pull in the day's catch.

We glanced over at *Mamusah* to see if they were as miserable as we were, but Sara and Mubs had disappeared down below. A surge of envy rose from *Heritage*'s cockpit as we sat sweating, imagining them sitting comfortably in their spacious, air-conditioned salon.

When my father and Max returned, we learned the extent of our suffering. The port captain told them it was the hottest day in seventeen years.

On the third morning, my father announced he was sick of the smell of diesel and the mess it was making to our waterline. Informed of a better anchorage, he and Max agreed to move the boats to the north end of the bay.

As we neared the new anchorage, an amazing sight greeted us. Curved into the hillside and rising straight up from the beach was a newly built Arabian palace straight out of *One Thousand and One Nights*. Men were busy running back and forth, like worker ants, with the last bit of construction. As soon as my father laid eyes on the hotel's brilliant, white-washed façade and beautiful Moorish arches, he could hardly wait for me to row him ashore so he could investigate.

In a letter to my grandparents, my father described his first impression of the hotel's final construction:

*I went ashore this morning to view the effort, and it is considerable when you see them moving concrete by five-gallon bucket-loads. They do have bulldozers and trucks for the excavation, but most of the moving is done by two legs and a strong back.*

His observation was laughable, as this was no different from what he'd had my sisters and me do when he added a studio at the top of our steep backyard in Oakland. After concluding that hauling a cement mixer up the hill was too arduous, my father used my sisters and me as his bucket brigade. While he ran the mixer in our carport, we lugged buckets of wet cement up the steep hillside. He'd never marveled over our "two legs and a strong back" as we hauled five hundred bucket-loads up the hill.

Later that night, I rowed my father ashore again, this time with my mother, who sat perched in the bow, tightly clutching her skirt as we surfed the waves to shore. Max and Mubs had invited them for cocktails at the bar, which overlooked the anchorage. When my father and Max had visited the hotel earlier, they'd discovered it was called Las Hadas, built by an eccentric tin-magnate from Bolivia as a hideaway for the rich and famous. One more hotel to add to my checklist, I thought, when I make it in Hollywood.

After a day and a half, we moved back to the south end. Not only was the anchorage too choppy, but *Mamusah* had to remedy a failing water pump.

At our new anchorage, Max was now just a short taxi ride to the airport and then a quick flight to Guadalajara, where he was hoping to locate a new pump. At the last minute, Sara went with him, leaving Mubs, as she told us, "to get some peace and quiet from those two."

The next morning, Mubs shouted over an invitation to Pam, Gayle, and me to be her lunch guests in town. My father grudgingly allowed us to accept, so we quickly changed from our bathing suits to shorts and T-shirts. Being invited anywhere by either Mubs or Max was always a treat. Unlike our parents, both exuded a sense of *joie de vivre*, which drew us to them like moths to a flame. Mubs continually complimented us girls and, craving the attention, we basked in her kindness.

After depositing Pam and Gayle at the Navy pier, I rowed back to pick up Mubs. I could see my father out of the corner of my eye watching me as I helped her into the unstable dinghy, hoping he wouldn't embarrass me by yelling over directions. Mubs was used to the flat bottom of the Whaler, where she could stomp aboard with her stiff gait and sit without it rocking. Getting her into our rice-paper float was a greater challenge. After a couple of scary moments where we almost capsized, she settled in the stern, and I rowed us back to the pier.

"I found the loveliest old hotel and courtyard restaurant when Max and I were in town the other day, and I couldn't think of better company than you girls to share a nice relaxing lunch," she said, as we started the short walk to town. There it was again, the stroking and the compliments. *She couldn't think of anyone better than us.* We three leaned toward her, stopping just short of purring and rubbing ourselves against her legs, as if we were adoring cats.

Sweating through our clothes by the time we reached the center of town, we welcomed the Hotel Colonial's cool, dark interior. With its painted cathedral ceilings, arched doorways, and patterned, hand-tiled floors, it was a place I imagined a wealthy person would frequent. My father would have complained about the darkness, the broken tiles, and the patched plaster, but we saw it through Mubs's eyes, as a place with an elegant history of a bygone era—lively with patrons, fully booked, and freshly stuccoed. It elevated Mubs even higher in our estimation.

"*Señora y señoritas,*" the waiter said, smiling as he escorted us to a table in the center courtyard. Though we were outside again, the four walls of the three-storied hotel and the table's wide umbrella shaded us from the direct sun.

"Anything you girls want," Mubs said, as she ordered a Scotch on the rocks for herself.

"I'll take a Virgin Mary," Pam said. Gayle and I both nodded.

"Give your Spanish a try," Mubs suggested and smiled encouragingly at her.

Blushing, Pam looked up at the waiter and said haltingly, "*Uh, tres Vírgenes Marías . . . para mis hermanas y yo . . . por favor.*"

The waiter grinned and said, "*Habla espanol muy bien! Tres Vírgenes Marías para tres señoritas bonitas!*" He performed a little bow, handed each of us a large menu, and left to get our drinks.

While everyone was studying the menu, I admired the white table-cloth, polished silverware, and freshly cut flowers adorning each table. Along the periphery of the yellow-and-blue tiled walls were potted palms and hanging down from the center of the arches were baskets overflowing with lemon-yellow trumpet vines. In one of the far corners sat a large birdcage where a scarlet macaw swung sleepily on its perch.

Catching my wonderstruck expression, Mubs said, "Lovely, isn't it?" Embarrassed by her keen observation, I wondered if she was also aware of the turmoil churning within me. It seemed so easy for the Frasers to eat this way, a simple and mundane occurrence, rather than the extraordinary experience it was for us. Even at sixteen, I could see a connection between a sense of ease and wealth. Living on the lower end of the middle-class spectrum, our harried parents forever worried about travel funds and how to stretch our dollars, while the financially secure Frasers exuded something entirely different.

Although both boats traveled side by side, from port to port, we couldn't have been more different—the six of us, uptight, confined on a narrow, leaky vessel, and the Frasers, relaxed, moving freely on a roomy, dry ship. We lived the stripped-down version of their fully equipped life.

Enjoying my shrimp cocktail, I wondered if money was the sole factor separating our life and theirs. I considered the fact that even at Mexican prices, my father couldn't afford to take the six of us to a restaurant like the Colonial, but I knew the difference was deeper than that. Sitting here with Mubs, we were eating, laughing, and relaxing, and not just inhaling our meal in silence with our stomachs tied in knots. We were *dining*.

I realized it wasn't their money I was envious of, but how it had given them a deep sense of place in the world. It was a state-of-mind I yearned for, a feeling of *all is right with the world*.

"Well, what do you girls see that you'd like?" Mubs asked.

Pam and Gayle ordered *tacos de pesca*, but I took advantage of Mubs's invitation and ordered *carne asada*, the most expensive item on the menu.

"I just love it that you tall, skinny gals have such a good appetite," she laughed.

Hearing my father's voice chastising me over my less than stellar manners, I suddenly felt ashamed, and stuttered, "I can just g-g-g-get the fish tacos, too."

Mubs smiled at me and then turned to the waiter, "Make that *dos carne asadas*."

Five days passed and Max was still without a water pump. Because he didn't want to rely on only one engine, he decided to wait in Manzanillo until the part arrived. We were running low on money and were now officially in hurricane season. Assured by information we'd read in Babe's letters that our next destination was one of the most protected harbors along the coast, and only 125 miles away, my father felt confident we could manage by ourselves.

We said goodbye to the Frasers and headed out to sea on June 25th. With our bowsprit nosing its way back and forth like a blind man's cane, we ventured forward into unseen waters, guided by our desire to reach our next anchorage, Zihuatanejo.

Clearing the harbor, my father ignored the approaching gray skies and increasing swells. *Heritage* pushed onward.

# 16

## *Chubasco!*

### *Zihuatanejo, Mexico*

**June 26–30, 1970**

Two days out of Manzanillo, we realized we wouldn't make it to Zihuatanejo until well past dark. Worried about attempting the harbor's entrance at night, my father corrected our course and headed closer to shore, hoping to anchor on the lee side of Isla Grande, some twenty miles north of Zihuatanejo. This way we could enter our next port by mid-morning.

What we didn't count on was that the clean air and clear sky made Isla Grande appear closer. Even with the engine at full throttle, we seemed to stand still as *Heritage*'s bow dipped and buried beneath each wave. We should have realized that along with the current, the swells were increasing and slowing us down.

We reached the northern end of the island before dusk, but with fading light and faced with dangerous low-lying reefs and submerged rocks, my father decided that entering between the island and mainland was no longer an option. Our only choice would be to bear off and spend the night at sea.

Rounding the windward side of Isla Grande, the weather abruptly changed. An approaching squall, accompanied by a powerful gust, sent Pam and me scurrying to drop the genoa.

"Get that goddamn thing down!" my father yelled. Pam and I fumbled to loosen the cleated halyard. The line zipped through the block as we both grabbed wildly at the blue canvas. Before we could pull it all the way down, a second gust hit and whipped the lower half of the sail up and off the deck and over the side.

We clawed at the canvas as it dragged in the water, hearing my father rant from the stern, "Get that canvas out of the water before it fouls the propeller!" Rain pelted us from all sides as Pam and I leaned over the lifelines straining to pull in the waterlogged sail.

We pulled more than half of it back on deck, but the wind gusted again and threatened to blow it all back over the side. "Tie it down while I keep pulling it in!" I yelled to Pam. She crouched in front of the forward hatch, tying off the sail, as I clipped myself to the lifeline and leaned out as far as I could, jerking and tugging at the leaden sail.

In the time it took to wrest the genoa out of the water and lash it down, the dusky sky turned a greenish hue, and the wind whistled an eerie tune. A storm was approaching.

Safely in the cockpit with the rest of my family, I thought about the weather and a game my sisters and I used to play in the barn in Livermore. We memorized nautical rhymes in anticipation of one day sailing the ocean. I recalled the one I liked best, "Red sky at night, sailor's delight; red sky at morning, sailors take warning," but realized my father's favorite, "Mares' tails and mackerel scales make tall ships take in their sails," was the one we should've heeded. It was now apparent to all of us the high cirrus clouds that had formed earlier in the day had given us fair warning.

Bare-poled and engine roaring, *Heritage* turned seaward. As Isla Grande fell astern and a starless night enveloped us, the seas mounted. When the first line of squalls hit and the troughs turned deep and far apart, we realized it was too late to turn around and head back north, and impossible to head seaward and wait it out.

"We're going to have to make it to Zihuatanejo, girls, before this weather turns any worse," my father said. Aware his initial decision to avoid a night entry had resulted in two alternative and ultimately unsuccessful actions, we understood the gravity and risk. I suddenly thought about Joe Eklund, and for the first time, worried that maybe the reason we hadn't heard from him was that he'd faced a storm like this. What if

Joe, who'd made several transatlantic crossings from Norway and was a seasoned sailor, had forged ahead in bad weather, as we were doing, but had not made it? I tried not to think about the possibility because compared to him, we had no business out here in rough weather. To calm myself, I imagined Joe anchored in a warm, safe cove somewhere south of us, throwing back a beer and chatting with his pet parrot.

With each plunge forward, the weather worsened. *Heritage* was now sliding down each trough with increasing speed and making a slow, hellish climb back to the top while we sat terrified, anticipating it happening all over again.

Shackling ourselves to the lifeline, we huddled in the cockpit in our harnesses and float coats. My mother gripped Nancy with all her might, and Pam, Gayle, and I grabbed each other. With his face lit by the binnacle's red light, my father rode the helm like a possessed cowboy. The seas raged all around us, and he gripped the wheel as if seated on a wild bull that wanted nothing more than to buck and stomp the living daylights out of him.

"Looks like we're in for a full-blown *chubasco!*" he shouted above the sound of the screaming wind and churning waves. Little did he know this was nothing compared to what lay ahead in the rising black seas.

Plummeting like a stone, the boat dropped with such speed there was no time to look around and figure out what was happening. My peripheral vision narrowed until the only thing I could see was my father's unlit wet cigarette hanging from the corner of his mouth.

*Heritage* smashed and hit bottom, shuddering from bow to stern as she struggled to climb back up. Against the blackness, a bright, white luminescent line of phosphorescence appeared and just before *Heritage* reached the top, the wave broke and crested over the bowsprit. Water tore along the decks and cabin top in an avalanche of spray drenching us and filling the cockpit.

There was no time to react before *Heritage* began her next wild descent, smashing and shuddering before climbing again. The troughs were increasing in length and the climb back up them was longer, so when *Heritage* had only made it two-thirds of the way up, we could see the phosphorescence forming.

"Oh my god," my mother cried, shielding Nancy. We watched the wave crest and race toward us. It roared along the cabin top, under the main boom and over the dodger, smashing into my father with such force that it pushed him back against the stern railing. He slid back up on the seat and lunged for the wheel, catching his breath.

No sooner had he taken control of the helm than we dropped again, so fast and precipitous, it was only when we looked up could we understand the enormity of what was happening. We had stalled at the very bottom of the trough. Too terrified to even cry out, we watched the top of the wave crest.

"Hold on!" my father yelled. I closed my eyes and waited to hear the splitting of timber and the sound of the mast crashing onto the cabin top and deck. When I opened my eyes, I saw a wall of water, its phosphorescent crest frothing and foaming like a rabid animal.

I instinctively ducked, pressing against my sisters and mother. Water barreled headlong into us with such force that it lifted us off our seats. *Heritage* groaned under the weight of water submerging her stern. I was certain this was it and that the next wave would sink us, but as *Heritage's* bow plunged down into the trough, the stern emptied, and we rose back up and over the next crest.

Suddenly, we saw an offshore light in the distance. A few minutes later a second one on shore was visible. As soon as they lined up, my father turned *Heritage* straight toward them. With all of us holding our breath, we approached the entrance, hoping to slip through before another wave struck.

*Heritage* was finally inside the harbor. My father grabbed the flashlight and checked the navigation chart. With harbor depths recorded at several fathoms, we cautiously made our way in the dark until we reached the inner harbor. Just like Babe's letters had promised, we were in calm, protected waters.

We motored slowly between the anchor lights of other boats, backing away just in time from an unlit trimaran. Clear of it, we set anchor, paying out plenty of chain. It was 2:00 a.m. Sleep deprived since departing Manzanillo and thoroughly spent, we stumbled below, making our way through the dark, dank cabin to our bunks.

I could have slept all day, but for the wind whistling through the rigging and the loud scraping from the anchor chain against the bow. Unable to fall back asleep, I swung out of my berth and in my bare feet gingerly stepped onto the wet floorboards. Emerging from the companionway, I got my first glimpse of Zihuatanejo. High winds and leaden skies had replaced the previous night's calm and windless conditions. I suddenly felt queasy as I steadied against *Heritage*'s bucking. I wondered how great this anchorage really was. But even as conditions in the anchorage deteriorated, something far more menacing was happening out at sea. A *chubasco* with its center sixty miles offshore was slowly making its way northward. The hills on the harbor's south side shielded us from the worst of the wind, which was raging just beyond the harbor's entrance.

When my father awoke and assessed going ashore, he warned us the rough surf increased the chance of broaching. Given the choice of being seasick onboard while, in my father's words, *Heritage* "danced at the end of her chain," or braving the waves and the possibility of getting doused, my sisters and I unanimously chose the latter. Spared of making that choice, the crew of the trimaran we'd almost collided with the night before offered to take us to shore in their large, flat-bottomed dinghy.

The *Triton* crew's friendly smiles and easygoing style reminded us of how much we missed the company of Max and Mubs. Single and good-looking, they were our first "south of the border" crushes. Don, long and lean, with blond tousled hair and an easy smile was the obvious winner, with Tony, slightly shorter and more muscled coming in second, followed by Ian, a fireplug with a mop of coal-black hair and a thick, Cockney accent, trailing in third. Even though Ian was English, all three had sailed together from Australia, so we crowned them "the Aussies."

Immediately, we each laid claim to our crushes, but it was not as if the Aussies, who were at least a decade older, were aware they were the objects of our affection. They were never less than polite, kind, and respectful, and an invitation to board *Triton* was made with the friendly intent to join them, as Ian was wont to say, for "a spot o' tea." To them, just like the rockers in San Diego, we were nice girls who knew more than the average female about boating. The other stuff they could find elsewhere.

Since the normally calm inner harbor had turned into a choppy anchorage and the town into a mud hole, Mama Elena's, with its twelve-cent cervezas and eighty-cent meal, became the town's social center. It was here, under the thatched roof cantina, where everyone congregated.

Two young women, just a few years older than Pam, who had taken the bus from Cuernavaca for a short beach vacation, also joined us. Mary Lou and Cathy hadn't expected to spend their time sipping beer and watching the rain pour down, but it gave Pam a chance to get acquainted with Cathy while Mary Lou concentrated on wrestling an invitation from the Aussies to crew with them.

We also met Bill, Keith, and Keith's friend, a reticent young woman named Sonja, who'd arrived in their trimaran, *Mercury*, a day before us. Keith and Bill fit the classic description of what my father considered "hippies," with their shoulder-length hair, leather and puka-shell neck-laces, and stoned smiles, but they were also friendly and helpful. And with his laid-back attitude and guitar playing, Keith entertained every-one while we all waited for the weather to clear. My father grudgingly admitted that, despite their appearance, they were decent guys and so nicknamed them "the nice ponytails."

While Mary Lou was successful in her quest for an invitation from the *Triton*, Cathy had enough of the rain and decided to return to Cuer-navaca. When my father learned Acapulco was on the bus's itinerary, he departed with Cathy that evening. He'd wanted to scope out the harbor and pick up our mail, and Cathy, who was fluent in Spanish, was the perfect traveling companion.

Returning to the boat the next evening, my father groused about Acapulco's high prices, his sour stomach from too much coffee, and the long, bumpy ride back. But none of us minded his complaining. Pam was ecstatic because my father told her Cathy had invited her to Cuernavaca, and Gayle and I were happy because he'd brought a sack full of mail and news that he'd seen *Tolaki*'s owners, Laddie and Tony Duff, whom we'd met in San Diego.

The next day, the swells within the harbor calmed, and it was now safe to venture out into the Pacific. It would be a long trip, but we were looking forward to Acapulco and were curious about meeting up with the

*Tolaki* again. Along with Cathy's invitation to Pam, my father surprised us by promising to take my mother, Gayle, Nancy, and me to Mexico City. More than learning about the Aztecs or climbing the pyramids, what I really wanted was a hotel room with a real bed and the chance to stretch out and sleep under fresh sheets.

# 17

# Mexican Riviera

## *Acapulco*

**JULY 2–15, 1970**

For two days and a little over one hundred miles, we sailed by a continuous ribbon of green. If there were villages along the coast, they were too small and far away for us to detect any inhabitants. On this leg, my mother resorted to her anti-nausea remedy and holed up in the galley; Nancy, with her iron stomach, moved freely in and out of the cabin; Gayle, unable to overcome her stomach's adversity to the ocean's motion, hung over the rail; and both Pam and I remained queasy but functioning. Because my father handled the helm during the day, Pam and I split the night watch.

Since the engine was off and we were sailing, we encouraged our father to leave his usual bed in the cockpit for the quarter berth below, so we could at least enjoy the evening without him snoring or sitting up and lighting a cigarette.

It was on the first evening, with a steady breeze and manageable waves, that Pam and I came up with a way to ease the boredom during our watches. I'd vowed after my father had made me swim with the snakes, I was going to get my revenge.

Reemerging from the cabin, I whispered to my sister I had a surprise. Pulling a carton of my father's Salems from behind my back, I said, "Payback time!"

By the end of our watches, the two of us had managed to empty the carton, not by simply chucking the whole carton over the side but by carefully unwrapping every pack, pulling out each individual cigarette, and meticulously twisting and emptying all the tobacco before tossing it with Machiavellian glee into the water. Methodical in our counting, we decided to keep a running tally to see how many of my father's beloved Salems we'd have to flick overboard before he noticed something was amiss. Pledging to one another that neither would rat the other out, we agreed that if questioned, we'd both give him the same answer, that he'd simply smoked way more than he'd imagined. Better for him to question his sanity than for us to lose ours.

By early evening on the second night, we saw the glow of Acapulco's city lights. Happy that soon we'd be at anchor, we didn't realize the lights were over thirty miles away. But because he'd successfully navigated Zihuatanejo at night and in a storm, my father continued on, steering *Heritage* toward Acapulco's harbor.

Relying on his memory from his recent bus visit, my father was able to distinguish between the island at the north end of the harbor and the headland dotted with hotels. Once inside the harbor, however, we realized we'd entered an obstacle course. Dozens of small fishing boats were working the water with nets, each silhouetted by a small lantern. *Heritage* carefully wove her way through the small boats and headed to the northwest corner of the harbor where the yacht club and the small-boat anchorage were located.

By 3:00 a.m., *Heritage* was anchored, and we were asleep in our berths.

The next morning, we motored over to the yacht club and paid the usurious $8 per day berthing fee for the convenience of getting on and off the boat, and for use of the club's 110-volt electricity, freshwater showers, and pool.

That afternoon, we all traipsed downtown, trying to ignore the stifling heat. First, we stopped at Sanborns, a fancy tourist restaurant, where we ordered grilled cheese sandwiches and Cokes. Then we took the bus to the port captain's, where we picked up more mail and my grandparents' latest letter, which was filled with complaints about how my parents had saddled them with piles of paperwork.

Next, it was off to *Mercado Central* to buy some fresh produce, where we discovered tomatoes the size of grapefruits, papayas as big as footballs, and limes the color of the bright-green parrots we'd seen roosting in the trees.

Loaded down with groceries, Pam pointed out that at least we didn't have to fight our way back through a treacherous, thorny goat path like in Cabo.

With the harbor filling up with north- and southbound boats, my father cut our stay at the yacht club to snag a mooring. My sisters and I grumbled as we collected our towels from the pool and took our last freshwater showers before motoring out.

To ease our disappointment, my father announced that *Tolaki*, moored close by, had invited us to join them for cocktails. I thought about my brief time aboard *Tolaki* in San Diego, when Laddie invited my family, and my aunt, uncle, and cousins onboard for a tour of their spacious steel ketch. That event had thrown my father into a foul mood, and I hoped that now, with nobody to impress, he'd have a better time. Besides, I wanted to hear all about the Sea of Cortez, where Tony and Laddie and their two toddlers spent several months before sailing straight for Acapulco. My father wrote about our trip down the coast:

> *Actually, we are the luckiest of the lot. While boats holed up in the Gulf of California or sailed non-stop to beat hurricane season, we had no destination, so we were able to enjoy many of the interesting spots along the coast.*

We might have stopped in a lot of places, some interesting, some not, but enjoying? I don't think so. And the luckiest? Who were we kidding?

When a speedboat pulling water skiers zipped by in the harbor, one of the young instructors, who appeared no older than I, offered to give me a lesson.

"Quick, Pam, what's 'free' in Spanish?"

"*Gratis*," she said, dryly.

"*Es gratis?*" I shouted at him.

"*Si, es claro*," he replied, waving me over to his stern's ladder.

"I'll be back in a minute," I said to Pam and Gayle as I jumped over the side and swam to his boat.

He then jumped in alongside me with a couple of single skis while his partner kept the engine idling.

"I help you," he said, attaching his ski after he fitted mine. "*Arriba*," he said, pointing to my ski and pulling the tip out of the water.

He signaled to his partner, and the boat roared to life. He grabbed my waist, and before I knew it, we'd popped up out of the water and were riding the boat's wake. I grinned and waved to my sisters each time I passed them, zipping around the harbor. I'm not sure why he let me ski for so long for free, but I was happy and grateful he did.

Having to row back and forth several times a day, we missed the convenience and luxury of docking at the yacht club. We didn't realize, however, that during our brief stay there, we'd taken on some stowaways.

Less than a week after our arrival, I was lying in my bunk one afternoon reading, and upon finishing my book, I stretched out and stared at the ceiling, contemplating life.

I thought about all the letters I'd written since the start of the trip and how desperately I'd waited for mail as we entered each new harbor. In the few letters I'd received, compared to the amount I'd mailed, I realized my expectations were far greater than my friends'. They were busy going to school, learning to drive, and making new friends, while my sisters and I had to make do with one another. Neither Pam nor Gayle wanted to talk about Grandma, or that the captain was worse than ever, or that our mother had retreated permanently to the galley. Instead of interacting with me, Gayle was content to spend hours memorizing her entire French book and Pam used every chance to run errands to practice her Spanish.

Except for Sara from *Mamusah*, Tony and Laddie's two toddlers, and two kids we'd just met on *Scheherazade*—a stuck up nineteen-year-old, whose much older boyfriend was accompanying her, and her bratty younger brother—the rest of the cruising community was mostly young men in their twenties and thirties or older, retired couples.

I didn't want to admit it, but I knew my sisters didn't like me. I knew they blamed me for my father's foul moods, and that life aboard *Heritage* would be so much more tolerable if I'd stopped pissing him off so much. I wished I didn't care, but I did. I wanted my sisters to like me; I wanted my friends to remember me; and I wanted my father not to hate me.

As I stared up at my ceiling wondering how I was going to accomplish all these things, I suddenly detected the tiniest of movement from behind the holes in the pegboard. What in the world is *that*, I thought? At first, I wondered if I was imagining things but then, out of the corner of my eye, there it was, running across the hole. Whatever was in there was, without a doubt, *moving*.

"Oh, shit!" I rolled out of my bunk, hit the settee, and landed hard on the floorboard before scrambling up the companionway to where my father was snoozing under the awning.

"Dad! Dad! Wake up!"

"What?"

"We've got cockroaches!"

"Christ, if it's not one thing, it's another," he huffed, making his way down into the cabin. "Where did you see them?" he asked, shifting my mattress.

"No, not under the mattress . . . in the ceiling!"

He stuck his head near the peg hole and suddenly jerked away. "Get me a screwdriver," he said.

I watched as he unscrewed the board above my bed, ready to bolt in case there was more than one. As he fumbled with the last screw, one side of the pegboard dropped onto my bunk, sending hundreds of giant roaches skittering in every direction.

"Ahhh!!!" my father and I both screamed.

He tried to stab them with his screwdriver, but they were too fast, wedging themselves behind the bulwark and down below the bunk into the back of my drawer. "Oh my god, oh my god, oh my god," I repeated to myself. I'm gonna leave my underwear on forever, I thought. I'm never opening that drawer again.

"I've got to row over to the yacht club and see if I can locate an exterminator," my father said, as he threw down the screwdriver and walked faster than usual out of the cabin.

"Stay out of the cabin," he said as he shoved off in the dinghy.

No shit. Did he actually think I was going back down?

While my mother and Nancy were enjoying a swim at a nearby hotel, Pam, Gayle, and I crouched together on the foredeck, sweating in the blistering sun.

When my father returned, he told us to pack a change of clothes.

"Make sure you shake out anything you take so you don't bring any with you to the hotel," he said.

As my sisters and I vigorously shook each article of clothing before stuffing it into our canvas bags, I imagined what my father might do if one got loose in the dinghy.

Thanks to the *cucarachas*, my sisters and I slept in real beds for two days while the exterminator wrapped the boat in plastic and bombed it with insecticide, making sure our unwanted stowaways and their future progeny would never expose their hairy legs onboard again.

All too soon, we checked out of our luxurious rooms, and our high life at the hotel reverted to the cramped pedestrian life onboard. To make matters worse, after promising to take my mother, Gayle, Nancy, and me to Mexico City, my father informed us that because of the purchase of a new alternator, the unexpected cost of fumigating the boat, and our subsequent hotel stay, he was canceling the trip. The best I could hope for would be that Pam shared her experience with us, which was better than nothing.

On the morning of July 9th, my father dropped Pam off at the depot, where she bought a ticket and boarded the bus for the five-hour ride to Cuernavaca. While she enjoyed sightseeing in Mexico City, we spent our time bored and moored, watching cruise ships steam into the harbor and deposit passengers for the day.

When Pam returned, she was so pumped from her five days of freedom she generously shared her adventure, and I clung to her every word. As she recounted people she'd met and the places she'd been, her eyes shone, and it was the first time she looked genuinely relaxed and happy.

It made me wonder if she thought a better life existed beyond our family and *Heritage*. And, if she did, was it possible that I might feel the same?

While Pam had been away, a big storm had blown through, so we waited another two days before deciding it was safe to depart. The Frasers had just arrived, but busy with our imminent departure, my sisters and I didn't get the chance to say goodbye to them. We'd have to wait until we met up with them again down the coast.

My father checked one last time for mail and left our Costa Rican forwarding address with the port captain, while my mother, sisters and I made a last trip to the *mercado* for fresh fruit and vegetables. Then we motored over to the dock to refuel, and fully loaded, we motored out of the harbor.

# 18

# Four Short Hops and a Skip

*Puerto Marques, Puerto Angel, Bahía Huatulco, Bahía
Chipehua, and Tehuantepec*

## July 15–22, 1970

It was *adios* to Acapulco, high prices, and flying *cucarachas* as we cast off
in the late afternoon on July 15th. Our new traveling companions, *Tolaki*
and *Scheherazade*, had departed a day earlier, and both boats were waiting
for us at our first stop, Puerto Marques, a little over six miles south of
Acapulco.

After a short sail across Acapulco Bay and around Punta Bruja, we
entered Puerto Marques Bay. In sharp contrast to Acapulco's bustling
tourist atmosphere and crowded beaches, the bay was serene and devoid
of people. Besides *Tolaki* and *Scheherazade*, we had the beach to ourselves.

After anchoring, everyone on *Heritage* jumped in and swam the short
distance to shore, or in Pam, Gayle, and Nancy's case, dog-paddled wearing their floats, to join the other boats for a few hours of fun. Before the
sun set, we all swam back to our respective boats to ready ourselves for
the two-day, two-hundred-mile stretch to Puerto Angel.

Unable to sleep and eager to depart, my father woke us before dawn.
"Let's get a move on," he said as he came through the cabin, shaking our
shoulders. Groaning, my sisters and I rolled out of our bunks, trying not
to bump into each other in the dark cabin while we struggled into our

shorts and T-shirts. Fortunately, it was nearly a full moon, so with the deck well lit, we weighed anchor and motored out.

My father looked pleased, sitting at the helm, smoking his cigarette, as *Heritage* passed the bay's opening. He'd decided with no place to stop along the rugged shoreline we'd motor seven miles west into deep water, before making a straight course south to Puerto Angel. I also knew he wanted to get a head start down the coast to prove *Heritage*'s mettle; I recalled how he'd put up with the friendly jabs from other boat owners over *Heritage*'s sloth-like speed. But before we could cover the distance, we caught sight of *Tolaki* approaching our stern. Just as the sun rose over the mountains, we watched Tony and Laddie wave and pass us. My sisters and I shouted and waved back, but I noticed my father barely looked up, choosing to focus straight ahead.

*Scheherazade* was the last to leave Marques, but with her sleek, fiberglass hull and main and genoa drawing the light air, she shot past both boats. By the time we turned south, *Tolaki* and *Scheherazade* were mere dots off our bow, and before long they'd disappeared beyond the horizon. We'd pass the next two days in choppy seas, alone, staring at one another as we sailed along the rugged, barren coastline.

Just before dawn on the third day, we picked up the beacon marking Puerto Angel and slowed our approach to the harbor, waiting for the morning light. As the sun rose, we passed *Tolaki*, which lay hove to, and *Scheherazade,* which tacked back and forth outside the entrance. Arriving hours ahead of us, they'd had to wait all night before they could safely enter at dawn. I caught my father smiling as he slid past them and guided *Heritage* through the bay's entrance. Motoring past the one-hundred-foot-high rocky islet to our port and the three-hundred-foot bluff off our starboard, I heard him chanting, "Slow and steady wins the race."

Inside the tiny harbor, we tucked in behind a large outcropping and anchored. Shortly after, *Scheherazade* and *Tolaki* arrived. Puerto Angel was nothing more than a hole in the wall with steep bluffs rising above its shoreline. Normally a safe shelter for small craft from November to May, in the middle of July a southerly wind buffeted the harbor and made for a rolly anchorage. After a disastrous attempt to make it to shore, my father radioed *Tolaki*, requesting a ride on their Whaler.

A few minutes later, Tony zoomed over and picked up my father. Bored and complaining about being stuck onboard with nothing to do, we noticed three heads bobbing in the choppy waters, moving toward us. Passing by the other boats, they swam up to our stern.

"*Est-ce que nous venir à bord?*" one of the young women asked, looking up at us while she treaded water.

Pam and I looked over at Gayle, who answered excitedly, "Oui."

Gayle turned to us and said, "They want to come aboard. Hurry, get the ladder!"

I pulled the ladder out from the locker underneath the cockpit seat and Pam helped me attach it to the stern railing. We stepped back as the three swimmers climbed up and jumped into the cockpit. The two young women, one a brunette and the other blonde, and a raven-haired young man, looked like they could've stepped right out of a fashion magazine.

"*Vous etes françaises?*" the brunette asked.

"*Nous sommes americaines,*" Gayle replied.

"You are studying French, no?" the blonde asked.

"*Oui!*" Gayle enthused. "*J'étudie le français tous les jours.*"

The young man turned to Gayle and said, "*C'est merveilleux! Votre français est excellent!*"

Gayle blushed.

Before our guests could catch their breath, my sister barraged them with questions about all things French. This was the most animated I'd seen her during the entire trip. It was as if she was one of those wind-up toys that, after being hand cranked, takes on a life of its own. Instead of being put off, our new friends were so flattered by her enthusiasm, they stayed and talked to us for most of the afternoon.

Before we knew it, they thanked us, waved goodbye, and dove over the side. My sisters and I watched as they swam easily and effortlessly, like mermaids, through the choppy waters back to shore. Gayle stared out over the water with a dazed expression pasted on her face. I knew later on she'd scribble everything down in her notebook.

When my father returned soon after our visitors' departure, we motored over to the dock for fuel. While we waited for the tanks to fill, the workers casually revealed we'd anchored off *Playa de los Muertos*, the beach of the dead. Besides the rough surf, it was one more reason we were glad we'd never stepped foot onshore.

Since the next anchorage was only forty miles away, we left mid-morning. By early afternoon we reached Huatulco Bay, by far the most beautiful port we'd seen since Cabo's Los Frailes. After swimming off the stern and snorkeling near the boat, we rowed ashore to the pristine beach right before dusk, content to spend a few minutes on firm ground. The last time my sisters and I had been ashore was four days before in Puerto Marques.

We left Bahía Huatulco the next morning bound for Bahía Chipehua, our last resting spot, before crossing the Gulf of Tehuantepec. My father chose the open roadstead, instead of sailing on farther south to Salina Cruz, where he heard they charged high port fees. But after anchoring and pitching and rolling all evening, not only were we extremely seasick, but *Heritage* sustained damage to her hull and trail boards from the anchor chain. A little past midnight, my father announced we were leaving. Weighing the choice between working the windlass or hurling over the rail, I concluded it was far better to stand out to sea than spend another night in this hellhole.

Passing Salina Cruz around 3:00 a.m., I wondered if we were going to make it across Tehuantepec. Both *Tolaki* and *Scheherazade* had departed from Huatulco and had set a course straight across the gulf. They were only six hours ahead, but with spotty radio contact, we couldn't rely on them for weather updates.

This was the crossing my father had secretly worried about after he'd heard harrowing stories like that of Sid Wallace, a well-traveled yachtsman who, in his 102-foot schooner, *Constellation*, was caught in Force 9 winds. I couldn't imagine another storm like the one we experienced on our way to Zihuatanejo, especially if we were in the middle of a 260-mile-wide body of water with no safe harbor in sight.

Crossing the gulf at any time of the year was potentially dangerous. Because of the isthmus's narrow but mountainous topography, winds formed in the Gulf of Mexico and blew west over the Sierra Madres, barreling down through Chievela Pass with hurricane force into the Gulf of Tehuantepec.

Superstitious sailors follow certain protocols of the sea and crossing the Gulf of Tehuantepec was no exception. My father decided to follow convention and stay as close to shore as humanly possible, sailing the coast as he would jokingly admit using his preferred navigational style of "one foot on the beach." It added fifty miles, compared to sailing straight across, but if a storm brewed, it was far safer than getting blown out to sea.

By morning, we'd reached the low-lying beaches and spent the rest of the day sailing less than a half-mile from shore. It had been as flat as a millpond, and we had a hard time believing the gulf warranted its violent reputation. Whether it was Lady Luck or blissful ignorance, we sailed along with our genoa up and the engine running, and by late afternoon, were confident it would be smooth sailing during the night.

At dusk, however, the calm weather ended. Replaced by headwinds, our progress slowed to three knots. We didn't give it a second thought until the sun dropped over the horizon and the sky filled with an other-worldly palette of pinks, purples, and reds. The sunset was the most glorious any of us had ever witnessed, but there was also something strange about it. To the west, the colors continued to intensify, but to the east, a dark black line had formed.

As night approached, the increasing wind carried the familiar metallic scent of an approaching storm. Within seconds, lightning and thunder surrounded *Heritage*. Rain pelted down, beating the sea's surface into foam. I sat at the helm, terrorized, yet awed by the force of nature surrounding me. The sky flashed bright, blinding us, and the black night thundered, shaking us. It was as if we'd sailed into the end of time. I thought about Sister Mary Joseph, the nun who grudgingly taught catechism to all of us wayward, public-school kids. I remembered the day she'd opened the Bible to Revelations. As if she were in a Charlton Heston movie, she dramatically raised her arms as her voice rose to a crescendo. "Then the angel *TOOK* the censer, filled it with *BURNING COALS* from the altar, and *HURLED IT* down to the earth!" If she could only see how scared-shitless I was now, she'd be one satisfied nun.

Even though our topmast was equipped with a lightning rod, my father sent everyone below except for the crew member standing watch.

As each of us finished our time at the helm, we passed a pair of sunglasses to the next person to protect against the blinding light.

With increased headwinds, we crawled along at two knots. But the Starrett kept on chugging, and by morning we'd successfully crossed the gulf. Under clear skies, we sailed past political upheaval in Guatemala and on to El Salvador.

# 19

# Birthday Blues

## *Acajutla, El Salvador*

**JULY 24–AUGUST 2, 1970**

"Goddamn mother fuckin' engine!" my father shouted from the engine hold. So started the day of my seventeenth birthday.

With the cockpit hatch removed and engine exposed, the overpowering odor of burnt rubber and diesel fumes sent Gayle heaving over the side. Perched on the cockpit seats, Pam and I sat on our haunches like two howler monkeys, peering down at our father, following his every move.

"Son of a bitch!" he yelled, as he jiggled various wires, tightened nuts and bolts, and checked several gaskets. Sweat poured down his back. With only a pair of cutoffs to protect him from the hot casing, my father straddled the Starrett trying to figure out how to restart the engine.

In desperation, he loosened the injectors, and a thin stream of hot oil shot skyward. Pam and I watched in horror as its trajectory, reversing course, rained down in greasy, fiery droplets onto his bare back. "Shit, shit, shit!" He twisted back and forth as he tried to wipe the hot oil away with his hands. "Don't just sit there with your fingers up your butts! Throw me a goddamn cloth."

Jolted from our paralytic state, Pam and I sprang into action, almost knocking each other into the engine cavity, as we frantically tried to locate something to wipe the oil. Spying my father's T-shirt, which he had placed near the stern seat, Pam grabbed it and flung it back at me. I balled it up and leaned over to wipe his back. "Just give it to me! I'll do it myself!" he said.

Throughout all this, my mother manned the helm, furiously spinning the wheel, first to starboard and then back to port, as if her futile gesture on a flat and windless sea would somehow fix the mess we were in. It was obvious why my father limited my mother's time behind the wheel and had assigned her to galley duty; she had no idea what she was doing.

Today, though, she'd insisted on taking the wheel, announcing that until further notice, she was on strike and would only return to galley duty when we stopped criticizing her culinary skills. She could only create as good as she got, she said, demanding we understand there were only so many variations one could create from chipped beef and canned ham.

Crouched on the cockpit seat, I looked toward shore and through the dancing, shimmering heat, I could see Acajutla and the green hills rising above it. If we didn't make it into the anchorage by sundown, we'd have to heave to and spend the night offshore because the harbor was littered with debris—concrete blocks, cables, and sunken boats, all casualties of poor navigation, illegal dumping, and bad weather.

Despite the chaos surrounding us, I believed my family had planned something special for me. That's why no one had mentioned anything; they were going to surprise me! At this very moment, I had only warm and fuzzy thoughts for everyone, including the "motherfuckin'" engine.

"All right, Lorraine, turn her over!" my father said. She reached over to the binnacle stand and turned the key. The engine miraculously started, and we all breathed easy for a moment, until the green hulk coughed and died, this time for good.

Reeling off his favorite expletives, my father grabbed the crowbar that lay next to the engine and started banging its top and sides, as if beating it would somehow force it back to life. We remained silent, hoping his tirade would eventually cease. As he whaled on the engine, however, his rage escalated, and he uttered the one word no father should ever allow to pass his lips.

"You motherfuckin' CUNT!" he screamed.

The king of profanity had gone too far and crossed the line.

Pam let loose. "You bastard!"

My father pretended not to hear but immediately stopped.

Shocked and disgusted, I should've said something, but I also knew he was looking for a fight and now was *not* the time. It was my birthday, for crying out loud.

My mother, who had, up to now, remained silent, said, "Jim . . . ?"

Oh no, I thought. She's going to use *this* moment to stick up for us? Please, please, don't say anything! You'll just get him riled up again.

"WHAT, GODDAMMIT?" my father said, shooting my mother a look like he wanted nothing better than to bash her head in with the crowbar he was holding.

"Well, I know this might sound a bit silly . . .," my mother said. *Where is she going with this*, I wondered? She cleared her throat and continued, "But I noticed the fuel gauge didn't move when I turned the engine on . . ." Oh god, of course she's not sticking up for us . . . she's making it worse! She's suggesting we're out of fuel!

Then as if out of a movie, *Tolaki* appeared on the horizon, like the Lone Ranger, galloping straight for us. "The *Tolaki!*" my sisters and I shouted. In no time, with their twin engines at full throttle, they were aside us.

"Yo, what seems to be the problem, Jim?" Tony said.

"Well, I think we've run out of fuel," my father replied, sheepishly. Exchanging glances, my mother, sisters, and I were all thinking the same thing: *All that anger, swearing, and fury, just because we're out of fuel?*

"I'll move off to starboard so you can drop your dinghy in, and we'll get some fuel to you," Tony said. He stood there, casually puffing on his pipe, looking like Errol Flynn, in his spotless white shorts and a navy and white striped shirt. Laddie, in a flowered bikini, stood next to him, smiling, as their two naked, tow-headed sprites, Paul and Amanda, grabbed onto each of her thighs.

"Okay, let's get a move on here, girls!" my father said, suddenly energized by an audience and a chance to give orders. I looked over at Tony, who, suppressing a smile, puffed away on his pipe. I suspected he and the other yachters were bemused by my father's histrionics, viewing him as some sort of blustery Captain Bligh caricature and his kids deserving of their pity. But neither my sisters nor I wanted anyone to feel sorry for us. All we wanted was to be normal.

"Get that hatch lowered," my father said. The three of us struggled with the bulky door, straining to drop it squarely over the engine. "I need you to row over with these five-gallon cans," he said to me, as if he'd asked me to run down to the corner grocery for some milk. My father was a great one for volunteering others, I thought.

I grabbed the cans and lowered myself into the dinghy, eyeing swells that with one slight dip could swamp my stamp-sized vessel faster than I could set the oarlocks. The brilliant idea of buying a dinghy light enough for one of us girls to launch singlehandedly now seemed foolhardy. Instead, I longed for an Avon raft like *Faraway*'s and *Scheherazade*'s, or *Tolaki*'s and *Mamusah*'s sturdy Boston Whaler. My father's take on our gas shortage:

> *Getting the dinghy over the side was easy on the smooth sea, and Tolaki quickly pumped twenty gallons from their generous tankage, which was then ferried over in our five-gallon jerry cans.*

Once I made it safely over to *Tolaki*, I passed the empty jerry cans to Tony. As he siphoned the fuel, I suctioned my feet and butt, like a starfish, to the bottom of the bobbing dinghy to steady myself. So much for a "smooth sea."

Loaded down with four five-gallon cans of fuel, the dinghy sat so low in the water it resembled a canoe. Reaching our stern, I tied a line through the cans' handles, so that my father could safely pull them aboard.

With twenty gallons of fuel in our port tank and *Tolaki* fading in the distance, my mother turned the key and the green carcass coughed to life. But, because of our limited fuel supply, we throttled back, motoring along the glassy sea at barely three knots. With the current running against us, we could expect to drop anchor in the middle of the night.

As the sun began its fiery descent, a terrible truth sank in. My family had forgotten my birthday. While they all sat admiring a blood red sky, I was planning their murders.

With a full moon, an unexpected pickup of wind, and radio assistance from *Scheherazade*, we motor-sailed into Acajutla a little after midnight. Since *Tolaki* and *Scheherazade* had claimed the two available moorings, we dropped anchor in the middle of the harbor, hoping our chain wouldn't tangle with any submerged debris.

Anchored and engine off, I sat in the cockpit, stunned by the sudden silence around me. I leaned back and closed my eyes, too exhausted to bring up my forgotten day. Instead, I breathed in the earthy scent of rich, dark farmland and of Brahma cattle and wondered what this moment of solitude meant to each of us. I imagined for Gayle, happiness over the cessation of motion; for Pam, dreaming of a future escape; for my mother, relief from galley duties; for my father, temporary reprieve from engine repair; and for me, an understanding of self-reliance and the pitfalls accompanying high expectations. If there was going to be a celebration, it would have to spring from me, so I wished myself a happy seventeenth and called it a day.

20

# Bottoms Up

*Bahía Elena, Costa Rica*

**AUGUST 4–9, 1970**

It had been a year since the Soccer War between El Salvador and Honduras had ended, but political tensions between the two countries were still festering. Mr. Smith, our American friend from Acajutla, advised my father to bypass Golfo de Fonseca and sail on to Nicaragua. The war had created a strong sense of Honduran pride embraced by local villagers who, Mr. Smith warned us, "wielded very large machetes." That's all we need, I thought . . . machete-armed farmers chasing us in our pea-pod-sized dinghy.

Crossing the border into Nicaragua, however, proved no better. Nicaragua was in the midst of its own revolution and civil war and, after several terrorizing fly-bys from military jets and warnings from a naval ship, we decided to forego any stops along its coast. No need for them to think our little ship was in cahoots with rebel forces.

Forced to fall back from the well-patrolled shoreline, *Heritage* headed out to sea. Although the storm that had kept us in Acajutla had passed, its violent aftermath was still visible in the gray skies and murky swells as we battled our way past Nicaragua. For two days, everyone, except for sea-hearty Nancy, hung limp and listless like rag dolls over the taffrail.

On the second night, the seas calmed. Exhausted, my father had retired below, leaving Pam and me to split night watches. Around 2:00

a.m., Pam stepped into the cockpit to relieve me. Taking her place at the helm, she held up what she'd been hiding behind her back.

"What are you doing with that?" I asked. It was one of my father's *huaraches*.

"This is the equivalent of the 'C' word," she said. And with that, flung his sandal overboard. Hearing it splash, we looked at one another and burst out laughing.

"You're lucky it's night," I said. "With those rubber-tired soles keeping it afloat, you'd be able to see it bobbing behind us. Maybe there's a one-legged fisherman who'll find it."

"Exactly," she said as she settled back and checked the compass reading. "Dad will be looking high and low for that left shoe."

"Between his sandal and his Salems, we're gonna drive him over the edge," I said.

Although I experienced an infinitesimal grain of remorse for what I'd done, I loved giving him a taste of his own medicine.

At dawn on the third day, the lush, emerald peninsula of Costa Rica's Cabo Santa Elena jutted out from the rugged coastline. We were now well below the hurricane belt and had passed safely through the unprotected waters of Guatemala, El Salvador, Honduras, and Nicaragua.

Sailing into this verdant paradise, it was as if we'd reached Oz's Emerald City. Maybe here we'd finally find what we'd been searching for. My father would get a heart, my mother would get some brains, and my sisters and I, some courage.

*Tolaki*, *Scheherazade*, and *Mercury* had arrived a few days before and were anchored close together near one end of the beach. With no sign of the boats' offshore crafts, we figured they were off exploring the nearby coves and islands.

As soon as we erected the awning over the cockpit, my sisters and I rowed to shore. After we beached the dinghy, the three of us hiked down the beach to a freshwater stream, where we cooled off. The feel of the cool, silky water brought back memories of our time at the waterfall in Yelapa, but with no one around, I wished I could strip off my shorts and T-shirt and let the water rush over me. I wondered if my sisters felt the same way. Never having seen one another with less than a bikini or bra and a pair of underpants, though, the thought of splashing around in the buff was as implausible as imagining my parents having sex.

Refreshed, we walked a little farther down the beach when we noticed a modest house tucked into the volcanic hillside and shaded by banana trees. Off to its side was a small truck farm, where a woman and two children were crouched between rows, picking squash.

"*Hola!*" Pam said. The woman looked up, momentarily startled, before breaking into a wide smile. The kids, like two bunnies, hopped out of the vegetable patch and over to us. "*Como te llamas?*" Pam asked them.

The smaller of the two, a tiny girl with the assessing eyes of an old woman, stared at my sister. "*Maria,*" she said solemnly, and then pointed to her brother. "*Jesus.*" Then she spread her arms wide as if to encompass the entire beach. "V*ivemos solamente en bahía.*"

"*Es verdad?*" Pam said. Maria nodded and backed into her mother's colorful skirt.

Stroking the girl's hair with work-worn fingers, the woman said, "*Es cierto. No hay que otras familias por veinte millas.*" She took a few steps back to her basket and pulled out a gargantuan zucchini, holding it as if it were a newborn, and handed to Pam.

My sister cradled it awkwardly, and said, "*Gracias.*"

"*De nada,*" the woman replied, and with Maria and Jesus in tow, she returned to her garden.

"What did she say?" I asked.

"She says, besides them, there are no other families living within twenty miles. Right, Pam?" Gayle said.

"How would you know? You've had your nose stuck in your French book ever since we left San Diego," I said.

Unfazed, Gayle coolly replied, "It's easy. They're both romance languages."

"Gayle's right," Pam said. Then, with a slight smirk, added, "If you studied harder, you wouldn't have to ask." I noticed their sly exchange and thought about wiping it off their faces with a fistful of sand. How could my sisters understand languages so easily? What good was being fearless and athletic if you couldn't string together more than *hola* and *gracias?*

"I'm going back," I said. "Let's see if your romance languages will help you on the long swim back to the boat." I sprinted down the beach while Pam, weighed down by the giant zucchini, and Gayle, chased after me.

By the time I reached the dinghy, with my anger spent from running, I waited for them. I didn't want them tattling. The place was too pretty to have it ruined by my father's yelling. I figured it was better to endure their low opinion of me rather than end up grounded on *Heritage*.

The beauty of Costa Rica had temporarily loosened my father's iron grip, and the next evening, he let me row over to *Mercury* by myself. We hadn't seen Bill and Keith since Zihuatanejo and although my father still considered them "the nice ponytails," they'd gained a few new habits as they'd made their way down the Central American coast. Every evening, Bill, Keith, and Sonja would sit *au naturel* in *Mercury*'s cockpit, enjoying their version of cocktails by passing around a big, fat blunt while they strummed their guitars. All my father had to say was, "whatever they do on their boat is their business." When he'd heard Laddie and others were joining Keith for free guitar lessons, my father assumed proper attire would replace *Mercury*'s "clothing optional" preference.

Reaching *Mercury*, I tied off the dinghy and hopped aboard with my guitar. As I made my way over to the companionway, I noticed the silence and wondered if they'd all moved to another boat. Before calling out to see if anyone was onboard, I leaned down and saw Keith sitting with his back to me. Lit by the glow of the kerosene lamp, and unaware of me, he stood up and, except for his guitar strap and guitar, was buck naked.

Staring at him, I realized it was one thing to witness nudity from afar; it was another thing to be up close and personal. Worse yet, when he turned sideways, I caught sight of the biggest erection I'd ever seen. To be accurate, the *only* erection I'd ever seen.

Backing up, I leapt into the dinghy and cast off.

As the oars dragged in the water, I drifted and tried to forget what I'd just seen. All I thought about was what I was going to say to my father when I returned to the boat. I remembered the look he gave Pam and me during our stay at Southwestern Yacht Club when he'd caught us staring at the bronzed, muscled backs of young guys as they bent over, fine-tuning their boat engines. "Just remember," he lectured, "if you don't exert any self-control, when those urges surface, you could end up with . . . a baby." Pam and I were so embarrassed we could barely look at him.

I thought back to the few times boys had asked me out during my sophomore year. All I'd wanted to do was go to the movies with a boy I liked, but my father's excruciating exchange with my dates made it appear there were darker forces at play. And the cross-examination I'd faced when I returned home made me feel that with one slight misstep, I'd find myself compromised and headed toward teenage motherhood.

As I drifted along in the dinghy, I wondered why my parents, especially my father, viewed anything relating to sex as sordid. If I hadn't learned about the birds and the bees from outside sources, I'd probably be thinking right along with Nancy that the sea turtles were playing piggyback.

Whether the day or time was wrong or plans had been changed, it was obvious Keith had not been expecting any guests. And, as my father had said, "what they do onboard is their own business." I knew once I recovered from the shock at seeing my first hard-on, I'd live. It was not that big a deal, and it certainly didn't elicit any "urges" in me. I refused to believe that it was something to hide, like a dirty secret, when I knew it existed. If my father had been smart, he'd have taken us to frigid Alaska instead of the hot, steamy tropics. Sex was everywhere—in the warm, languid breezes; in the dark, predatory jungles; in the sensuous riot of colors; in the fresh silky streams; and in the deep salty waters—enveloping the dark nights and dazzling stars in a voluptuous embrace.

Nearly back to the boat, I felt something thump against the dinghy's thin fiberglass shell. Another sharp thump sent the oars popping out of their oarlocks. When I leaned over to grab the oar, I saw the dark fin cutting through the moonlit surface and knew it could only be one thing: a shark.

Setting the oars carefully back in the oarlocks, I rowed toward *Heritage*. The shark circled and swam past and was now between *Heritage* and the dinghy. Without warning, the bow rose and landed with a slap, just as if I had ridden over a small wave. The shark was under the dinghy, and I wondered if it had mistaken the small hull for a big fish. I rowed faster.

Thankfully, the next thump was not the shark but the dinghy striking *Heritage*. My father, who was sleeping in the cockpit, awoke. "Pipe down, will ya!" he said.

"Dad, there's a big shark out here!"

In less than a second, he leapt out of the cockpit and was on deck, extending his arm.

"Let me pass my guitar up to you first," I said.

"Jesus Christ! You gotta be kidding!"

"Okay, okay, I'll get it in the morning."

"Wow, will you look at the size of that thing!" my father said, as the shark brushed against the dinghy.

"Dad!"

"Quick, grab my hand." With one powerful jerk, he pulled me up on deck. "You okay, Sport?" he said, hugging me. I nodded and leaned in.

We stayed in Bahía Elena for a week, reluctant to leave our idyllic life. And, except for our moment near the stream and the occasional tussle over laundry duties, it was the first time I could remember my sisters and I enjoying time together.

My father wrote:

*All in all, the week we spent here will go down in our memory to be remembered when things are not quite so good.*

# 21

# A Disappearance

## *Playa del Coco, Costa Rica*

### AUGUST 9–15, 1970

*Heritage* slid noiselessly out of Bahía Elena as an orchid-colored dawn rose and slowly spread across the dark, volcanic hills. With the engine off and only the forestaysail up to catch the light morning breeze, the only sound heard was the quiet swish of water along the boat's prow and the chattering of dolphins riding our bow wake.

By mid-morning we passed the outermost island of Islas Murciéla-gos, a chain of eight bat-like formations that stretched, like webbed wings, across the water. A school of bull sharks zipped by us in the aqua-colored water and closer to shore, a school of eagle- and cow-nosed rays soared above the waves. This, even more than my first sighting of Cabo San Lucas, was what I'd always imagined Neverland to be: a pristine necklace of volcanic islands, covered in rich, lizard-green vegetation and small, curved coves with tiny slices of blindingly white sand. I wanted to sail over and explore but my father had other ideas.

"We've got to get across the Papagayo Gulf before sunset," he said. It was always the same excuse and sense of urgency that traced back to my father's failure to complete his celestial navigation course. Had he finished it, we'd be sailing by starlight, no longer slaves to the coastline or prisoners to the setting sun.

Although we missed our chance to explore Murciélagos, we were fortunate enough to catch a steady downwind breeze, and under the mainsail and genoa we arrived at Playa del Coco, a picturesque retreat for wealthy Costa Ricans, in plenty of time to anchor and enjoy a meal at one of the several restaurants lining the beach.

But I also knew my father had been eager to reach Playa del Coco for other reasons. He'd asked about Joe at every port south of Cabo, hoping someone had news of him or his boat. While a few northern-bound boats remembered Joe's unusual double-keeled vessel and his towering presence, one yacht owner told my father there'd been talk of Joe's disappearance somewhere north of Playa del Coco.

After we anchored in the horseshoe-shaped waters of Coco Bay, I rowed my parents and Nancy to shore, dropping them off on the dirt-colored volcanic sand before returning for Pam and Gayle. Word had spread quickly down the coast that a family with four girls, three of them teenagers, would soon arrive at Playa del Coco, home to a family with four boys.

We'd no sooner finished our meal at the beachside cantina when Mr. and Mrs. Bragg and their four sons—all with varying degrees of red hair and freckles—walked up to us and introduced themselves. "We've been eagerly awaiting *Heritage* to arrive with her legendary all-girl crew," Mrs. Bragg said, smiling at us.

Joining us at our table, we learned the Braggs had spent the last three years running a boutique hotel in Playa and homeschooling their sons. After more than a year of no contact with any boys my age, I found myself tongue-tied and painfully shy. Pam hit it off with eighteen-year-old Rusty, when she discovered he could speak fluent Spanish. Fourteen-year-old twins Roy and Robert were immediately smitten with Gayle. Even Michael, who was my age, was drawn to my younger sister. While all four boys were polite and well mannered, it was painfully obvious that none were interested in me and preferred my sisters' company over mine. I shrugged off the sting of rejection, but deep down I feared they'd recognized the same deficit my father saw: that I was unworthy of anyone's attention. Adding to that sense of unworthiness was my own heaping serving of self-criticism and judgment, which magnified what I perceived as my sisters' perfections. At fourteen, with her platinum hair, ice-blue stare, and coquettish smile, Gayle was becoming more beautiful every day. And, at nineteen, Pam, who was smart, bilingual, and beautiful in her own right, was becoming more independent. Sandwiched between two golden-haired siblings, I was dark-haired, quick-tempered, and tough.

Pretending not to care I'd been slighted, I turned my attention to the far end of the beach where *Triton* and her crew, who we hadn't seen since Zihuatanejo, were anchored. Sailing down the coast from San Francisco to Costa Rica, we'd traveled with boats mostly owned and crewed by young men. This demographic had been a royal pain-in-the-ass for my father, but a boon to me. The brotherly advice they'd given and platonic interest they'd shown made me feel safe, and appreciated. Pam and Gayle could spend time with those boys; I was going to spend my time with Don, Tony, and Ian, who made me feel as if I could accomplish anything I set out to do, and become anyone I wanted to be.

I thought about the slim volume of short stories my sisters and I had discovered among a box of paperbacks gifted to us in Acajutla by Mr. Smith. After we'd worked our way through the box of pulp fiction, detective novels, and a few classics, the only one remaining was a book with nine short tales about teenagers who exacted revenge on the adults controlling them. My favorite story among them was about a boy who dreamed of doing great things, only to have his mother repeatedly remind him, "You might think you are a pine in the forest, David, but you will always be just a little bush in the valley." One day, after years of listening to her, he took an ax and killed her. The macabre tale made us laugh out loud every time we read it. With a sporadically working radio, a tape deck devoid of batteries, and no access to TV, we passed the time acting out the scenes under the glow of the kerosene lamp, while my parents, unaware of the dark humor taking place below, relaxed and sipped their beers in the cockpit.

Even though I knew my father thought I was "just a little bush in the valley," I needed to believe I was more than that. One day, I'd prove him wrong and become a pine in the forest.

The next morning, my father rowed ashore to make inquiries at the port captain's about Joe. When he returned, I noticed his eyes were red, as if he'd been crying on his way back to the boat. "There was a terrible storm where Joe was last seen and they believe, after an unsuccessful sea and air search, he either capsized or the boat broke apart," he said.

We all started bawling over the news. I couldn't imagine our Kris Kringle and gentle giant had been lost at sea and we'd never see him again.

Because Joe had planned on sailing solo, he'd built a boat with a double keel, which allowed him to beach it singlehanded should the bottom require repair. Unfortunately, this also created a potentially serious issue if the boat was ever involved in a sudden knockdown. Unlike a single-keeled boat, which, if flipped, could right itself, a double-keeled boat could not. And Joe's mainmast was deck stepped rather than keel stepped. If a wire parted during a storm, like the one he was in, the whole rig could fall, leaving him with a broken mast and without sail power. And equipped with only a small outboard to guide him back to shore, he'd have become a victim to the current, pushing him out to sea.

As traveling yachts learned of Joe's disappearance, opinions floated freely over what might have happened. Many cited "design flaws," or assumed "pilot error." My father, believing in Joe's seamanship, was convinced otherwise. No one who cruised wanted to believe they had no control over the ocean. But, if any boater ever took time to ruminate, they'd realize boats were just little corks floating along, waiting for disaster to happen. All these people who'd rejoiced at having left their stifling and messy land lives in the belief that freedom and mastery defined their ocean lives were going to find out the only captain in command was the deep, blue sea.

Accepting Joe's death exposed the harsh reality that with one bad storm, we could easily face the same fate. Losing him had chipped away at our naïveté and exposed the fact that now, more than ever, *Heritage* held our lives in the balance. My father resolved to make sure she remained seaworthy and safe, and decided our next stop should be Puntarenas, which had a shipyard. Once there, he planned to haul *Heritage* out of the water and check for existing damage and future issues. If we were going to die on the high seas, it would be from a force out of our control and not because we hadn't replaced a rotten plank.

# 22

# Reality Bites

## *Puntarenas, Costa Rica*

**AUGUST 17–NOVEMBER 2, 1970**

After a two-day trip, we entered the Gulf of Nicoya and anchored at Isla Jesusita. From the water's edge to the treetops, thick vines crisscrossed the island like a giant chartreuse spiderweb, and under its entanglement, we could hear the screeching of monkeys and parrots.

Eager to get off the boat and explore, my sisters and I claimed first-dibs on the dinghy.

"Don't fool around too long," my father said as we rowed away. "Remember, other people want to get off this boat."

"No shit," I said, under my breath.

"You're lucky Dad didn't hear you."

"You think I care?" I said. Pam may have established leverage with her Spanish, but I was confident no one would climb the mast to fix a block or hang from the bow during a storm to pull in a sail. "It's not like he can kick me off the boat."

"Just try not to aggravate him," Pam said. "He's already in a bad mood."

He'd been out of sorts ever since he'd had to ration his smokes to two packs a day after discovering his low inventory. When he'd mentioned he couldn't believe he'd smoked that much, Pam and I assured him he had. "At this rate," he'd groused, "I'll have to load up with local ones." I remembered Pam and I exchanging side-long looks. We'd emptied so many Salems overboard, we'd come dangerously close to getting caught. Looking at him from the safety of the dinghy, I thought, if he's this crabby about his cigarettes, how's he going to react when he discovers he only has one shoe?

As I rowed toward the island, the dinghy cut through the smooth, bottle-green surface as easily as a water strider on a pond. How I wished my father's acknowledgment of me could have been as easy. I'd proved my worth countless times under the most treacherous conditions, but his tirades of "dealing with you goddamned women" canceled the smallest of achievements. What difference did it make doing the work of a man, if I never rose above the disappointment of being a girl? I thought things might change after Bahía Elena, where we'd had a wonderful time as a family, but when the initial shock of Joe's death wore off and we left Playa del Coco, he'd reverted right back to his old self.

"If I have to spend one more minute with him grouching, I swear I'll push him overboard," I said.

Gayle and Nancy were quiet, but Pam stifled a laugh. I looked at my older sister, who sat facing me. We might have had nothing in common, but the one thing we agreed on was how we felt about our captain.

Motoring over the next morning to Puntarenas's outer harbor, we side-tied to a steel barge connected to the main pier and waited for customs to board. It wasn't until the customs officer arrived, though, that I remembered my bag of marijuana in my drawer. While my father handed over our passports and ship's papers, I slid down the companionway in a panic.

Grabbing some panties from the laundry bag and an open box of tampons from the shelf in the head, I raced over and opened my drawer, threw them on top, and slammed it shut just before the officer descended the stairs.

"*Hola, señorita.*"

"*Hola,*" I said. I tried to smile, but my lips quivered as I watched the officer's eyes sweep the cabin.

"*Ya sabe, estamos buscando contrabando,*" he said, and then turned and faced me. When he realized I didn't understand, he said, "We are looking for contraband." He smiled, and then systematically lifted the bunks' mattresses, tapped on floorboards, and rummaged through lockers and drawers. I stood, frozen, in front of mine. *"Por favor,"* he said as he waved me aside. I held my breath. When he opened it and saw the crumpled underpants and loose tampons, he cleared his throat, muttering something in Spanish, and slammed the drawer shut.

"Are you keeping the officer from doing his work?" my father yelled from the cockpit.

Noting my distress, the officer smiled and raised his hands as if to say, *fathers, they're all alike.* Letting him misinterpret my reaction as one of teenage embarrassment, I smiled back with what I hoped looked like a grateful, conspiratorial grin.

The customs officer shouted up to my father, *"No problema, señor. Esta completo!"* Then, with a wink and a quick salute, he turned and ascended the stairs.

I stood there shaking and decided, the first chance I got, I'd throw the bag overboard. No reason to tempt fate, I thought, imagining what might have happened if my dirty laundry and feminine products hadn't deterred him. Better to get rid of it. Besides, I'd learned I could always bum a far superior joint from other yachts.

Once the customs officer signed off and cleared our entry, a pilot hopped on board to accompany us up the tricky channel and uncharted estuary to the Costa Rica Yacht Club. Since we were low on food supplies, my father reluctantly offered the pilot cigarettes from his depleted cache. Instead of taking a couple of packs, as my father thought, the pilot smiled and grabbed the entire carton.

Barely a quarter-mile into the estuary, the pilot, busy smoking on the foredeck, promptly drove us up on a sandbar. After surveying the situation, he shrugged, and said, *"Tenemos que esperar la marea,"* and then made a sweeping motion with his hands to show an incoming tide. Stepping into the stern, he tapped his watch and rubbed his stomach, and announced, *"Creo que es hora de almorzar!"*

Frustrated at the pilot's incompetence but unwilling to offend him, my father barked an order to my mother. "You and the girls . . . rustle up some lunch for our hungry guide."

While our pilot enjoyed his meal and a short siesta, two fishermen motored up and offered to pay out our chain and anchor. With their help and the incoming tide, my father winched *Heritage* toward deeper water.

Clear of the sandbar, *Heritage* continued up the freshwater estuary. Children raced along the muddy bank laughing and shouting at us, while, on the opposite side, cream-colored Brahma cattle and the snow-white egrets perched atop them ignored us, as they lunched on grass and flies.

Nearing the yacht club, the pilot pointed to a mooring near the main dock and said, "*Esta aqui!*" My father steered *Heritage* over and idled, while I leaned over and hooked the line.

As soon as we moored, the club's launch arrived to pick up the pilot. With his belly full of corned beef hash and carrying his cigarette carton, the pilot gave us a friendly wave as he motored off. Still seething over *Heritage*'s running aground and losing his beloved Salems, my father acknowledged the pilot's farewell with a flick of his hand and then turned his attention to us. "The launch will be back soon, so let's hustle."

In no time, my mother and sisters were ready and waiting in the cockpit. Meanwhile, our captain was busy tearing apart the cabin, opening and slamming locker doors and drawers. "Where the hell is my other sandal?" he yelled up.

"Gosh, Dad, I dunno," I said. "It must be around somewhere."

"Have *you* seen it?" I asked Pam, loud enough for my father to hear. I didn't dare look at her for fear of laughing.

"Nope," she said, leaping into the launch.

When my father emerged from the cabin wearing his old, moldy leather topsiders—the only other pair of shoes he owned—his expression made it crystal clear. He was going to murder whoever had misplaced his comfortable *huarache*. Life in the tropics had done nothing to ease the pain from his plantar warts, with the exception of his urine-cured, tire-soled sandals—and now he had only one.

When we made our way over to the club's pool, we found Laddie and her kids relaxing in chaise lounges. The *Tolaki* had beat us by a week, leaving Bahía Elena before us and sailing nonstop to Puntarenas. "Hey, guys, welcome to Poon-tah-ray-nas!" Laddie yelled. Laddie never just spoke.

Everything was always a couple of decibels too loud and punctuated with exclamation marks. Her energy and enthusiasm, we'd witnessed, was like a car with no brakes on a downward slope with no one at the wheel. Once she got started, there was no stopping her.

"Look at this mar-veh-lous saltwater pool, girls! . . . and the wait-staff is ab-so-lute-ly fabulous! Let's all celebrate your ar-ri-val!" she sang. "What do you guys want? I'm having another gin gimlet!"

"We have to go into town to get supplies and might not be back until late," my father said. We all knew it was an excuse to avoid her; there was nothing in town we had to buy that couldn't wait until morning. Pam, Gayle, and I stared longingly at the pool but didn't dare contradict him. Nancy, however, had no problem speaking out. "I want to go swimming, Daddy," she announced. She shrugged off her ragged cutoffs and T-shirt to reveal a blue, one-piece swimsuit. Unlike us, who'd not thought to wear our suits under our shorts, my youngest sister learned early on that preparation plus opportunity made for a perfect afternoon in the pool.

"Oh, puh-leeze, Jim, you can borrow whatever you need for tonight and go into town in the morning!" Laddie said, waving her hands dramatically. She had a way of pronouncing rather than conversing, which stifled any opportunity my father might have had for redress. He stood there, furious but tongue-tied.

Laddie's ability in silencing him rendered her, in my father's estimation, as a "pants-wearing female" with "nakedly aggressive tendencies." But her husband appeared to adore her and was more than happy to bask on the sidelines while she commanded center stage.

From the first encounter in San Diego, Laddie's unapologetic, bossy, and brassy behavior had rattled my father. But it wasn't until now that I realized it wasn't as one-sided as he'd purported. It was true she relished her punchlines, throwing back her head and braying like a donkey, but she was also undeniably feminine, floating about in her colorful, flowing caftans or in her tiny bikinis that were barely bigger than her flirtatious smile. She possessed in equal parts both yin and yang and navigated easily from one to the other, which threatened my father. After all, what would he do if his crew adopted Laddie's modus operandi? He was lucky that neither my sisters nor I had the expertise Laddie possessed or he might have faced a different crew.

Except for *Tolaki*, most of our traveling companions had stayed behind in Playa del Coco, so when a tiny twenty-four-and-a-half-foot cutter sailed up the estuary and moored nearby, it intrigued us. The next morning, we met *Seraffyn*'s owners, Lin and Larry Pardey, while we were having breakfast at the club's poolside cantina.

After my father and Larry exchanged boat-building stories, Lin and Larry invited us to board *Seraffyn* that evening for cocktails. Eager to show off *Heritage*, my father suggested they stop by our boat after lunch.

When the Pardeys rowed over in their dinghy, my father brought Larry below, while Lin remained in the cockpit with us. As we sipped our iced teas, made with ice my mother had pilfered from the club's outdoor ice-making machine, Lin enthusiastically dispensed beauty tips. "I never go anywhere without my mascara wand because it darkens *and* combs my lashes and eyebrows," she told us. Checking out the two unruly brows nestled like a pair of large furry caterpillars above her deep-set eyes, I could see why she considered it indispensable.

Larry appeared from below and wriggled in next to Lin, slinging his arm around her and pulling her close. After taking a long deliberate sip from Lin's iced tea, he turned to my father and said, "How much does she draw?"

My father proudly replied, "A little over six feet."

Larry whistled and said, "Wow, that's deep. Seems a little tough sailing a boat with her design in these shallow waters." He took another long sip before adding, "You must have had plenty of issues running aground."

Trying not to sound defensive, my father replied, "One or two, but nothing major."

"What made you decide to build a Gloucester schooner, designed for offshore fishing in New England, for cruising down here?" Larry asked.

"Guess I just liked the look of her lines," my father said.

"Well," Larry sighed, giving Lin a squeeze and a conspiratorial grin. "Too bad you'll be missing out on some magnificent spots along the way."

Even though my father ignored Larry's slightly smug expression and subtle jab, I couldn't. I recognized a setup from years of being bullied, and my father had stepped right into it. But I was a kid and so were my bullies. My father and Larry, however, were adults. Why did my father allow someone to insult him? If it had bothered me, it had to have bothered him. But as the Pardeys pushed off in their dinghy, my father simply reiterated he was looking forward to boarding *Seraffyn* at sunset.

That evening, the six of us and Larry crammed ourselves into *Seraffyn*'s cockpit, while Lin, busy in the galley, passed up crystal goblets filled with wine for my parents and Coca-Cola for me and my sisters. While my mother fawned over the stemware, Lin invited my sisters and me down to look around the tiny, compact, but well-appointed cabin.

At twenty-six and only seven years older than Pam, Lin acted more like a prim schoolteacher than a contemporary, as she instructed us on how to store dishes and stemware. "Larry built these wine racks for rough weather, and not one piece of crystal or plate from my service of eight has broken since we left Newport Beach!" she said, proudly showing us a perfect chipless plate. I tried to look interested but could have cared less. If being married was all about plates and glasses and storage compartments, I'd decided I'd rather be single for the rest of my life. When she pointed out the marriage benefits of having a double berth, it was all my sisters and I could do to not laugh.

After our tour, Lin joined us in the cockpit and blushed while Larry gushed about her culinary talents. "Lin cooked for a crew of six hungry men for almost three weeks, to and from Cocos Island," he said. "Show them the shells the crew gave you when they pulled the nets in." She obediently popped down below, brought up a cloth bundle, and unwrapped it.

"This one is very rare," she said, picking up a cone-shaped shell covered in an exquisite tortoise-shell pattern.

"Here, feel it," she said, handing it to me. I turned the shell over in my hand, exposing its creamy, translucent inner lip, and felt the same rush I'd had as a kid when I'd hammered off a piece of glittering mica in the arroyo behind the barn. I was at a loss to explain why I was so drawn to this shell and that piece of mica. Maybe their immutable beauty comforted me, unlike feelings or people, which could be fleeting and fickle.

When we returned from our evening on *Seraffyn*, we were unusually subdued. The self-confidence the Pardeys exuded exaggerated our own hidden insecurities. What we found annoying in them was what we found wanting in ourselves. Joe's death had revealed nature's overpowering force and had made us realize how little control we had. It had forced us to reexamine and even question *Heritage's* ability to protect and keep us safe. And Larry's intimation of *Heritage's* unsuitability in Central American waters and the conviction his Lilliputian-sized cutter was far superior, only added to our doubts.

To break the gloomy spell, my father announced, "Tomorrow I'm going to order a new butane stove to replace the outmoded kerosene one you girls and your mother have been using." As the boat's official cook, my mother brightened over the news, but my sisters and I remained unimpressed. Detecting our unenthusiastic reaction, my father pumped his arms as if warming up for a pep rally and said, "We're going to make the galley a proper cook's delight, with a new stove and fridge. We're also going to give the ol' gal a facelift and change her colors."

I looked at him and thought, let him flap his arms. It won't change a thing.

By the middle of September, Sammy Manley's shipyard pulled *Heritage* out of the water. After spending a month in the freshwater estuary, worms had attacked the planking along the waterline and *Heritage* would have to remain dry-docked longer than planned.

While my father fashioned replacement planks, the rest of us painted *Heritage's* cabin top and sides with her new colors: forest green for the hull and buff for the cabin top and masts.

It had been a while since we had crossed paths with Lin and Larry. They'd made themselves scarce, sailing *Seraffyn* out in the Nicoya Gulf for day and weekend trips. My sisters and I were relieved to be rid of them, but it seemed to bother my father that they'd avoided us.

One day, when Lin and Larry were back at the yacht club and near *Heritage*, I tucked my chin down, intending to barrel past them.

"I see you changed *Heritage*'s colors," Larry called out.

"Yup," I replied, rushing by them.

"Just curious, but . . ."

I wanted to keep walking, but he kept talking.

"Did your dad order the masts that way, or did he shape them himself?"

"He made them himself," I said. The setup was palpable, but I just stood there.

"Too bad," Larry paused before adding, "'cause he made them all wrong. They're way too skinny for the size of your boat. Those masts will never hold in rough weather." He exchanged knowing looks with Lin.

I stared at his pudgy, bearded face, which reminded me of the garden gnomes squatting in my neighbors' yards back in Oakland. I don't know why, I thought, but I hate this guy.

"They did just fine in the hurricane off Zihuatanejo," I said. I turned on my heel and walked away, barely controlling the urge to run back and punch him in the face.

What made things worse was the underlying fear that for all his arrogance, Larry Pardey might have been right. I wondered if any other boaters felt the same way but, unlike the Pardeys, were too polite to express it. Was *Heritage* considered flawed like Joe's boat? If so, was there a consensus that, like Joe, we deserved whatever outcome might befall us?

Then again, maybe Larry was just being an asshole. Adults were way worse than teenagers for being dicks. I wished I'd been brave enough to tell him what I thought. But I'd learned it was hard to be brave as a kid. If there was fallout from my actions, there was no place I could run to. The only home I had was on the boat.

With the help of a local carpenter, my father finished rebuilding the galley, installing a new freezer compartment, and an Italian-made butane stove, which he'd purchased in San José. This was all done while *Heritage* was dry-docked to avoid further work after she was back in the water. In fact, we had so much work, my sisters and I took a break from our studies.

Finally, the day arrived for *Heritage* to go back into the water. We were the third boat scheduled to reenter after two eighty-foot shrimpers launched. When it was our turn, we watched as the twenty-ton travel-lift slid and hovered like a giant insect over *Heritage*. After shipyard workers strapped thick belts around *Heritage's* keel, the travel lift raised her and made its way over to the ways. Once the lift positioned her, my father and I climbed up on deck to handle the lines needed when she slid down to the water.

*Heritage's* narrow ten-foot beam required three different wood shims on each of the four locations between the hull and cradle, on both starboard and port sides, fore and aft. But when the rollers, which moved the cradle down to the water, suddenly jerked, I felt the shim on the starboard bow pop, destabilizing the hull.

"*Jesus Cristo!*" a worker shouted from below. "*Miro! Miro! El barco esta inestable.*"

"Jim, the boat's slipping," my mother shouted.

Standing on the foredeck, I stared down at the pandemonium taking place on the ground. Men were yelling and pushing my mother, Gayle, and Nancy out of the way. I felt the boat sway, and without thinking I grabbed the nearest line, lassoed it around the dock's piling, and hitched it to the cleat and forward bit. I jumped back and held my breath as the line stretched out and took the boat's full weight.

"*Su hija es muy valiente!*" the men cheered.

Ignoring their shouts and whistles, my father pushed me aside and yelled down, "Someone get a goddamn block and shore up this vessel."

"I should have let the boat slide off and crash," I told my mother later that evening.

"You know your father is grateful," she said. "He just doesn't know how to show it."

Salvaging the day, my father showed up with mail. Since arriving in Puntarenas, I'd posted so many letters to the States, I was hoping a few friends had written back. But I stifled my excitement because my father was always snapping at us to "cut the ties" with our old life back in California. "We're never going back so why prolong friendships you'll never rekindle," he'd utter every time we pestered him about mail. "We have more important problems to focus on than worrying about your past," he said to us.

The problem was he never talked about the future, so I clung to the familiar and the life I'd known. While *Heritage* continued to sail in a southerly direction, my father hadn't planned past Panama or, if he had, didn't share it with us. Depending on his mood, he'd say we were on our way to Tahiti or if he changed his mind, on our way to the Caribbean. Either way, it didn't bring me any closer to knowing the endgame, so I found comfort in looking back rather than forward.

For me, my father's insistence on cutting ties was more about his guilt rather than us letting go. His decision to leave my grandmother behind, which, I believed, hastened her death, and the chastisement by relatives who reminded him he'd left a steady job, made *him* want to cut ties with not only colleagues, friends, and family, but everything else connected to our land life.

Announcing a boat was no place for animals, he gave away Pam's Siamese cat, Nutmeg, and Gayle's wire-haired terrier, Beau. My sisters had been pragmatic about relinquishing their pets, but I mourned their loss as if they'd died.

When I thought about *Faraway*'s four-footed crew members—their Sphinx-like and fierce-looking shepherd and their loud and sassy Siamese—I knew my father had made a mistake. Spending time in Yelapa with John and his elderly mother, Hilke, I'd asked them if it was hard traveling with their pets, to which John had laughed and replied, "Why, Schatzi and Tinkerbell are better sailors than we are. They don't even get seasick!"

What seemed effortless to other people—taking their pets and loved ones with them as they sailed from country to country and across the sea—had been an impossibility for us. I'd observed Hilke, who was not only surviving but thriving. If she could live on a boat at her age, why couldn't Grandma have done so? Why didn't I try harder to convince my father to take her and our pets? Maybe then, we'd be more like the *Faraway*, whose crew didn't have to cut their ties, because they'd taken it all with them.

"There're letters for everyone," my father said. He handed three to Pam, two to Gayle, and only one to me. Disappointed I hadn't received more, I ripped open Sara's letter and learned she was still in Acapulco. Their deckhand, Mike, had returned to the States, and while they waited to find a new one, she and Mubs were busy exploring Acapulco and Mexico City. They'd celebrated Max's birthday by giving him a big machete and a tiny green parrot named Chico. Since she had the boat to herself, she'd studied hard and was now a semester ahead of me. After reading this, I almost wished she hadn't written to me.

"I noticed Mubs Fraser sent you a note," my father said to Pam. "After you've finished reading it, maybe you'll share it with the rest of the family." He also announced he, my mother, Gayle, and Nancy would leave in the morning to ride the narrow-gauge train to the consulate's office in San José, so Gayle could take her semester exam.

That night I slept fitfully, dozing off in the early morning and missing my parents' departure.

"What's the matter with you?" Pam asked, when she saw me curled in my bunk.

"I'm sick, goddammit." My head was pounding, and I could barely swallow. "I can't believe that the one time they leave, I feel like shit."

"Well, I'm going to sit by the pool. It's too hot down here. And it's so still I'm sure the mosquitoes won't wait until evening to feast on us," she said. "Why don't you come with me? At least if you get too hot, you can jump in the pool."

I shivered. "I'm just gonna lie here for a while."

Pam shrugged and said, "Suit yourself." She gathered her towel and a paperback, climbed up the companionway, and blew the whistle for the launch.

For only the second time in a year, I was alone onboard. No parents, no siblings. It should have been a moment to celebrate; instead, I lay in my narrow bunk, sweating and shivering, and scratching the hundreds of mosquito bites on my arms and legs.

When I turned over and faced the settee, I noticed Pam's letters sticking out of her notebook. I knew I shouldn't, but I was sick and itchy, so I retrieved them.

Settling back in my bunk, I reread Mubs's letter and discovered Pam had omitted the last sentence in which Mubs had written, "Naturally, we all send our very best to everyone on the slave ship *Heritage*."

It seemed as if everyone, including the generous and understanding Frasers, saw us for what we were. My father might as well have clapped us in leg irons and raised a skull and crossbones flag atop the mast. His behavior toward his crew had fooled no one. I hated the thought everyone either felt sorry for us or pitied us.

I refolded Mubs's letter and opened the next one, which was postmarked Playa del Coco, and was from Rusty, the eldest of the four Bragg boys. "Dear Pam, Gayle, and I forgot-the-other-name," it began. It couldn't get any worse. Not only was I considered a slave, but I was also nameless. At the end of his letter, Rusty asked if she still planned to study at the university.

I glanced at the third letter, which included an application form. Was Pam planning to escape? Why hadn't she said anything? She had a savings account back in California, just like I did, started with money she'd earned from babysitting. But how was she going to get ahold of it with no one knowing? Even though I reassured myself that she couldn't just pack up and leave, I worried what life would be without her. Already, I'd had to work twice as hard for half the respect. With the remaining crew too young, too seasick, and too nautically challenged, my father would saddle me with all the work.

I folded the letters and inserted them back into her notebook. I could only hope it was a passing interest, piqued by her week in Guadalajara with Cathy.

When my father returned from San José, he was short tempered and depressed. "Your father discovered a few things while we were in San José," was all my mother would say. When I pressed her, she admitted he'd gotten his hands on an American newspaper to check on his stock investment. Unable to locate the company's ticker symbol in the stock section, he'd sent off a telegram to his stockbroker in California.

While he paced the deck, awaiting news from the States, I recalled the day the stockbroker first visited us after we'd moved onboard in

Alameda. My father had encouraged my mother and sisters to sit and listen as the broker talked about "a guaranteed home run." Before departing, he'd convinced my father to invest all of our college savings in what he touted as the next great American venture, the Alaska pipeline.

My father assured my mother he'd made the right decision, by reminding her that "after all, the guy's an ex-priest," as if having worn the collar meant we'd receive celestial attention and a godly guarantee we'd never get screwed.

Unfortunately for us, the broker-ex-priest's "guaranteed home run" struck out.

After my father received news of the company's bankruptcy and delisting, I overheard him say to my mother, "We still have cash from our funds in the savings and loan to draw upon."

But right on the heels of that revelation, he received a letter from my grandparents. The CEO of the savings and loan in California, which held our travel funds, had embezzled and absconded with everyone's cash. My grandfather insisted we return home.

My father read the letter, then tore it up, sending the pieces fluttering overboard. "We're not going back," he said to us, "but there's going to be a slight change in plans."

## 23

# Chiquita Banana

### *Golfito, Costa Rica*

**NOVEMBER 2–9, 1970**

After nearly ten weeks in Puntarenas—two weeks longer than expected—we freed *Heritage* of her mooring, waved goodbye to *Tolaki*, and motored down the estuary and into the Nicoya Gulf. Under clear skies, we crossed over to Isla Jesusita and anchored for the night.

Right before dawn, a front moved in, and as I lay in my bunk listening to the downpour, my father yelled down from the cockpit, "Up and at 'em! And get your slickers on!" My sisters and I groaned as we rolled out of our bunks. I opened the locker where we kept the foul-weather gear and passed them out to Pam and Gayle.

"Ugh, it smells and it's sticking to my skin," Gayle said, slipping hers on. I couldn't tell her to shut up because it was exactly what I was thinking. I could only hope the skies would clear, and I could rip off the stinky jacket. But after weighing anchor, the weather worsened, and as we huddled in the cockpit, water funneled into our foul-weather gear, soaking us to the bone. When my father sent us below to dry, I couldn't decide what was worse, the wet cockpit or the stifling cabin.

For two days, we pushed forward down the coast on a flat sea through unrelenting rain. As we passed Bahía de Coronado and reached its southern end, my father decided to anchor at Bahía Dey for the night.

The rain had finally stopped, but the anchorage, an open roadstead and unprotected from northerly winds, kept us from rowing ashore. Our navigational chart showed the black-sand beach was only accessible by sea, so it surprised us when two long *pangas* filled with men suddenly materialized from shore and paddled toward us.

My father stood watching them approach, and I wondered if he was thinking of the warnings from northbound yachts of the dangers of desolate anchorages. Incidents of night intruders had increased following the disappearance of a yachtsman, whose boat, ransacked and crewless, was discovered floating off the coast.

During our stops along Baja, and the Central American coast, we'd successfully traded canned goods and staples for freshly caught fish or fruits and vegetables. So, we didn't worry until they reached our boat and noticed that their canoes, except for the men in them, were empty.

When several of the men grabbed onto our railing and tried to hoist themselves on board, my father strong armed them, forcing them to drop back in their canoes. Although they complied, the men grinned wildly, thrusting out their hands, and speaking rapidly in a dialect Pam couldn't understand.

"Go below and tell your mother to rustle up a bag of rice and some canned ham," my father said. I shot down the stairs and returned shortly with the items and handed them off to a man in the first *panga*. Pam pointed to the goods and then said, "*Todos,*" to show it was for both canoes.

"*Dinero!*" one of the young men from the second boat said, as he held out his hand. My father turned to Pam and said, "Tell them we have no money."

"*No tenemos dinero.*" They looked at Pam and then at my father, who shook his head and repeated, "*No dinero.*" Again, they grinned at us. I hoped it was a friendly grin, but the look in their eyes belied something else, as if they were weighing the veracity of our words.

If I could have, I would've invited them on board to check out our less than luxurious conditions. Rather than the *Americanos ricos* they assumed we were, we were closer to *los Americanos pobres*. As it was, it was our last bag of rice until we could replace it in Golfito, and even though I hated canned ham, it had been a great trading item, and we'd given them the last one. More worrisome was that an empty *panga* meant they had nothing to trade because they were surviving on very little, or they were desperate and looking for something worth more than food or supplies.

That evening, while dining on coffee-can bread and beans, my father told us we'd have to stand watch. Pam relieved me at ten, with my father relieving her at midnight. Instead of waking me at two, my father continued his watch until he woke all of us around 3:00 a.m. "Okay, folks, let's get a move on. Now!"

Pam and I rolled out of our bunks in a panic. I looked around for my shorts, but my father yelled down, "No time to change. Get up here now and get the goddamn anchor up!" By the time Pam and I scrambled on deck and were hauling up the anchor, my father was ready, with the engine idling. For a moment, the full moon shone through a break in the clouds, and I could see movement on the beach. I worked the windlass even faster until the anchor popped up.

"Anchor's up!" I said. With that, *Heritage* pulled away and headed into the black night.

We sailed along the coast until, lining up with Isla del Cano, we altered course and rounded Punta Llorona at the northern end of the Oso Peninsula. All morning, under steady rain, I stared out at a wall of dark-green jungle that extended directly down to the sea. Somewhere inside that dense rainforest, scarlet macaws, white hawks, and keel-billed toucans flew under its thick canopy; squirrel and spider monkeys leapt from its branches; jaguars, cougars, and ocelots stalked its forest; and tapirs and peccaries rooted around its forest floor. But all I could see on this rainy day was an endless line of green.

While my father helmed *Heritage*, the rest of us sat chilled, wet, and silent in the cockpit. My sisters and I had run out of things to say to each other and were cranky because everything was cold and wet. And the captain was in pain because of his plantar warts and miserable over the cigarettes he'd purchased in Puntarenas. As he blew smoke rings in my face, I almost regretted throwing his Salems overboard. I didn't know what kind of tobacco they grew in Central America, but it smelled as if he were smoking dried cattle dung.

By the late morning, we entered Golfo Dulce, named Sweet Gulf for the four freshwater fjords pouring into it. The skies finally lightened, and we enjoyed a fast motor-sail across the gulf, keeping to the edge of the shipping lane to avoid banana-laden freighters steaming by us on their way out to the Pacific.

Approaching Golfito, we could see it lay nestled on a narrow strip of land between the bay and the steep, evergreen forested hills rising behind it. The port was a company town, where locals who weren't bar or restaurant owners worked for the United Fruit Company—picking, transporting, and boxing bananas, which were then stacked on pallets and loaded onto freighters that delivered the ubiquitous Chiquita Banana brand all over the world.

Once we'd secured *Heritage* to the dock with double bow and stern lines and fenders at her midships, my father suggested we all take a short walk to town and on to the banana plantation where he'd promised we'd get a tour. But, when we reached the plantation's manicured lawns and freshly painted, colonial-style bungalows, an executive stepped out from one of them and politely informed my father they no longer gave tours. Disappointed, we turned around and headed back.

Unable to deliver on his promise, my father suggested he make it up by taking us to a late lunch at the Chinese cantina we'd passed in town. Although sick of eating *camarones con arroz fritos*, the mainstay on every menu in every cantina along the coast, we also knew it was a hard meal to screw up. Since it had rained again, we were happy to delay our return to *Heritage* and her hot, stuffy cabin.

By the time we finished our meal and returned to the boat, we were drenched. Rain pounded the cabin top and deck, and unable to crack open the portholes, we lay in our bunks and tried to ignore the stifling conditions, and one another. My father confined himself to the quarter berth, which ran parallel to the engine compartment and opposite the head. It was not the most ideal spot in which to catch a few winks, especially if you possessed a queasy stomach and delicate nose. I guess that was my father's justification for lighting up. The smoke, though, drifted toward us rather than up through the crack in the hatch. To avoid its dung-like odor, I buried my face in my pillow. Rivulets of sweat ran down my neck and soaked the back of my T-shirt, and I wondered how I could put myself out of my misery. Wishing I hadn't smoked the rest of my stash in Puntarenas, I buried my head even deeper into my pillow, hoping I'd suffocate.

For the next two days, it seemed the sky dumped all the world's precipitation directly on Golfito. On the morning of the third day, the rain let up enough for my father to sneak off while we were still sleeping. He's likely nursing a *café con leche* and enjoying a smoke at the cantina, I thought. Trying my best not to wake Nancy or my mother in the forepeak, I whispered over to Pam and Gayle. "Hey, wake up, you guys. Dad's gone, and I've got an idea how we can get off this boat for a couple of hours."

Pam propped herself up on one elbow and Gayle rolled over on her side.

"Let's check out that freighter that came in last night." Although Pam, Gayle, and I had sworn we'd never freighter hop again after boarding ships in Acajutla, we were all dying to do something other than sit on the boat all day. "I think it was flying a German flag. They gotta be more civilized than the guys we had to deal with on that ship from Monrovia or the drunk officers on the Scandinavian one."

"I'm in," Pam said. Gayle nodded, which I took for a yes.

We grabbed our rain jackets, scrambled up the companionway, and hopped off the boat, hoping we'd be beyond the pier before my father returned.

Slinking along the main street, we made our way to the loading dock. Cranes were busy lifting and moving pallets over to the freighter and lowering them into the hold.

"Uh oh, I think we might be in trouble," I said, eyeing the uniformed man walking toward us. In Acajutla, we'd simply rowed over and climbed on board, but here, they probably considered our mere presence as trespassing.

"Hello zehr. Are you Americans?"

"Uh, yes, we sailed in last night with our *parents*," Pam said nervously.

"Ya vell, very goot," he said, in a light German accent. "I zee you are interested in our ship. Vood you like a tour of zah bananas being loaded?"

"Yes!" we said in unison.

"Goot, follow me." He turned and walked toward the steep gangway. We quickly followed behind, ready for a new adventure. Reaching the top of the gangway, the young officer turned to us and smiled. Surely, he's trustworthy, I thought. He doesn't look much older than Pam.

After taking us through a quick tour, he brought us to the ship's salon, where he introduced us to the captain and his fellow officers. They stood up, shook our hands, and invited us to join them for coffee and cake. As we devoured our dessert, the junior officers told us the ship was German, as were they, but joked that they could all sing English better than speak it because the captain only listened to American rock music.

One officer excused himself and returned shortly afterward, carrying three cassette tapes. He set them down in front of us and pointed to two of them. "Zis are some of my favorite groups. Zere are zah Beatles, Simon and Garfunkel, Bob Dylan, and so many more." He picked up the third tape and shoved it in the cassette player.

"You vill like zis group. Zeh are called Mungo Jerry. Very snappy songs." He was right. They were catchy tunes. Gayle immediately fell in love, especially with a song called "In the Summertime," and claimed the tape as hers.

Having finished our desserts, we clasped our tapes and stood up, ready to leave. Just then, the port captain burst through the door. A small, greasy-looking man with dark, darting eyes, he spoke in rapid Spanish to the ship's captain. I elbowed Pam. "What's he saying?"

Before she could answer, the port captain motioned us to follow him. "Where is he taking us?" Pam asked one officer. The officer's complexion colored as he stuttered, "He is thinking zat you girls are vanting more zan to witness loading bananas."

"*Ahora!*" the port captain snapped. We stared at the embarrassed officers.

"Don't worry. We follow you out," the second officer said, trying to reassure us.

Pam and I, thoroughly humiliated, pulled Gayle out the door and followed the port captain through the boat's corridors and down the ramp to the dock. The officers followed quickly behind and ushered us over to a jeep. On the drive back to the pier, they invited us to dinner at the Chinese cantina, as their apology for the port captain's behavior.

Neither my sisters nor I had any intention of joining them, but when we returned to the boat, my father had taken over the cockpit now that the rain had stopped, leaving us to hunker down in the cabin. Dinner with the officers suddenly looked like the better choice.

After spending the afternoon hours sweating in the stuffy cabin, my sisters and I could hardly wait to jump ship and make our way over to the cantina. Almost instantly, though, I regretted my decision. While my sisters and I ate, the officers guzzled bottle after bottle of cheap Costa Rican beer, until they could barely string two sentences together. Skipping dessert, we informed our very inebriated hosts it was past our curfew.

"Boy, was that uncomfortable," I said, as we headed back to the pier. "How come they didn't defend us to the port captain? Did they invite us to dinner because they felt guilty for being douchebags?"

Pam sighed. "Look, it was dinner with the Germans or Captain Bligh. I'll take the Germans any day."

"He's not Captain Bligh all the time," Gayle said.

I laughed. "You're right. He's a bastard, the rest of it."

"Don't talk about Dad that way!"

I could understand why Gayle defended him. Maybe it was because she was seasick most of the time, but he never yelled at her the way he did with me.

"Cut it out, guys!" Pam said.

I shrugged. "Why? It's the truth."

"I wish I hadn't come," Gayle whined.

"Well, I can understand that. I mean . . . we can't take you anyplace," I said. "What in the world . . . did you forget to close your mouth, or what? You sprayed fried rice all over everyone." Gayle stuck her tongue out at me.

"Gawd, don't remind me. I was so embarrassed!" Pam said. "This whole evening was a disaster."

"Well, I thought they were nice," Gayle said. She held up her hand, waving the cassette tape. "And, I have Mungo Jerry."

"Oh, what do you know? You're clueless," I said to her. "You don't even know why that sleazy port captain escorted us off the ship."

"Just stop," Pam said.

"I hate we can't go where we please," I said. "I'm done freighter hopping."

"Let's just get back to the boat," Pam said.

To lighten the conversation, I said, "Here's some interesting trivia for you guys. Did you know that on this last leg, Dad barfed forty-three times?" My sisters both laughed. "Oh, and I almost forgot. On the thirty-seventh time, he almost lost his teeth overboard, 'cause he forgot to take them out before throwing up and they shot right out of his mouth. He had to chase them along the deck before they disappeared through the scuppers. Can you imagine giving us orders with no teeth?" "Geth thoth thails, up now, girlths!"

"It wasn't his fault. It was the oatmeal's," Gayle said.

She was right. "I have to admit, when I'm seasick, it tastes like paste," I said.

"I couldn't even look while he was eating it," Pam said.

"I know. It's the raisins. They look like little black bugs drowning in cement. Just thinking about it makes me nauseous," I said.

"Mother gets an F minus in the cooking department," Pam said.

"Which brings us back to what's worse: Chinese food with boozers or a disgusting meal with Dad?"

By this time, we'd reached the end of the dock, where *Heritage* rocked quietly in the dark.

"Uh oh," Gayle whispered. "Dad's asleep in the cockpit."

I whispered back. "Where's Mom?"

"Where do you think? She's sleeping in the forepeak as usual," Pam said.

"Great marriage, huh? Remind me to kill myself if I ever end up like them, okay?" I said.

Pam snickered. "How are we going to crawl over without waking him?"

"I'm tired. I want to go to bed," Gayle said.

Ignoring her, I turned and whispered to Pam. "We have to be careful. He'll be mad as hell if we wake him."

"Gawd, you'd think I'd have gotten used to crawling over him by now, but I haven't. I just hate it. I'm afraid my foot will slip and land on his face," she said.

"Are you kidding? You *wish* your foot would land on his face!" I turned back to Gayle. "Okay, since you complained, you're first."

"I'm afraid," she said.

"Okay, then you go, Pam."

"Uh, no thanks. After you."

"Man, you guys are unbelievable! Just remember who you call pushy in the future." I grabbed the stanchion and jumped on board. I tiptoed down to the stern, ready to make my move. But the second I leaned over and wrapped my arms around the boom, I knew I'd made a mistake. Stored in the folds of the mainsail were a couple of gallons of ice-cold rainwater.

A blood-curdling scream filled the night air as my father shot up, completely drenched and wild-eyed, from the cockpit floor. Spying my sisters cowering on the wharf, he leaped onto the deck, shaking his fist. In unison, they pointed their fingers at me.

"Uh, Dad, I can explain . . . ," I said, peeking out from the hatch, trying my hardest not to laugh.

He turned back to my sisters. "You two, get on board and get below. NOW!" They scrambled on deck and tumbled past me into the cabin. My father shoved his face close to mine. "And wipe that goddamn smile off your face!"

By this time, my mother and Nancy were awake and were sitting at the settee. I was explaining what had happened when my father, still fuming, came below.

"Daddy, you're all wet!" Nancy exclaimed.

"You can thank your sister for that!" He rummaged around for some dry clothes and stomped back up the companionway to change in the cockpit.

"What on earth happened?" my mother whispered.

"It's all her fault," Gayle said, pointing to me.

I laughed and then caught myself. "Look, it was an accident. How did I know so much water was under the cover?"

As I lay there in the dark mulling over the evening's events, my father called down from the cockpit. "Go to sleep! We're departing before dawn."

Sick of the rain, we were all ready to move on.

It was still dark when my father roused us. As soon as I dressed and was on deck, he ordered me to clear the dock. I threw the bow line to Pam and the stern line to Gayle and hoisted myself on deck, as my father threw the engine into reverse and *Heritage* cleared the dock. As she made her way out of the harbor, I watched the twinkling lights of the United Fruit Company recede. Between the freighter adventure, bad weather, and pissing off my father, it was a relief to turn my back on this strange little town.

## 24

# Between the Sea and Sky

### *Limones and Islas Secas*

From the moment we left the open roadstead at Limones and sailed into the jade-green waters of the Chiriqui Gulf, something shifted. With the engine off and a light, steady breeze filling the genoa, *Heritage* cut through smooth seas, where pods of dolphins surrounded us, and magnificent frigate birds flew above the rigging.

No one, including Gayle, was sick. In fact, we all had appetites. Without the constant assault on our stomachs we'd experienced since departing San Francisco, we sat together in the cockpit, enjoying a meal and actually conversing. Civility had replaced churlishness. It wasn't until its absence that I could see how debilitating and incapacitating the effects of seasickness had on us, especially on my father and Gayle. My younger sister had spent the bulk of her time over the rail. And when she was not there, we could find her curled in her bunk. For thousands of miles, she'd emptied her guts, only regaining her appetite when we reached port. While she rarely complained, it had taken a toll on her physically. As for my father, the change would have been remarkable, if not for the unnerving reaction it elicited. For the first time, he joked and kidded around with us as if his Captain Bligh persona had been an illusion. It was even more disconcerting when, adding to the mix, his dream of sailing to the South Pacific was over now that our funds were gone.

"Well, kids, we can now sail the Caribbean, where the water is just as blue, if not bluer," he said. "And just think of the adventure we're going to have transiting the Panama Canal."

I wasn't sure what to think of this change in him or how long it would last, but decided it was better than what he'd been before. I made my way up the deck to sit in my favorite spot between the forward hatch and cabin and stared out over the ocean. Far beyond the coastline, I could see the faint outline of Panama's Baru Volcano, and closer to *Heritage*, my favorite mini-cetaceans rollicked in the waves, twirling, cartwheeling, and leapfrogging over one another. Even now, after hundreds of sightings, I never tired of their play. If only I could be as they were—with no desire to be anywhere but right where they were. Unlike them, I struggled, finding it easier to embrace what had been or what might be. Looking back at my family, I realized it didn't matter if this would last; the only thing that mattered was, it was happening.

Suddenly, the pod I'd been watching shot out of the air as the sea boiled around them. "Hey guys!" I shouted. "Something's happening off the port!" I jumped up and leaned against the rigging as the first humpback breached. Right next to him, another breached. Excited, I swung onto the ratlines and climbed halfway up for a better look. "They're coming closer. And there's a baby!"

By this time, everyone was leaning over the railing to get a better look. A whale surfaced directly behind the stern, blowing a stream of pungent mist from its airhole and spraying everyone.

"Oh, man, that stinks!" Gayle said.

"The mama and baby are right at midships," I said. The water was so clear, I could see the two clearly as they followed alongside us. Then, off to our starboard, the second whale breached high out of the water before it plunged back, slapping the water with its flukes and pectoral fins. They played alongside us, swimming under our keel and surfacing until finally, the threesome disappeared at our stern, heading northward.

I climbed down and made my way to the cockpit.

"This was even better than our sighting off San Diego," Pam said.

All the envy I'd felt over having missed that experience dissipated, and the separation I felt between my sisters and me lessened.

By late afternoon, Islas Secas appeared off our bow. Named for the long stretches of beach that were exposed during extreme tides, the volcanic Dry Islands were wild and uninhabited, surrounded by pristine beaches and coral reefs.

By the time we reached Isla Cavada, the largest of the islands, and found a safe anchorage in one of its coves, the sun dipped below the horizon. After three attempts to set the hook, it was too late to row to shore, so we sat in the cockpit and enjoyed the warm breeze and the sky's changing colors. The farther south we traveled, the more intense the sunrises and sunsets, and tonight was no exception, as we watched a spectacular spectrum of reds, oranges, yellows, pinks, and purples saturate the sky.

Just when I thought the evening couldn't get more glorious, I looked over the side, where a dazzling display below rivaled the technicolor show above. With darkness descending, the turquoise waters turned black, and the sea burst in bioluminescence. Millions of microscopic organisms and one-celled plankton pulsed with an otherworldly glow as schools of fish darted through the inky water, leaving phosphorescent swirls and spirals and zigzags in their wake.

The next morning, my father announced the anchorage was too beautiful not to stay an extra day and suggested we enjoy our time swimming and exploring the beach. When his back was turned, we all exchanged glances. It was as if he'd swallowed a magic potion that erased all the meanness. He even snorkeled with us in the turquoise shallows around the boat, counting sea turtles, eagle rays, and a few whitetip sharks, as they swam below us. Leaving my sisters to float on the surface, buoyed by their life vests, my father and I swam down to the bottom, where a green moray eel poked its head out from a coral head and schools of neon blue parrotfish swam by, while purple starfish moved slowly across the sandy bottom.

In the late afternoon, we rowed ashore and built a fire out of piles of driftwood scattered on the beach and watched the sky morph from blue to pink to orange to red to purple as the sun disappeared into the sea. Rowing back under the stars, I forgot about everything, except the sound of the oars dipping into the water and feeling the night air against my skin.

Back in the cockpit, my father talked about how once we reached the Canal Zone, we'd transit and make our way to the Windward and Leeward islands to enjoy the Caribbean before sailing to Florida, where he'd look for work and we could go back to school. The promise of a new adventure replaced thoughts of crossing the Pacific. "The Caribbean will be as beautiful as this," he said. I couldn't imagine anything more beautiful than where we were right now, and I couldn't imagine being happier.

Back in my bunk, I lay in the dark, listening to the soft lapping against the hull. I thought about all the times I'd spent waiting to be happy. As far back as I could remember, back to when I was five and sitting on the porch steps, I'd been waiting. Throughout elementary, junior high, and high school I'd waited. Throughout the years spent working on the boat, I'd waited. And having sailed over three thousand miles, I'd waited.

Just as my father promised he'd be happy once we started on our trip, I'd promised myself that even after losing Grandma, I'd be happy. But along the way, we'd both failed, miserably. I'd been as unhappy as he was. But today was different. I didn't look back or ahead. As I drifted off to sleep, I dreamed I was leaping and twirling in a sapphire sea. Like the dolphins, I had no desire to be anywhere but here, with my family, aboard *Heritage*.

# III

# ABEAM OF THE ARROW

## 25

# Honking for Slim

### *Balboa, Canal Zone*

**NOVEMBER 14–DECEMBER 15, 1970**

After a three-day sail from Islas Secas and dodging freighters all night in the Gulf of Panama, we reached Isla Taboga and anchored in its crystal-clear waters. The "Island of Flowers," so named for its colorful blossoms and natural beauty, was our last stop before the Canal Zone. If I could have imagined the Spanish Riviera, it would have been this small volcanic gem, with its sun-drenched beach, turquoise waters, and pleasure craft anchored offshore. Maybe it was the wealthy Panamanians who zipped in and out of the small bay in their powerful speedboats, or the proximity to Panama City, or the sight of massive ships steaming by, but there was an electric atmosphere surrounding the island. Our arrival and the last seven days we'd spent sailing to Panama had shown me that even though we'd lost our savings and our itinerary had altered, we'd been the happiest since starting the trip.

Following a quick trip onshore for freshwater showers and lunch at the nearby hotel, we weighed anchor and made our way to the channel to rendezvous with customs. Although we were going only as far as the Balboa Yacht Club, which lay six miles away, a pilot was required to help us navigate around the heavily congested canal traffic.

When customs pulled alongside us two hours later, the pilot jumped down onto our deck and made his way to the stern. "Let's get y'all over to the yacht club," he said brusquely. He handed a sheaf of papers for my father to sign and took command of *Heritage*.

Manning the helm, he steered toward the Thatcher Ferry Bridge, the gateway to the ten-mile wide, fifty-mile-long strip of land known as the Canal Zone. Operated by the Panama Canal Company and protected by the United States Military, the CZ housed civilian and military Americans and their families. That meant, besides stateside movie theaters, libraries, ice cream parlors, bakeries, and grocery stores, there were American kids. I wasn't sure how long we were staying before we transited, but maybe it was long enough to meet some of them.

I grabbed the camera from below and made my way to the foredeck where Nancy sat tucked between the cabin and the forward hatch, conversing with her redheaded best friend. She looked up just in time for me to snap a picture of her gap-toothed grin with the expanse of bridge in the background.

"Y'all better come back and sit in the stern!" the pilot yelled to us. Nancy held my hand, dragging Raggedy Ann behind her as we made our way down the deck. When we settled in the cockpit, Gayle turned to the pilot and asked him where Rainbow City was. He looked at her and after a beat asked, "Why on earth do y'all want to know?"

"Sounds like a cool place," she said.

"I don't think y'all want to go there," he drawled.

"Why?" Gayle asked.

"It's where all the colored live."

I stared at the pilot. He was like a character straight out of Harper Lee's *To Kill a Mockingbird*, one of the last paperbacks I'd read from Mr. Smith's box of books.

"That's why it's called *Rainbow* City," he said, looking at us as if we were dimwits.

Confused, Nancy asked, "Like my crayons?"

"No. Colored . . . like *Creoles, Indians, Panamanians*," he said, enunciating each name. The antebellum South was on full display.

Undeterred, Nancy turned to my mother. "Mommy, those aren't colors."

Embarrassed, my mother said, "No dear, he means black."

"Rainbows don't have black in them," Nancy persisted.

The pilot cleared his throat and adjusted the collar of his shirt.

Saved from further cross-examination by my youngest sister, he steered *Heritage* to the edge of the yacht club's anchorage and throttled down, spinning her wheel. "Get your hook ready. Mooring's coming up on your starboard," he said to my father.

As soon as we tied off, I looked around and noticed we were so far from the club's pier that it seemed as if we could reach out and brush the sides of the freighters steaming to or from the locks. "Is this the only available mooring?" my father asked, as a huge, passing wake from a Chinese freighter smacked our midships, sloshing the deck and causing *Heritage* to lurch to port.

"Well, there's a lot of y'all cruising folks, and it's hard to get y'all to leave," the pilot said dryly. "Maybe when some of these boats transit, y'all can move in closer." It was hard to tell if he was helping or insulting us.

Suddenly, the boat swung sharply on its mooring and jerked us around.

"Ship's coming south out of Miraflores," the pilot said. The outgoing tide, strong current, and fifty-two million gallons of water emptying from the locks into the Pacific rushed past us like a mighty river.

"Ride's here," the pilot said, as a motorboat approached our stern. He tipped his hat and said to no one in particular, "It's been a *real* pleasure."

Manning the rough-hewn, square-nosed boat was the fattest man I'd ever seen. His impressive girth, though, in no way impeded his graceful moves. Like one of the dancing hippopotami in the *Sorcerer's Apprentice*, he performed a delicate *jeté*, making room in the bow for the pilot. Grabbing the railing to steady his boat, he grinned, flashing us a blinding-white smile. "Yeh, Mon, name's Slim an' I takes ev'rybody in. You blow your horn, an' I come get you. Dem's dat take care of me, I take care of dem," he said.

Watching Slim speed away with the pilot, my father said, "He's not gonna get a goddamn dime from me."

Considering Slim had the advantage and controlled the only means to disembark, it surprised me that my father didn't shower him with money. As far as I was concerned, we couldn't pay him enough. When

Slim picked us up and brought us to shore, my mother slipped him some cash when my father wasn't looking.

I should have taken my father's reaction to Slim as a sign that even with the brightest outlook, things could turn sour. Once we reached the Canal Zone, the euphoric feeling I'd experienced in Taboga would all but disappear. The day after we arrived, everything we'd planned changed. After disappearing for the entire morning, my father returned to *Heritage* and announced he'd applied for a job with the Panama Canal Company. And the day after, Pam told us she was leaving within the week to start school at the Instituto de Lengua Española in San José.

Although I'd rifled through my sister's mail in Puntarenas and read the application letter from San José University, I realized Pam must have applied to the institute when she, Gayle, and I visited the capital. I recalled her sudden headache and insistence that Gayle and I browse the shops and streets near our pension without her. When we returned, she was sitting in the lobby, gulping down a tall glass of papaya juice, red-faced and sweating, as if she'd just run a marathon. Her story that she'd awakened in a sweat and went searching for something to quench her thirst was suspect, but I ignored it.

She could have revealed her plans earlier, but she'd waited until she'd received her acceptance letter and a job offer to teach English. Whereas I was impulsive, Pam was cautious and thorough. The tortoise to my hare, my sister was far more resourceful than I.

Neither my father nor my mother resisted. My father even made a special trip to Fort Amador's package store to root around for a cardboard box to use as a suitcase.

Two days later, Pam climbed into Slim's launch. With her cardboard box of belongings wedged between her knees, she motored off to her new life in Costa Rica with barely a backward glance.

It had all happened so fast we were still adjusting a week later. United more by misery than by love, we were still a family. Now Pam had left. My father sat in the cockpit, smoking, and watching the endless succession of ships steam to and from the locks. My mother sat below, catching up on letter writing and reading to Nancy. Gayle and I tried to get off the boat as much as we could. Even though Pam had reassured my parents she'd return when school ended, my father moped around as if she'd left for good.

I wasn't sure how I felt about his reaction. I expected him to be angry or feel betrayed; instead, he withdrew and smoked more than ever. Although I understood why Pam had been surreptitious, I was also pissed she'd waited to reveal her plans. I wondered if she'd done that not because she'd worried about my father forcing her to stay, but so she'd have the courage to leave. When she drove away with Slim, had she not turned around because she was looking ahead to the future, or because it might have revealed how uncertain and scared she was?

I tried to imagine myself in her place, but when I did, there was terror. Pam had figured out a plan and a way to survive. How could I entertain the thought of leaving when I had none?

With her departure, I lost my only ally. I worried that when my father was tired of grieving over her absence, I'd once again find myself in his crosshairs.

My father wrote to his parents as if nothing had changed:

*The trip has been most enjoyable, and the family and I are still eager to push on.*

*Here at Balboa, we are moored to a buoy and must depend on the club launch to haul us back and forth. Sometimes when the wind is in the wrong direction, they can't hear our horn and we have an uncomfortable wait.*

"Where is that goddamn lazy son-of-a-bitch Slim?" my father shouted, sounding the air horn again and again. Gayle, Mom, Nancy, and I stuck our fingers in our ears as the sound of the horn shattered the air. We prayed Slim wouldn't torture my father too much by performing his usual routine of picking up yachters on the south side and zigzagging back and forth to the pier before swinging around to us on the north side. When this happened, my father would growl and leap into the launch and leave without us. Deciding Slim's suggested donation was a small price to pay for a few hours of freedom, my mother tipped him only when he agreed to make two trips in succession.

Once on shore, we explored the grounds of Balboa and Fort Amador, the military base that surrounded the yacht club. After five thousand miles of barren landscapes, open roadsteads, and tropical jungles, it was relaxing to walk along sidewalks bordered by clipped hedges and manicured lawns.

While we could shop at the bakery, eat at the cafeteria, and read at the library, we still had to take the torturous bus route into Panama City to buy groceries. Being able to purchase from the CZ's commissary was reason enough for my father to apply for a job. If he didn't get the job, we'd only have time for one or two more trips, before our thirty-day stay was up. With our bank funds frozen and our education money sucked into the black hole of a failed oil company, we would need to transit as soon as possible.

In the meantime, our living expenses were soaring. The cost of food was exorbitant, and my father needed to pay for fittings he'd ordered from the States and the extra lines other transiting boats told us we'd need. So, he wired my grandfather for the last of our reserves, reassuring them he'd applied for a job and was waiting to hear whether we would stay or push on. Without fail, along with the check, they included a vitriolic note expressing their continued disapproval and the fiscal burden my father had placed upon them.

Well into December, we watched as a succession of boats arrived, flying flags from as far away as New Zealand, Germany, Canada, Brazil, and France. But it was the Swedish flag of the *Susie II* that made an impression.

I was studying at the yacht club, when *Susie II*'s owner, a rugged, good-looking Swede, named Ulf Peterson, entered the crowded room, and asked if anyone had seen his wired-hair terrier, Susie, who'd disappeared after jumping out of Slim's launch. Distraught, he asked all of us to keep a lookout in case she showed up while he searched the club's grounds. Looking for an excuse to avoid studying, I volunteered to look outside with him.

While we scoured the grounds, he shared he'd just finished transiting from the Atlantic side and was taking two weeks to stock up on stores, refuel, and make any repairs before he and Susie headed across the Pacific to continue their three-year circumnavigation. I could see why he was so upset about losing her; she was not only a beloved pet but his first mate and sailing companion.

"Aren't you worried about her falling overboard, especially in bad weather?" I asked.

"Ya, but she's an expert sailor, and I made her a little harness, so in case she falls over I can reel her in like a big fish," he said, laughing.

Must be nice, I thought, that, unlike aboard *Heritage*, the only one barking on *Susie II* had four legs and a tail, and the only ones getting barked at had feathers or fins.

"There she is!" I said, spying her digging a hole near the edge of the pristine golf course that bordered the club grounds.

"We've got to get over there before anyone sees what she's doing," he said. "You circle that way and I'll come around this way, and one of us will catch her for sure." As I cut a wide swath around Susie, hoping to surprise her from behind, I couldn't believe Ulf's good humor about a situation I was sure would've driven my father crazy.

As we closed in on the little terrier, she looked up at Ulf and bolted in the opposite direction, heading straight for me. I lunged, grabbing her by the collar. She tried to wiggle from my grasp, but I scooped her up and pinned her against my chest.

"Ah, you are my hero!" he said as he hooked the leash onto her collar and set her down on the ground. Having had her fill of fun, Susie looked at me with what I could only describe as a sly grin, reminiscent of Slim's, before casually trotting after Ulf. As we walked back to the clubhouse, he said, "You have no idea how much this naughty girl means to me! Ya, for sure, I'd be lost without her. I'm in your debt."

I looked down at the ground as we walked, embarrassed by the praise and attention. He placed his hand on the small of my back. "Did I say something to upset you?" His momentary touch was enough to release the strife within, and I felt a lump form at the back of my throat.

"I'm . . . I'm just glad we caught her," I said. Whether he was unaware of his effect or aware of my discomfort, he changed the subject.

"You are my guest for lunch tomorrow, ya? It's my thank you for finding Susie," he said as he rubbed the terrier's ears. "And I won't take no for an answer!" he added as he walked away.

All evening back at the boat, I rehearsed what I was going to say. But the next morning while I was still asleep, my father hopped on Slim's launch to spend the day in Panama in search of an engine part.

"Why didn't you mention this to your father last night?" my mother asked.

"I was going to ask him this morning, but he left."

"How old is this . . . *Ulf?*" my mother asked.

"I don't know. I didn't ask," I said. Why was she so concerned when I'd hung around family friends and fellow yachters who were years older?

"Is there going to be anyone else there with the two of you?"

"Mom! I told you, other than his dog, he is sailing solo."

She raised her eyebrows and said, "I'm not sure how it might look."

"Oh my god, it's lunch! I'll tell him to bring Susie as our chaperone!"

"People may get the wrong idea," she said.

"About me or him?" I asked.

"What do *you* think?" she said. Why did my mother always make me feel that if things ever went south, it was all on me?

"It's just a simple thank you for finding his stupid dog. Just forget it!" I said.

Whether she had second thoughts or she was tired of arguing, she relented a few minutes later, warning me to make sure I returned before my father. Thanking her, I raced up the companionway and blew the air horn for Slim.

When I reached the restaurant, Ulf was already there, sitting at one of the back tables. He stood up and waved me over when he saw me. After he pulled my chair out for me, he handed me a menu. "Order anything you like."

Like Mubs, Ulf was well versed in the art of dining. Between leisurely bites, he asked me about myself. It seemed easy to reveal to him all the things I'd kept inside me. I spent the entire afternoon telling him how much I'd missed my grandmother, how lonely I was, how my sisters didn't like me, how miserable our family was, and how my father never acknowledged me. When I stopped to catch my breath, I realized how much time had slipped by and, after apologizing, excused myself and left. Running down the pier, I prayed Slim would be there waiting.

With Ulf's stay nearly over, I drummed up any excuse I could think of to join him on morning walks around Balboa. With Susie and Ulf walking beside me, I felt almost happy. Almost because although I'd done nothing more than take morning strolls, I was enjoying it under an umbrella of duplicity and subterfuge and somewhere, deep inside, a tiny seed of doubt had sprung. So, while I'd felt something akin to happiness, I was also relieved Ulf was leaving.

On his final evening, I agreed to meet him for one last walk. Convincing my family I needed to study at the club, I waited for Ulf. When he arrived, I left my homework sitting in a pile on the table and joined him. As Susie stopped to sniff every blade of grass, the sun soon dipped below the horizon and set the sky in a blaze of yellows, oranges, and crimsons.

When we reached the far edge of the golf course, Ulf suggested we stop and watch the sunset. As we stretched out on the grass, Susie plopped down between us and fell fast asleep. Soon, the sky darkened, and the stars emerged. Pointing out each constellation, Ulf explained how imperative it was to master the stars, especially when crossing an ocean. I thought about my father's aborted navigation course and how he'd planned on crossing the Pacific.

"That's Orion's Belt over there," Ulf said, pointing to the telltale row of three stars.

"I see it," I said. Gazing at the sky and feeling the soft, warm evening breeze on my skin and the intoxicating scent of jacaranda and frangipani in the air, I wanted to remember this moment.

As if he'd read my thoughts, he turned to me and said, "I won't forget this night!" Then he moved closer, and in one smooth movement, deftly unbuttoned my jeans and slid his hand inside.

My heart raced. While I wanted to close my eyes and let go, my father's face rose, like a goblin, before me.

"No. No. No! Stop!" I said, grabbing Ulf's hand.

While he stopped, he didn't remove it.

"I'm a virgin!" I blurted. Unsure why I assumed *that* was a deterrent, it worked as well as if I'd admitted to having a venereal disease.

He immediately yanked his hand out. Then he sat up, cradling his head in his hands. "Oh, no . . . no . . . no . . ."

I sat up and buttoned my jeans. After he stopped moaning, he turned to me and said, "You seemed so mature."

I didn't understand why he apologized but was relieved he wasn't angry.

He held my hands and searched my face with a look of earnestness I found unnerving. "You promise me to save yourself for your husband, ya? If you don't, you'll regret giving it away." He jumped up, startling Susie. "We must get you back." His demeanor had changed, and I felt, as he placed a protective arm around me, that I was walking back to the yacht club with an older brother.

I struggled to understand Ulf's sudden about-face. What was it about my virginity that needed such protection? And why was it so important I wait to give it to some future husband? That might be a little difficult, I thought, since I'd already decided I was never getting married.

When we arrived in Slim's launch alongside *Heritage*, it was so dark I could see nothing but the glowing end of my father's cigarette.

"Where the hell have you been?" he said in a voice thick with rage. His accusation rendered me speechless. What should I say? What was the truth, and what was a lie? Had the small bit of pleasure equaled guilt? Had I asked for it? Who was at fault? Was I guilty or not?

"Sorry, Dad, the time . . ." In one swift move, my father leapt out of the cockpit, flew down the deck, grabbed me by the arm, and yanked me out of the launch.

Lit by Slim's lantern, Ulf steadied himself and gripped the railing. "Please, if there is anyone to blame, it is I," he said, attempting to assuage my father. Good luck, I thought. Try reasoning with a man who, like Ahab in his quest, was lying in wait, harpoon ready. There's nothing Ulf can say or do that will change that, I thought. He's only going to make it worse for me.

"Just get your goddamn hands off my boat before I kill you," my father said.

"Nothing happened," Ulf insisted, still under the impression he could straighten out this misunderstanding. I turned around and stepped forward, hoping to place myself between them, but my father strong-armed me.

"If you are going to hit anyone, let it be me. Ya?" Ulf said. "She did nothing wrong!"

"Get away from my boat, now! Slim, if you know what's good for you, you will move your launch away from my boat!"

"You got it, Captain. Don't want no trouble," Slim said, as he backed the launch up with Ulf still standing in the bow.

Shoving me back to the cockpit, my father pushed me toward the companionway with such force my foot slipped, and I landed headfirst at the bottom of the stairs.

"Get up!" he said. I lay there hoping he'd maimed me, so I could hate him even more than I did. As I tried to get up, pain shot from my neck, down my shoulder, and all the way to my fingertips.

"How could you?" my mother said.

I crawled on all fours until I reached the settee and hoisted myself into my bunk. Turning my back to them, I lay there and ran my fingertips along the gash in my forearm. My shin was also on fire, where my jeans had ripped, but I didn't want to move from my bunk. I just wanted to disappear.

The next morning, I awoke to a stiff shoulder, a bruised and bloody shin, a large gash that ran from my wrist to my elbow on my inner fore-arm, and the disapproving stares from my entire family. Even Nancy, confused but taking a cue from both Gayle and my mother's reactions, shook her head and wagged her finger at me.

I'd spent the entire night rehashing the previous evening, concluding I'd done nothing to warrant their contemptuous reaction. Still wearing my clothes from the night before, I hobbled over to the stairs.

"Where's the air horn? I'm calling Slim," I said when I stepped into the cockpit. "I'm leaving."

"You're not going anywhere, young lady," my father spat.

"Why don't you just call me what you think I am?" I shouted. "Go ahead! Let's share it with the rest of the world!"

"Keep your voice down!" my father hissed.

"Whaddya gonna do?" I said. "Throw me down the stairs again?" I climbed up on the helmsman's seat and stood with my arms spread wide, and shouted, "Hey, all you out there, my father thinks I'm a big fat ugly whore!"

"Fer chrissakes, sit down!" my father said, pulling me down into the cockpit.

"Don't you dare touch me!" I said. "Remember, I'm a dirty whore!" I wanted to embarrass and humiliate him as he'd done to me. A wild panic rose in me, making it difficult to catch my breath as I fought the urge to leap overboard and sink to the depths of the bay.

I knew I'd stayed out too late, kept company with a man who was too old for me, and let his experienced hands travel a little too far. But I also knew these actions didn't deserve the punishment meted out to me. What part of me did they hate so much?

"Did it ever occur to you what other people might think?" my father said. I stared at him, open-mouthed. It wasn't about me at all; it was about them. Their rage had sprung from a perceived humiliation. My actions had made *them* look bad. Guilt or lack thereof was of no consequence.

"You just don't get it, Dad, do you? After thousands of miles, you still don't trust me to do the right thing. Sure, you trust me to fix a block fifty feet in the air, you trust me with your lives when I'm on watch, you trust me to work my ass off on this godforsaken boat, you trust me to save this fucking boat, not once but three times, but you can't trust me to *behave* correctly?"

"It's not that we don't trust you," he said.

"But what?" I cried.

"It's just that he's a *man*."

"Meaning what, Dad? That you would have reacted differently had he been a boy?"

"No, I don't mean *that*," he said. "That's also bad."

"So, both boys and men are bad, but I'm the one thrown down the companionway? Sorry if I don't quite see the logic." If I had to face condemnation, then so should they. Why should girls shoulder all the blame? "Men are pigs," I said.

My father took a long drag on his cigarette and avoided my gaze. Disgusted, I turned away and started down the stairs.

# 26

# Coming of Age

## *Pedro Miguel, Canal Zone*

**DECEMBER 17, 1970–MARCH 31, 1971**

The day we reached the thirty-day limit at Balboa Yacht Club, the Panama Canal Company hired my father. Along with the use of a commissary card, enabling us to purchase American groceries and just about anything else, we'd be moving on land. Life wouldn't be so bad, I figured. There was even the possibility I'd get my own room.

In a letter to my grandparents, my father wrote:

> *Just a note to let you know I've been accepted for employment, so it looks like it will be a merry Christmas after all! They're letting us extend our stay here at the yacht club for two weeks, and then possibly over to another club for a short period before they offer housing to us.*

"I want you kids to know I won't get my first paycheck until after the New Year, so Christmas aboard *Heritage* will be skimpy," my father announced.

"Does that mean Santa won't stop at our boat?" Nancy asked, her green eyes brimming with tears.

"Nah," I reassured her. "Santa knows exactly where *Heritage* is. And he knows who's been naughty or nice, and you've been very, very nice. He'll be bringing you lots of presents." I glared at my father, and added, "Of course, he'll be leaving a couple of lumps of coal for others."

On Christmas Eve, Nancy handed my mother one of her little socks to hang up. "Gosh," I said. "That sure is a small Christmas stocking. Don't you want to use one of mine or even Dad's?"

She shook her head vigorously. "If I put out a little sock, Santa will see I'm a good girl."

I tried to suppress the smile spreading across my face. Despite what had transpired between my father and me, Nancy's innocence made me believe all was not lost. While my world crumbled around me, she was the magic sprite who kept hope alive.

Flying out of her bunk on Christmas morning, Nancy squealed. Her tiny stocking had been replaced by a huge, multicolored one—refashioned by us from the Mexican and Costa Rican flags we no longer needed—and Santa had stuffed it with presents. She ran over and hugged my father. "I just knew Santa was coming, Daddy, because I heard reindeer on the cabin top." Even though I loved my youngest sister, I felt a pang of envy as I watched my father's delight and their effortless exchange.

After six weeks moored at the Balboa Yacht Club, we readied *Heritage* for her next anchorage as promised by my father's new employer. To reach it, though, we'd have to transit the first set of locks.

"The pilot will be here any moment, girls. Let's get a move on!" my father said, as he double-checked the four coiled lines needed to keep *Heritage* centered in the chamber.

Soon, Slim approached and dropped off our pilot and a volunteer boater, who, along with me, Gayle, and my father, would comprise the four required handlers. This would be the last time we'd see our big, friendly, enterprising water-taxi driver. My father even managed a smile and farewell wave to Slim, now that he no longer needed to blow the air horn a hundred times to attract attention. Why hold a grudge? We were moving on.

The minute Captain Haff stepped onboard, we all relaxed. Unlike our previous pilot, he was as affable as he was competent. A big bear of a man, Captain Haff lumbered over to my father and shook his hand. "You know you're a lucky captain to have such a beautiful crew," he said. My mother practically melted from the compliment while my father simply grunted and busied himself with freeing *Heritage* from her mooring. Gayle and I tried not to look embarrassed while secretly enjoying the attention.

Under Captain Haff's capable hands and watchful eye, *Heritage* quickly made her way to the Miraflores locks' entrance. "You see that?" he said to Gayle and me, pointing to a large, red, neon arrow on the center wall. "It's being activated a half-mile away in the Locks Control Tower, letting me know which set of twin locks to use. Today we're going to use the east side." He radioed to the tower, "We are abeam of the arrow." Then he turned to Gayle and me, and said, "When the arrow points to three o'clock, it means we can enter." The arrow moved. "We have the arrow," Captain Haff radioed. The seven-foot-thick, steel-gated leaves swung open, revealing the 1,000-by-110-foot chamber.

Captain Haff steered *Heritage* to the farthest end to make room for the massive freighter entering behind us. As soon as we reached the end and idled, workers threw down four lightweight heaving lines attached with monkey fists, two to our port and two to starboard. Stationed at the bow, Gayle and I attached our deck lines to the monkey fists, as did my father and our extra handler, who were astern. The workers then hauled the line in and tied it off. *Heritage* was now centered and ready. Poised at our stations, we watched as the freighter nosed her way forward until our stern was under the shadow of her massive bow.

When the lines were taut on *Heritage,* and the cables were secured between the electric locomotives or "mules" and the freighter, the gates closed. Within seconds, twenty-six million gallons of water churned and boiled beneath *Heritage.* While the boat rose twenty-eight feet in eight minutes, we pulled in the slack as fast as we could before repeating the process again in the second chamber.

After the water level equalized, the gates opened, and we motored across Miraflores Lake to the Pedro Miguel Yacht Club, where a lonely looking barge served as our new dock. As Captain Haff expertly backed *Heritage* between two unoccupied boats—an ancient daysailer and a mastless, half-built sloop—my father jumped onto the barge and secured the stern.

I stared at the rusty barge, muddy water, and surrounding dense foliage. The jungle seemed to press in on us. Thick vines snaked around the sides of the barge and onto the daysailer as if to remind us that if we stayed long enough, we, too, would fall into its suffocating embrace.

Shattering the silence the next morning, the alarm rang, waking all of us. A longtime adherent to the proverb misery-loves-company, my father decided if he had to rise at the crack of dawn to start an unpleasant day, so did we.

"Up and at 'em," he barked, before disappearing off the stern with towel in hand toward the clubhouse's outdoor shower.

"Jesus," I grumbled. "Why do all of us have to get up? Where in the hell are *we* going?"

"Just do it, will you?" my mother said, as she busied herself in the galley.

Gayle turned over in her bunk, pulling the sheet above her head.

"Mommy, it's still nighttime," Nancy said, rubbing her eyes and sitting up in the forward bunk.

"From the mouth of babes," I said.

"I know you girls were going to investigate school enrollment later in the week, but since we're up, why don't we take the bus into Balboa this morning?" my mother suggested brightly.

After my father disappeared over the hill to the bus stop, we grabbed our towels and walked over to shower. Because there was only one stall, Gayle showered first while my mother, Nancy, and I stood outside.

"Yoo hoo!" a woman's voice rang out. The three of us looked around, wondering whose attention the caller was trying to attract. "Yes, you ladies by the shower! Come on up and have some coffee while you're waiting." The voice came from behind the second-story, screened porch of the club's caretaker house. Unlike every other residence we'd seen in the Zone, this house sat by itself on stilts right near the water's edge.

I yelled out to Gayle. "Hey, we're going to have coffee in the caretaker's house. Come up when you're done."

The three of us walked down the path and up the stairs. The screen door opened, revealing a woman with piercing blue eyes set into a softly lined face, framed by gray hair fashioned in a loose bun. Ushering us in, a voice in the adjacent room screamed.

"Visitors!"

"Shush, Charlie," the woman scolded.

"Hello! Welcome!" the high-pitched voice screamed again. Nancy giggled. The voice sounded not quite childlike but not as mature as an adult.

"We can come back some other time, if it's inconvenient for you," my mother said. I could tell she was worried about who was in the other room. I thought the voice sounded friendly, though, and was curious to discover the child, teenager, or adult behind it.

"Charlie just loves to welcome guests," the woman said. "Go on in and meet him." Nancy ran to the next room. I followed her, while my mother remained rooted right inside the door.

"Hello, Charlie!" Nancy screamed.

"Hello, babe!" Charlie screamed back. I laughed when I spied him in the far corner, swinging on his perch. Stepping from side to side in a funny little dance, the huge blue-and-green macaw screeched, "*El viejo como el coco, poco a poco!*"

"He's speaking Spanish!" Nancy squealed, so excited she dropped her towel and Raggedy Ann on the floor.

I turned to the woman, who had followed us into the room, and asked, "What does that mean?"

"It roughly translates as 'Rome wasn't built in a day,'" she said dryly. "My husband has been building a boat in the large shed out by your boat for the past eight years and whenever I ask him when he's going to finish it, he always gives me the same answer, '*El viejo como el coco, poco a poco.*' Charlie has memorized it since he's heard it about ten thousand times."

Opening the screen door for Gayle, the woman invited all of us to gather at the kitchen table, where she set out coffee mugs. "I'm Ruth Kennedy, by the way. I apologize for not introducing myself, and I'm going to blame Charlie for all the ruckus he causes every time someone new comes into the house." She pointed to a tin can on the counter and said to me, "There are chocolate cookies in there. Why don't you bring that over to the table?" As she poured the coffee, she continued, "My husband, Dean, Charlie, and I have lived here for the past twelve years. We're originally from Oregon, but when we arrived here Dean encountered some health problems, and we sold our ketch. He's been building a cabin cruiser hoping it will be less taxing on him." Then she laughed and said, "We'll probably be dead and buried before he finishes. I truly think he likes the *idea* of cruising more than he likes the actual *doing* of it, hence the past eight years. But it keeps him busy and out of my hair, so who cares if he ever finishes it!"

She seemed to describe my father and not her husband. Ever since the beginning of our trip, I suspected my father had been happier building the boat rather than sailing it. During the years he spent building *Heritage*, watching her timbers rise toward the barn's rafters, I imagined he must have dreamed of all the places he'd sail to, of what he'd see, and how he'd feel. I remembered launch day when I was ten, and the look on his face as he described building the boat to the newspaper reporter. The dream back then seemed limitless as the twenty-six-wheel trailer winched the boat from the barn and revealed *Heritage*'s sleek, white hull and topsides, and oiled railings that gleamed in the morning sun. I thought about the ornately carved trail boards that had graced her snow-white prow, destroyed by the rough anchorage at Bahía Chipehua. And the boat's transom—a curved, teak name-board with *HERITAGE* carved in large serif letters and below it, a gold-leafed eagle with its wings outspread—torn away during the *chubasco* off of Zihuatanejo.

His dreams didn't have leaky, worm-infested planks or dirty, oil-filled bilges or violent hurricanes or engine fires or an incompetent crew or navigating with one-foot-on-the-shore. All these would come later, after we cut the dock lines in Alameda and sailed under the Golden Gate.

With our visit over, we thanked Ruth and headed down the stairs to take our showers. "Come back anytime, girls! The door is always open!" she said.

"Come back anytime! The door is always open!" Charlie screeched.

It was nearly 10:00 a.m. when we set out along the narrow dirt path leading to the bus stop. Huge cumulus rain clouds had formed, blotting out the blue sky. As the Pedro Miguel bus came to a stop, I ran ahead, yelling over my shoulder, "C'mon, everyone, let's get this over with so we can get home before the afternoon downpour." Every afternoon around three, the sky turned black and opened up, dousing anyone caught under it. No wonder there were no problems filling the locks, I thought.

As the bus bounced along the potholed road toward Balboa, I thought about being back in school with kids my age. What were they like? Were they friendly? Would I make friends, or would I be an outsider as I'd been in California?

The bus dropped us off in Balboa and we walked in the scorching heat until we found ourselves inside the cool halls of a massive, white, three-story building. Clutching our California school files, certificates, and test scores, Gayle and I, along with my mother and Nancy, entered the main office. While we sat waiting for the principal to call us in, I sweated, thinking about months of slacking off. Gayle sat poised and confident; I fretted and fidgeted.

When the principal opened his door, he introduced himself and motioned for Gayle and me to follow him into his office. Once we all sat down, he leaned back and studied us from across his desk. "Which one is Gayle?" he asked, holding up a thick file. Gayle raised her hand. He smiled and said, "Well, young lady, you've done an outstanding job with your studies, so I'm happy to say we can start you as a sophomore." Then he peered over his half-glasses at me and said, "But you, young lady, are four credits short, so we'll have to start you as a junior."

I stared down at my hands, unable to meet his gaze, fearful that if I did, I'd start bawling.

"Are you sure?" I stammered, unable to believe that Gayle, three years my junior, would only be one grade below.

Gayle had skipped second grade when we moved from Livermore to Alameda. I'd also had the good fortune to skip fifth but landed in a sixth-grade classroom run by an evil, black-hearted teacher by the misnomer of Mrs. White. Recalling her dark, beady eyes and raven black hair pulled into a low, tight bun, I remembered how she'd pointed her claw-like finger toward my face and said, "So you think you're going to skip a grade? Let's see how smart you really are! Get up to the chalkboard and write the answer to the math problem!"

Terrified, I'd buckled under the pressure of her and my classmates' scrutiny and wrote the wrong answer. It took only one trip to my desk at the back of the class, listening to their laughter and picking sticky spit-balls from my face, for me to return to my kind and nurturing fifth grade teacher rather than stick it out and prove the old witch wrong.

Because I'd taken the path of least resistance, the culmination of my seventeen years had brought me to this moment, where I found myself four credits short and a junior.

"I'm going to start tenth grade, and someone else is starting eleventh," Gayle piped up, as we exited the building.

"Isn't that nice, girls!" my mother said.

"It's not nice at all!" I said, seething. "It's completely shitty!"

"Dear, keep your voice down," my mother said.

"I don't care! I'm not going to this fucking school."

We rode the bus home in silence—me angry at an unjust world, and my mother angry at me. Ever observant, Nancy sat quietly, holding onto her doll and pressing herself against my mother. The only one happy was Gayle, who sat next to me, humming her favorite tune "In the Summertime."

I stared out the window, and even though I knew there was no one to blame but myself, I felt like punching a hole in the glass. If only Gayle hadn't rubbed my nose in it, I might've found the grace to accept the demotion. But now, it was too late. As the bus bounced along the road and the gray skies grew darker, I pondered what I could do to make her as miserable as I was.

A week later, Gayle was off to her first day of high school while I remained onboard. My parents had agreed I could stay out of school, with the provision I ramp up my studies and complete the missing courses. If I finished everything by May and we stayed here, I could enroll in summer school and graduate.

Saddled with an endless list of boat chores that lasted all morning, I snuck away in the afternoons to the high school's air-conditioned library to study. Although I was technically trespassing, I never thought to ask permission and no one, including the librarian, noticed me. So long as I was quiet, I was, as with my family, invisible.

My father had been working for more than a month when Ruth called out to my mother and me one morning. "Listen, girls, I just want you to know two men were snooping around your boat yesterday afternoon. They had on uniforms."

"Police?" my mother asked. I noticed the alarm in her voice.

"No, I think they're customs officers," she said. "After they finished poking around, they knocked on my door and asked if I knew your name. I told them no. The shorter one turned to his partner and suggested they come back tomorrow."

"What do you think they want?" I asked. "My father received permission to dock here."

Ruth shrugged and said, "They're just a couple of Southern rednecks trying to stir up trouble. The Zone's filled with them. They especially dislike anyone from the West Coast. Dean and I certainly have had our run-ins with them. Guess they think we're all hippies and potheads."

"Thanks for the warning," my mother said.

"Keep a lookout for them and duck when you see them coming," Ruth said. "If they're going to stir up trouble, make 'em work for it."

Not long after Ruth left, we were sitting at the settee in the cabin when we heard voices on the path that led onto the barge. "Hurry," I whispered, as I motioned to my mother and Nancy to crawl into the dark forepeak. While they curled up together in the port bunk, I crawled into the starboard bunk. The voices were closer and accompanied by the sound of footsteps as the men walked across the steel barge.

"Yep, that's where them squatters live," the voice said. I peeked out, hoping to glimpse their faces, but could only see their khaki-clad legs.

"Got to get rid of folks like these," the second voice said.

"Yup . . . nothing but white trash," said the first voice. "Probably from California," he added.

A wave of shame and anger washed over me. Were we trash? Why did they sound so confident describing us that way? Maybe they were just good ol' boys who hated Californians, like Ruth said. I wanted to run out and insult them like I'd done to the policemen who'd caught me when I'd skipped school one day from Skyline High. Back then, I thought I'd been fearless, even courageous, for questioning a punishment that did not, in my mind, fit the crime. But today, something stopped me. The men's smug tone made me think it was just a matter of time before they got what they wanted. With their heavy southern drawls, they reminded me of characters I'd read in *Deliverance* and were the type of individuals you didn't mess with. Even though I couldn't see what they looked like, listening to the sound and tone of their voices frightened me.

"Hey, anybody in thar?" the first voice called out. I flattened myself against the bunk's wall and motioned my mother and Nancy to do the same. We stayed hidden, sweating in the hot confines of the forepeak until their voices faded away.

Emerging from our hiding place, I turned to my mother. "I thought Dad's company gave us permission to stay here."

"As far as I know, they did," she said. "But I also know they've been pressing your father to move into Zone housing."

"What's the problem, then?" I asked. "I wouldn't mind getting off this pile of sticks."

"We can't afford it, that's why," my mother explained. "Until your father receives permanent status, we don't qualify for reduced housing costs, but they won't issue him permanent status until we move ashore. And without the reduced rate, we can't afford to leave the boat."

"So, these creeps are just going to come back every day?" My mother gave me a helpless shrug, affirming my fear. "Well," I announced. "I refuse to be the one left dealing with this. I'm leaving early with Dad and Gayle."

"Your father will handle this," she said, trying to console me. But my father, I'd learned, was just as ineffective as my mother. Instead of taking the bull by the horns, their way of handling a problem was to ignore it. I didn't think that these men who showed up today were used to being ignored.

When my father arrived home, my parents banished us to the barge. While we sat on the sagging, splintered bench listening to the rain hit the tin roof above us, we could hear my father yelling.

"What happened?" Gayle asked.

"Some jerks came down to the boat today and called us squatters," I said.

My mother's voice drifted up to us from the cabin's interior. "Jim, you've got to do something about this."

"Look, I don't know why it's such a goddamn problem. Jack Smith lives on board, and he's been working for the company for fifteen months. And another fellow in the design department is also a live-aboard. I can't understand why these bastards are targeting us," he said.

"'Cause we're a bunch of losers, that's why," I muttered. Gayle said nothing. Nancy sat between us and sucked her thumb, a habit that had returned with a vengeance, brought on by all the arguing. We'd even stopped telling her that at nearly six, she was too old to be sucking her thumb. If it comforted her, who were we to tell her not to do it?

The next morning, I left with my father and Gayle, leaving my mother to handle any further surprise visits from the *Deliverance* twosome. Gayle and I took the bus together but parted ways at the school's entrance, where she went off to her classes and I hightailed it to the library.

While Gayle had gained three boyfriends and Pam was making new friends in San José, I felt like an outsider. Spending my days isolated in the library and meeting no one, I'd board the bus, alone, back to Pedro Miguel. Even the group of girls I passed every morning in the school hall ignored me, as though I were a ghost drifting by.

The only time I didn't feel so lonely was time spent at the Balboa Yacht Club. When cruising friends sailed in, I was the one who reported the news back to my family. As soon as I told my father *Faraway* had arrived, he and my mother rode the bus down to the yacht club to invite John and Hilke to dinner.

John caught us up on news of *Tolaki* and the other boats, including the crew on *Triton*. John stuttered when he mentioned Ian had gone "native." We all laughed, imagining Ian buck-naked, pouring a "spot-o-hot-tea" for his onboard guests.

John and Hilke stayed a week before weighing anchor and heading west with Schatzi and Tinkerbell, toward their new missionary life in Papua, New Guinea. Watching them sail away, I wished I was on board with them. I'd never heard either of them raise their voices to one another or to their animals. I was used to sacrificing and suffering, and with an ocean to cross, I figured I could learn to pray.

In a letter to my grandparents, my father wrote about his new job, as if our lives did not differ from theirs:

*By now I'm getting well into my work, and I find it interesting enough. Right now, I'm involved in several air-conditioning designs for some of the company stores and some work at the high school on the Atlantic side. Eventually I'll be doing some redesign of the electric locomotives that tow the ships thru the locks.*

"If I have to continue in this goddamned boring job, I expect you to pull your weight and apply for one!" my father yelled at my mother one evening.

The three of us sat in the cockpit, not bothering to take refuge on the barge, while my parents continued their argument below. Their fights were so frequent, we'd become immune. Gayle ignored the discord by collecting boyfriends; Nancy comforted herself by sucking on her thumb; and I numbed myself by raiding the first-aid kit for Percodan.

"I'm sorry, Jim, but this is my 'me time.' I've earned this. My mother raised my first three, and I'm not missing out on my last one. When we get to Florida, I'll get a job, but not here. We'll just have to make do."

"Then we have nothing more to say to each other," my father said, speaking softly. Gayle and I glanced at one another, momentarily startled by his response. He'd stopped yelling and the change was unnerving.

"You're right. We have nothing to say to one another," my mother repeated. My mother's timing to take a stand stunk. Without her working, there was no chance we'd ever move ashore. I had to accept that, until we transited, my life was aboard *Heritage*, moored to a rusty barge, in a mosquito-infested swamp.

It was as simple as that. The family dynamic shifted. Gayle and I were now intermediaries for our parents. If my mother wanted to communicate with my father, she'd pass along the request to either Gayle or myself. Then my father would make us relay the message back to her.

I decided we were all fucking crazy.

Although I spent almost every afternoon in the school library, Gayle avoided me. By the time I returned home, one of her boyfriends had already picked her up. Ever since my parents' big fight, neither my father nor my mother seemed to care whether my younger sister came or went. I couldn't believe at fifteen, Gayle could have boys hover around her, right under my father's nose. Jumping into a souped-up car or on the back of a motorbike, she'd wave to him as she sped off. Instead of stopping her, he sat in the cockpit smoking, silently watching her departure through watery-blue eyes.

Life was not fucking fair.

The few dates I'd had when we lived in Oakland had quickly ended, when my father interrogated them as if they were war criminals. Either they never asked me out again or insisted they pick me up down the street.

"You're only getting away with this, because Mom and Dad are too busy fighting," I said, as Gayle waited on the barge one evening for her motorbike boyfriend to show.

A small smile formed at the corners of her mouth. "You're jealous," she said, as her ride arrived. She hopped on the back, and as the motorbike pulled away, her voice rang out, "*Tu aurais dû étudier plus!*"

Her smug rebuke ricocheted inside my head. *You should have studied more!* As she disappeared from view, I stood on the barge, alone, left with nothing but the bitter taste of regret in my mouth.

In March, my mother began her "me time" quest. My father would no sooner disappear over the hill for work than she and Nancy would quickly depart for their day's outing. Cast aside were work lists my father had compiled and left for my mother to complete. As far as she was concerned, the boat could have sunk right into Miraflores Lake. She'd turned in her first mate stripes and had fled the sea for a chlorinated pool, buying herself a season pass at Balboa's local community center and enrolling Nancy in swimming classes three mornings a week and spending the rest of the day lounging by the pool. What they did the remaining two days during the week was their secret, but whatever it was, it kept them away from *Heritage* until evening. Tightlipped, mother would only say they'd been out having a "jolly good time." It was only on the weekends any of us would catch a glimmer of my mother's former self, when a plate of tuna sandwiches materialized, or the smell of coffee-can bread filled the air, or a pile of fresh laundry lay sorted and stacked.

On the surface, everything appeared tranquil enough. My mother baked, my father turned a machine part on the lathe, Gayle came and went by motorbike or car, and Nancy played with her dolls in the fore-peak. But it was also eerily unsettling. We moved among one another in silence, as the humid air hung heavy with the sounds of ships' horns and rushing water, and of train whistles and afternoon rain.

Gayle finally brought her third boyfriend, a good-looking blond named Charles Gustafson, to see the boat. After boarding, she invited him below. Curious, I followed them.

"Whose guitar?" he asked, glancing at the case strapped above my bunk.

"Mine," I said.

"Can you play?"

"Not very well, but I try."

Gayle rolled her eyes. "She plays 'Leaving on a Jet Plane' and 'The House of the Rising Sun' until we're all going crazy."

"I need someone to teach me new songs, and then I wouldn't bore you so much," I said defensively.

"I'll teach you some new songs," Charles offered, clueless that he'd just started World War III. This was the moment I'd waited for, ever since the school registration incident.

"Great!" I said.

"I just learned how to play 'Alice's Restaurant.' Bring your guitar over to my house tomorrow." Glancing over at Gayle, he smiled and said, "I'd better get going. I'll see you at school."

"You can't go over to his house!" Gayle spat after he left.

"I can do whatever the hell I please," I said.

"He's my friend!"

"So?"

"Get your own friends!"

"Why can't he be my friend too?" I asked.

"Because I say so!"

Although I had no interest in Charles, it made it all the sweeter the invitation had come from someone my sister didn't want to share.

"Like this?" I asked as I strummed my guitar, moving the fingers of my left hand slowly along the fret through the progression of chords.

"Yeah, you got it," Charles said.

I'd been secretly taking lessons from him every day for a week and had finally figured out how to play the song's intro.

"You just gotta keep practicing," he said, after we finished the lesson and were walking toward the bus stop. While he waited with me, a Jeep roared by, screeched to a stop, and backed up to where we were standing. The driver, a blond-haired boy around my age, looked at us.

"Hey, Charlie, how y'all doin'?" he drawled.

"Hey, Mark," he replied.

Mark grinned, revealing a row of perfectly even teeth set against a rough complexion. "How come I don't know you?" he asked, studying me.

"Mark knows everyone," Charles said, explaining his friend's friendly interrogation. "She lives on a yacht over in Pedro Miguel."

"Is that so?" Mark said. I nodded, suddenly feeling self-conscious. Eyeing my guitar, he said, "I just got a sweet new Martin. You guys been playing together?"

"I'm teaching her 'Alice's Restaurant,'" Charles said.

Turning to me, Mark smiled, "Hey, when you learn it, you can teach me."

"It might take a while," I said. "It's a long song, and we're just working on the beginning."

"That's okay. I can teach you a new song I just learned by James Taylor called 'Sweet Baby James.'"

"Just so long as I don't have to sing along," I said. "I have a terrible voice."

"You play and I'll sing," he said. "I've got a great voice. Tell her, Charlie."

Charles shrugged and said, "Yeah, it's pretty good."

"Come on, hop in. I'll take you home," Mark offered, as casually as if he'd known me forever. I slung my guitar in the back and hopped into the passenger seat. "See ya later, Charlie," Mark yelled, as we roared off down the road.

Careening down the highway, with the warm wind blasting our faces, Mark turned to me and shouted to make sure I heard him above the Jeep's noisy engine, "You're mighty pretty!"

This was the first time a boy my age had said that to me. And I'd found him before Gayle.

## 27

# Jumping Ship

### *Pedro Miguel, Canal Zone*

**APRIL 1–SEPTEMBER 9, 1971**

It was now April and the beginning of the rainy season, which made life aboard in Pedro Miguel all that more uncomfortable. Mold attacked everything, spreading and embedding its mottled, musty-scented spores into our clothing, bedding, books, and anything else that absorbed moisture. Even the underside of my guitar case sported a carpet of green.

Gayle continued to ignore me, riding off with her boyfriends; my mother disappeared for hours with Nancy either to Spanish lessons or the pool; and my father expressed greater dissatisfaction with his job and a renewed reluctance to move off the boat and into company housing.

With no sightings of the customs officers, I switched back to spending mornings alone working on the boat, whittling down the endless list of jobs my father conjured up, before hopping the bus at noon to spend the rest of the day in the school library.

With my boat work and studying completed for the day, the late afternoons and early evenings were my own. I'd meet Mark at his Jeep in the school's parking lot and off we'd go. For a few hours, with the sunlight dappling the trees, the wind in my hair, and sitting next to a boy who liked me, life was good. I willed away what awaited me back at Pedro Miguel and pretended I was a normal teenager.

When the witching hour approached and it was time to drop me off, I'd make Mark pull over on the main road. Before he could protest, I'd jump out of the Jeep and scramble up and over the railroad tracks and down to the boat.

"Why don't you let me drive you all the way home?" he asked.

"It's fine right here," I replied. While I knew he liked me and I felt the same about him, I didn't trust his feelings would remain once he saw where I lived. Whenever I reconsidered having him drive me home, the image of the customs officers materialized. Recalling that, to them, we were nothing but squatters hunkering down in squalid quarters, I figured it was better to jump out and race over the hill. The less he knew about my circumstances, the better, I thought. To make matters worse, a Chinese freighter carrying a cargo of rice had sunk in Miraflores Lake, and as they worked to raise it, the putrid smell of rotting rice made it seem like we were living next to a pig farm.

Gayle didn't seem to mind being picked up at the barge by two of her beaus, but I knew there was a reason she hadn't brought Charles around a second time. I suspected she preferred him most of all and, like me, didn't want to risk being viewed in a less-than-flattering light.

"I told my parents I'm bringing home a dinner guest on Saturday," Mark announced just before dropping me off at my designated spot a few weeks after we met.

"Uh, I have a 9:00 p.m. curfew," I replied, hoping to discourage him.

"Don't you worry, we'll drive like the wind and get you back on time," he grinned. "I'll pick you up tomorrow around six."

On Saturday, I woke up early and rushed through the list of chores and my homework before announcing Mark's dinner invitation. Instead of a full-blown interrogation, my father merely grunted and asked if I'd done all my boat work. My mother ignored me. When Gayle heard about my invitation, she announced she was also going out.

As I made my way up the hill and over the railroad tracks, I heard the motorbike coming down the main road and waited to descend until it passed.

"Looks like your little sis is keeping busy. Just saw her whiz by on a motorbike," Mark said, when he picked me up. I didn't reply. All I could think about was meeting his parents. What if they asked about my family or my plans, like college? While I was proud that our family had built a boat and had sailed it five thousand miles to Panama, I also felt unmoored and disconnected from them.

Fifteen minutes later, Mark pulled into his driveway. Hollering a greeting as we walked through the door, his younger sister, Beth, and her hound dogs, Booger and Bird, came bounding down the hall, with his parents following close behind. It was as if I'd just stepped into a scene from *Leave It to Beaver*. Standing before me was the southern version of Mr. and Mrs. Cleaver.

Perfectly coiffed in a cloud of auburn curls, Mrs. Darden welcomed me in a warm, honeyed, North Carolina drawl, "Mah goodness, aren't you a tall drink of water!"

Mr. Darden smiled broadly and extended his hand. "Mark said you were a pretty gal."

The moment he spoke, I froze. My heart raced as I tried to maintain my composure. What were the odds that the one boy who had invited me to his house for dinner was the son of the customs officer scoping out our boat? I stood there, wondering how long would it take for him to realize his son had brought home a "squatter."

"Where do your folks live?" Mrs. Darden asked, as she handed me a Coke, assuming I'd say Gamboa or one of the other areas where new employees lived.

Unable to speak, I stared down at my sandals.

"She lives on this cool boat that's docked at Pedro Miguel," Mark said enthusiastically, unaware of my discomfort.

"Why, is that so!" Mr. Darden enthused. "Well, welcome to our home, young lady. Why don't you sit next to me?" he said, pulling out the dining room chair directly to his left.

"Pop's the chief of customs on this side," Mark boasted, as we filled our plates. "Maybe you're familiar with her boat," he said, turning to his father.

"Can't rightly say that I am," Mr. Darden replied. As he passed me the bowl of mashed potatoes, he winked. I realized he knew I knew.

Saved by Mark's entertaining monologue—riffing on everything from his new twelve-string guitar to his Jeep to school and everything in between—I made it through dinner without choking. When I thanked his parents for having me as their guest, Mr. Darden smiled and said, "Now, don't you go and make yourself scarce, young lady."

Confused over his warm and welcoming manner and what he'd said on the barge that day, I kept what had transpired between us at dinner to myself.

It had been two days since receiving notice from the Panama Canal Company that dredging would begin in Miraflores Lake when three uniformed workers arrived and announced we needed to move the boat immediately to the far end of the lake.

"Maybe we should just call your father before we do anything," my mother said.

"Are you kidding? He'll be like a rabid dog when he hears the boat has to be moved. He already hates the fact they want us to move off the boat, and he'll just think they're doing this to pressure us."

My mother stood facing me, nervously wringing her hands. "Well, what are we going to do? They told us they're coming in an hour, and if the boat isn't gone, they won't be responsible for any damage."

I shrugged. "So, the boat's gotta move."

"Who's going to do that?"

"Who do you think?" I said, sweeping my arm to point out the empty expanse around us.

"You mean you and me?" she asked incredulously.

"Who else is there?" I said. "Just pretend I'm Dad barking out orders and everything will be fine."

"What should I do?" she asked.

"I'm going to start the engine. Get Nancy settled below with some coloring books. I'll need you at the helm while I pull in the chain and bow anchor so that it's ready for you when we reach the far end of the lake."

"I'm going to throw the anchor?" she asked.

I laughed. "Don't worry . . . this time it'll be attached!"

My mother looked at me, perplexed. Then, her face lit up as she recalled the memory. "Oh, my goodness! I forgot all about the time on Angel Island. Your father was ready to strangle me."

"Well, you warned him," I said.

After my mother reemerged from the cabin, I threw the stern lines onto the dock and then slowly throttled forward to give a slight slack in the chain. "All you have to do is keep her idling," I said. Working the windlass as fast as I could, I pulled up the chain and anchor, piling it on the deck, and then raced back to the cockpit.

"Should I go up to the bow now?" my mother asked tentatively.

"Relax. Yes, you can make your way up to the bow." I watched my mother climb over the cockpit coaming and noticed a little spring in her step as she made her way forward.

As I neared the designated anchorage, where officials had assured *Heritage* would be safe from harm, I said, "Okay, Mom, throw'r over!"

She lifted the anchor up and heaved it over the railing. As it dropped to the bottom, the chain rattled through the hawsepipe. I threw the engine in reverse, slowly backing until the anchor caught and held. I turned off the engine, gave my mother a thumbs up, and waved her back to the cockpit.

"We did it!" she whooped, giddy as a kid riding a bike for the first time. I wondered how different she would have been if my father hadn't always pointed out her inadequacies.

After we wrestled the dinghy off the cabin top and maneuvered it over the side, I brought the painter around and tied it off the stern. I called out to Nancy to come up and pulled two beers and a soft drink from the ice chest, handing a Coke to my youngest sister, and a beer to my mother. She clinked her bottle against mine and said, "Just wait till your father comes home and sees *Heritage* out here."

Around dusk, after ferrying Gayle out to the boat earlier, I rowed across the lake to retrieve my father, who'd returned from work and was standing with his arms crossed, looking out beyond me toward *Heritage*. When the dinghy bumped against the end of the barge, his open-mouthed expression reminded me of the time in San Diego when I'd leapt onto the dock and cleated off *Heritage*. As he had then, he remained speechless.

I looked up and shrugged. "Mom and I moved her."

Without uttering a word, he stepped into the dinghy and settled in the stern. Then he lit up a cigarette, blowing smoke rings in the evening air, as we rowed back to the boat. I knew by his silence he was impressed. I didn't need him to tell me I'd done a good job because as I dipped the oars in the water, I could hear the crowd cheering.

As Easter approached, Pam wrote and asked if she could visit for her spring break. My father immediately sent money, and by week's end Pam arrived from San José exhausted, and sleep deprived, after a twenty-three-hour bus ride. Observing the look on her face when she stepped onto the barge made me wonder if she regretted traveling all those hours to spend it in a swamp. This was well before my father decided that with her home, she, along with Gayle and me, could wait on him while he treated his plantar warts.

On her first evening back, Pam asked me to accompany her to the outside shower.

"Gawd, it's dark," she said, clutching her towel, as we made our way along the path, lit only by the beam from the small flashlight I held.

At the stall, I reassured her, "Don't worry, I'll be right outside."

While she showered, I leaned against the wall, inhaling the heavy scent of jasmine and listening to the tree frogs and night crickets croak and chirp in the warm night air. I regretted the snide and inexcusable remarks I'd made to her when she arrived about her recent weight gain and wondered why I'd found it necessary to wound her. I didn't want to admit I was angry and jealous she'd extricated herself from our present mess without inciting ire or resentment. My mother and father bent over backwards for her, expressing their unbridled enthusiasm as she talked about her new life and second family in Costa Rica. They even agreed to call her Erica, the name she adopted right after she arrived in San José.

After Pam showered, we started back to the barge, which turned into a full run when we heard rustling in the bushes, especially since a few days earlier my father had crossed paths with a caiman—the Central American version and close relative to an alligator.

The next morning, Ruth invited us for coffee, and as we passed the shower, we saw two men with shovels filling up a hole.

"What are those guys doing down there?" I asked Ruth.

"You didn't hear all the commotion this morning?" she said. "They found a fer de lance hiding in the corner of the shower stall this morning. They think it crawled in there last night. Can you imagine? One bite from that and you're toast!"

Pam and I stared at one another, bug-eyed.

We spent the week watching my father stretch out and hog the cockpit as salicylic acid worked its way into the tangled ganglia on the bottoms of his feet. Pam was more than happy to end her nursing duties and catch the bus back to San José. Worried she might never return after her unsatisfying spring break, I made her promise she would come back after her classes ended in August.

Pam may have had a horrible vacation, but her presence helped me realize the only way out of my predicament was to study hard and get an education. I applied myself and completed my remaining correspondence courses and signed up for summer school at the Zone's junior college for geometry and English so I could graduate. If my father changed his mind and stayed at his job, I'd apply to the junior college in La Boca; if we pushed on, I'd apply to colleges, as Pam had, in the States.

Finally, I fired off a letter to Skyline High, addressed to my old guidance counselor and nemesis, Mr. Bianchi, to inform him my required coursework for graduation would be completed by August.

For the first time, I had a plan and a goal—study hard, graduate, and apply to college.

Now that I knew where I was heading, my responsibilities on the boat were tolerable. Although my mother stayed away from *Heritage* as much as possible, and she was still using Gayle and me to communicate with my father, she'd borrowed Ruth Kennedy's sewing machine and was helping me sew a replacement for the dodger. We were also stitching up

Dutch, French, British, Colombian, and Venezuelan flags to represent the new islands and countries we'd visit if my father decided to push on.

Whether the fight had left him, or he was simply too exhausted from trying to make us bend to his will, my father offered no resistance when Gayle and I took off, spending weekends with our respective friends.

Driving up with Mark to his family's cabin on one of the tiny islands in Gatun Lake, we swam and sunbathed while transiting liners, freighters, and private yachts steamed by in the distance on their way toward the eight-and-a-half-mile Gaillard Cut to the Pacific or to the Gatun Locks leading to the Atlantic.

At sunset, we'd hop back in Mark's little green boat and motor back to shore, passing herons and egrets roosting in the trees and osprey and vultures flying overhead, and if we were lucky, catch sight of a ringed kingfisher skimming the water.

Other times, he'd show me his favorite places, some only accessible by Jeep, like the beautiful waterfall that ran into the Canal along the Gaillard Cut, or take me on long drives through Panama's interior, passing through military checkpoints, to reach pristine beaches along the coast.

If we didn't feel like driving somewhere, we spent time in town at the Beldens' house, the local teenage hangout. Known to all the kids as Mr. and Mrs. B, the sixty-something couple were kind and welcoming, and their open-door policy and willingness to listen made it a desirable haven for any teen who needed guidance or just a safe place to hang out.

Some days, Mark and I were content to sit under the shade of a tree near Pedro Miguel's boatyard and talk. Although we didn't share the same opinion on certain topics, our conversation was easy. A self-described Christian, Mark felt it his duty to convince me to embrace Jesus. While I appreciated his conviction, I wasn't so easily swayed. He'd grown up in a safe environment, protected from the rest of the world, with friends he'd known his entire life. His parents and siblings all liked and loved one another. It was easy for him to be happy.

When he brought me to a Bible study class run by girls I'd passed in the halls at school, I found it difficult to reconcile their proselytizing when they were as mean as snakes, laughing at my clothes and snubbing me as I walked past them on my way to the library.

If there was a God, I told Mark, then He had favorites, and I wasn't one of them . . . and neither was my family. He wouldn't have let Joe Eklund drown in the middle of the ocean, or let Grandma die, or make my father hate me so much, or leave us penniless, or have made our trip so damn miserable. Jesus was supposed to teach love and tolerance, but from what I saw of those who claimed to believe in Him was smug satisfaction and an alarming willingness to pass judgment on those different or less fortunate.

I didn't need Mark or anyone else to save my soul. I'd been skating along on "the substance of things hoped for, the evidence of things not seen" for as long as I could remember. What I needed was not faith, but the here and now. I needed something that was real and tangible.

Summer school was almost over when the letter from Skyline arrived. I'd hoped time had softened Mr. Bianchi, but he was as nasty as ever, informing me that since I'd not kept the school up to date, the agreement between us was void and that I should find another school to accredit my courses. He closed his brief note by wishing me the best and hoping he'd never hear from me again. I imagined him smiling when he wrote the last line. He'd finally gotten his revenge.

Not even Mark could comfort me over this news.

"I don't want you to think I'm jealous, but you have a diploma!" I said.

"Maybe if you stay longer, you can get one here," he said. I knew he was trying to be helpful, but I doubted my father wanted to be here any longer than necessary. As much as I knew Mark cared for me, he'd be gone in a few weeks, on his way to college in the States. I knew I was on my own.

"Don't you realize what this means?" I cried, shaking the letter at my mother, who appeared as unfazed as my hateful guidance counselor.

"So, you finish school when we get back to the States," she replied, shrugging her shoulders.

"When will that be? A year? Two years? I'll be twenty and still in high school."

"Stop being so dramatic. Besides, you have no one to blame but yourself," she said.

"What are you talking about?"

"You spent all your time writing letters to those friends of yours back in California. A lot of good that's done you now."

"Just when, in between all the hours that Dad had me slaving away on the boat, did I have time to study?" I asked.

"Well, that certainly didn't stop Pam and Gayle."

"Pam has her diploma! And Gayle was in junior high when we left! I didn't see you or Dad trying to help me when I was struggling over geometry or my biology course."

"That was your responsibility. Don't put that monkey on my back," my mother retorted.

Seething, I pushed past her to get out of the cabin.

"Don't touch me! It's too hot in here!" she said.

It was an impossible request in the stifling heat of our cramped quarters. "I can't help that you have hot flashes!" I said. Ever since moving to Pedro Miguel, I suspected my mother was experiencing a difficult menopause. She'd scream at anyone who so much as brushed against her and had turned from a reticent first mate into someone who'd trample anyone she thought stood in her way.

I ran up the hill to the railroad tracks, swiping away my tears with the back of my hand. If my mother didn't give a shit about my future, I wouldn't give a shit about hers. Let her sit in the bosun's chair and get hauled up to the spreaders in the middle of the ocean or let her motor *Heritage* by herself to the far end of the lake.

I swore I'd figure out how to leave them.

While Mark had given me a chance to be the teenager I longed to be, and spending time with him had been a wonderful respite from life in Pedro Miguel, he was leaving. Without his presence, it left me with a family who ignored me and a father who viewed me as nothing more than "cheap labor."

When I returned to the boat, I went about completing my chores. Walking to the shower, I checked off the list in my head of all the things I'd need to do to accomplish my goal.

The next morning, I left for summer school, but when I got out of class, I headed straight to Mark's house.

"I have about a thousand dollars in my bank account in Oakland I can use once I get back to California. I just need to figure out who I can stay with and where I can get money for my plane ticket."

"Mr. and Mrs. B might help," he said. Mr. and Mrs. Belden had treated me with the same compassion and understanding they showed to all the Canal Zone kids. So when Mark drove me over and Mr. Belden encouraged me to sit down and talk, I found myself telling him everything.

After listening to me, he left the room to talk to his wife. A few minutes later he returned and sat back down, facing me. He smiled and said, "As soon as you find a place to stay in the States, Mrs. B and I will take care of everything on this end."

With my money issue settled, I wrote a note to my aunt and uncle, asking if I could stay with them and also wrote to my parents' boating friends, the Hookers, whose daughter, Lisa, was my age. Last, I wrote to my two great aunts in Minneapolis and offered housework and cooking in return for staying with them. If all went well, I hoped to be gone to either California or Minnesota by September.

As I plotted my course, my mother's behavior continued to worsen, and I chalked it up to hormones. In the meantime, I continued with summer school. Although I had the highest score in geometry, in English, my teacher handed back my latest paper with a handwritten note to see her after class. Mrs. Buehler had a stellar reputation among both faculty and her students, and all during the lesson I worried why she'd wanted to meet with me.

"I'd like to go over your essay with you," she said. I shifted nervously in my seat. "Did you ever think of becoming a writer?" I shook my head. "Well, consider it. This was a beautifully written essay."

All the way home, I felt as if my heart would burst through my chest. This was the first time an adult had told me I was good at something.

Continuing his daily tirade about his job, my father wrote to Pam he'd planned to quit at the end of August and that we'd leave the Canal Zone in September. In a letter two weeks later to my grandparents, he portrayed a fuzzier scenario, to soften the blow that, once again, their restless son would soon be on the move:

*The management down here is happy with my work and has talked about a reclassification, which would mean a raise, but I'm not holding my breath. What I would gain in salary, I would lose in boat value. Then too, the crew is growing up and soon I will lose all this cheap help.*

The day before my birthday, I received an answer from my aunt and uncle. Their rejection stung, but I still hoped the Hookers, or my great aunts, would reply favorably.

The next day, Mark had a surprise birthday party for me, which made up for my family forgetting it again. That night, before my father returned home, I told my mother I wouldn't be joining them for the rest of the trip. But instead of reacting with outrage or disappointment, she simply said, "And where are you planning to live during this grand adventure of yours?"

"Uncle Chuck and Aunt June already said no, but I wrote to the Hookers, and also Aunt Ethel and Aunt Ruth." When I mentioned my great aunts, she looked surprised and deflated, like a competitor who, after leading the entire race, suddenly finishes second.

A few days later, my great aunts' letter arrived, and I understood my mother's strange reaction. Confused about my request, my aunts wrote they had already given my *mother* permission to stay with them. Unwittingly, they'd revealed my mother's escape plan, and I, by announcing my departure, had foiled hers.

When the Hookers' letter arrived with positive news, I decided it was better to return to California rather than to a place I'd been to only once in my life.

"You're not only going to pay the Hookers' rent, but it's up to you to figure out how you're going to get there," my mother said. I knew she was confident that without money, it would be the end.

What she didn't know was that I had the Beldens on my side. What I didn't know was how much they would help. When they handed me an envelope, the next time I visited, I could hardly believe their generosity. I stared at the twenty-two $100 bills in disbelief. "How can I ever repay you?" I said.

"You don't have to," Mr. B said. "Just pay it forward by doing a good deed for someone else during your life."

The next day, I purchased my airline ticket and told my father I was leaving within the week. Unlike his grief-stricken reaction to Pam's announcement, he reacted to mine with contempt.

Overhearing my parents' conversation the following evening while they were in the cockpit, and unaware I was below, my mother said, "Don't you think we should, at least, know what her plans are?"

"Once she's gone, I don't give a good goddamn what she does," my father said.

"She's your daughter, Jim."

"Not to me, she isn't."

"She's more like you than you know," my mother said.

When I heard my mother say that to him, I knew she was right. Deep down, I'd always feared I was my father's daughter. I not only looked like him, but I feared I possessed some of his worst traits. I wondered if that's why he hated me so much. What better way to eradicate your reflection than to deny its existence? Whatever he saw in me was a constant reminder of what he wanted to forget.

Shunned by him, I worked in silence, fulfilling the long list of chores he'd given me to complete before leaving. As I cleaned the mold and mildew off sail covers, polished the brass fittings, mended sails, and washed and bleached the decks, the only thing that kept me going was, it would be the last work I'd ever do on *Heritage*.

The night before my departure, I emptied the contents of my drawer into a small canvas bag and then checked to see that my guitar was secure for travel. But when I did, I saw that the humidity had finally taken its toll; the bridge had separated and a crack ran from the bottom edge of the guitar's sound hole to its base. I snapped the case shut and rehung it above my bunk. It was one more memory I'd leave behind.

The next morning, with none of my family present, Mr. Belden and Beth picked me up and drove me to the airport. After a handshake from Mr. Belden and a quick hug from Beth, I checked my bag and headed to the gate.

When the agent announced the flight was ready for boarding, I made my way down the stairs with the other passengers and exited through the doors to the tarmac. Walking toward the plane's moveable stairs, I hummed along to my favorite tune, "Leaving on a Jet Plane."

# IV

# Coming Home

## 28

# California Dreamin'

## *Marin County, California*

**SEPTEMBER 9–DECEMBER 13, 1971**

Stepping into the chilly night air outside San Francisco's airport terminal, I'd forgotten how cold 55 degrees could be. After spending two years in the tropics, my blood had thinned, and I shivered in my jeans and T-shirt, waiting for the Hookers to pick me up.

When they pulled up in their forest-green VW bug, I was glad I had a small bag, as there was just enough room in the Beetle's front hood to stow it, and barely enough room to squeeze into the backseat, next to Lisa.

As we wound our way through the city and over the Golden Gate Bridge to Marin County, Mr. and Mrs. Hooker peppered me with questions about Panama, my family, and the flight back to California, but Lisa gave me the cold shoulder. The stocky eleven-year-old who'd shown me how to bake a bunny cake, soar on her tire swing, and slide down a hill was now older and unsociable. I wondered if she'd had second thoughts. From the disgruntled look on her face, I had a sinking feeling that was the case.

As soon as we arrived at the house, Lisa and her father headed upstairs, leaving Mrs. Hooker to show me around.

"Here it is!" she enthused, as she led me into a tiny room next to the kitchen. "I know it's small, but it's all yours."

"No, it's great," I said. After spending two years sleeping in the same space with five other people, even a closet was palatial. And after the chilly reception from Lisa, I was relieved my room was downstairs and far from hers.

"You must be tired after such a long trip. I'll let you settle in," Mrs. Hooker said.

I unpacked, stowed my suitcase, and crawled under the covers, still wearing the clothes I'd traveled in from Panama. The moon was waning, but bright enough to throw a shaft of light through the window and across my bed, illuminating the room in a cool, silvery glow. The wind rustled through the eucalyptus trees, and the old house creaked and groaned as if it, too, was settling in for the night. I squeezed my eyes shut and pulled the blanket over my head, hoping to calm the fear and uncertainty growing inside me. Separated from my family by thousands of miles, I realized I'd traded a life I'd known, to live with a family I barely knew.

While I'd made friends with Lisa during childhood sleepovers at her house, the only common ground our family had with hers was as fellow boat builders. I knew nothing about Lisa's parents, except for her mother's giddy laugh and her father's occasional outbursts. And even though I'd recognized the interior of their house from previous visits, surrounded on this night by bleak shadows and cool moonlight, it was as if I'd never known the place.

Sitting in the kitchen a few weeks later, cooling off from a sweaty, two-mile walk from school with a glass of milk and some Oreos, I watched as Lisa bounced down the stairs, scantily clad in a flimsy pink bra and panties.

"Look, I'll make this real fast 'cause I got company," she said, nodding her head toward the stairs to let me know her new boyfriend, Randall, was waiting for her in her bedroom.

"I need a favor."

I dunked an Oreo in my milk and took a bite.

"Well?" she said.

"It depends," I replied.

"What do you mean, it depends?"

"On what you want me to do," I said. I was already doing most of Lisa's chores so she could spend time with Randall.

"All you have to do is watch for my parents' car and warn me, so Randall can get out before they get home," she said. I stared at her pudgy figure, amazed at how relaxed and unself-conscious she was. I was still adjusting to her after-school uniform and the blasé manner in which she traipsed half-naked around her house. I wished I could be as uninhibited as she, but even on the hottest, most humid days onboard, my sisters and I would have preferred contracting jungle rot, rather than parade around in our skivvies.

"And if I don't?" I said.

"Listen, if you want to stay here, you're gonna have to earn your keep," she said, giving her hair a little toss to let me know she meant business. "Don't test me," she warned. My once-cheery, cherub-cheeked friend was now a beefy enforcer ordering me to pony up for her parents' generosity.

Like a teenage Patton, she marched me down the hallway, gripping my arm and propelling me toward a small window. "This is where you're gonna watch for their car," she said. I peered through the porthole-sized pane to the sloping yard and road below.

"Have I made myself clear?" Lisa said.

I nodded. What choice did I have? She'd made it clear my future was under her control, and I wasn't about to test it.

"Good. What's going to be our signal?" she asked.

"How 'bout 'land ho'?" I said, suppressing a laugh.

She wrinkled her nose, drawing her lips up to expose two over-sized front teeth. Standing there in her lingerie, she looked like a giant X-rated rabbit.

"Just whistle," she said.

From Monday to Friday, I stood by the open, portholed window, straining to hear the familiar chugging of the Hookers' VW Bug as it switch-backed up the narrow road to the house. Guard duty on Chapman Drive replaced any possibility of joining after-school activities. Instead of racing on the swim team, or throwing clay pots in pottery class, or perfecting my acting skills for my fantasy future in Hollywood, I was now privy to the sounds of Lisa's headboard banging above me.

One evening, lost in thought, I failed to hear the familiar chugging of the VW coming up the hill and only realized I'd missed it when I heard voices below the window.

Dispensing with my routine whistle, I raced down the hall and yelled up the stairs. I was afraid of Lisa, but her father, Kurt, terrified me. There was something predatory about him. When he arrived home, he never just entered, but burst through. In his dark form-fitting sharkskin suit, with his slick jet-black pompadour and glittering green eyes, he reminded me of a black panther waiting to spring and attack its unsuspecting prey. I tried to stay out of his line of sight until I was sure he'd decompressed from his day, suspecting he hated his job and was culling the herd as payback. If Lisa ever got caught, whatever punishment she'd receive, I worried mine might be worse.

I ran to the back door to intercept them. As I chattered on about my day, stalling them in the kitchen, I glanced toward the living room windows and watched the shirtless, shoeless Randall inch his way down the rusty drainpipe.

Later that evening, sitting cross-legged on my bed, I thought about the day's events. Away from my father's criticism and control, I'd hoped for a new beginning. Instead, I found myself in the same position as I'd been with him. I realized I'd just exchanged life on *Heritage* for *this*. What difference did it make watching for a rocky shore or listening for an approaching car?

I reached over and grabbed Pam and Gayle's letters off my nightstand. Filled with descriptions of their Canal Zone transit, there was no mention of anyone missing me. I thought about my mother and imagined she was still angry I'd foiled her plans and wondered if my father had regretted not saying goodbye. Maybe without a scapegoat, like me, they were better off, and my father would change back to the relaxed captain he'd been in Isla Secas.

Gayle wrote of Captain Haff returning to pilot *Heritage* through the rest of the Canal, and of hearing howler monkeys screech and flocks of green parrots fly overhead as they traversed the Gaillard Cut. When she described motoring across Gatun Lake, I thought about the times Mark and I swam in it, watching the yachts and ships pass by as we sunbathed on the tiny strip of sand in front of his family's cabin.

Reading their letters, I imagined being back with them, entering each chamber of the Gatun Locks and sinking eighty-five feet to the Atlantic. I still yearned for the chance to sail the Caribbean, but now, they would see it all without me.

While both Pam and Gayle expressed how excited they were to begin their trip to Grenada, they were worried about my father's decision to take the southern route to get there. Ignoring advice from more seasoned sailors, he planned to hug the Colombian and Venezuelan coast before heading north to the ABC islands of Aruba, Bonaire, and Curacao, and onto Grenada, rather than follow the shorter and more weather-friendly route from Panama straight across to Jamaica.

Refueled, and restocked with plenty of cigarettes and supplies, Pam wrote that *Heritage* would reach the San Blas Islands, home to the Cuna Indians, by the time I received her letter. We'd heard all about the Cunas from Ruth Kennedy, who collected their colorful hand-sewn, appliqued textiles they wore and sold. Back in Pedro Miguel, Ruth had shown us her prized *molas* and the photos she'd taken of the Cuna women. She laughed when she told us, "You know, it's a matriarchal society where the women are the breadwinners and handle all the money. Not only that," she added, "the women give the orders and have the final say . . . so it's their way or the highway!"

I remembered thinking, *these women have the right idea.* I could only hope my sisters would buy a *mola* for me.

Checking the dates of my family's itinerary, I figured they were close to Cartagena. If I wanted a letter to reach them in time, I had to mail it the next morning.

With pen in hand, I struggled over what to say. How could I tell them about life with the Hookers? I imagined my father's derisive snorting, and my mother's conclusive opinion, saying, "What did you expect? You made your bed, now lie in it." How could I fault her when I suspected she might be correct?

I'd blamed my family, especially my father, for crushing my soul, but I wondered if I might be my own worst enemy. The harsh memories of life aboard *Heritage* had softened, but I'd brought the same issues with me to California. Underneath the bravado, I feared I was still the lonely, angry young girl with two braids and a sailor's mouth. Was it better to lie and write I was having a grand time? Had I made my bed, and now needed to make the best of it?

*Dear Family,*

*Hope this letter finds you all well and safe in Cartagena. Life with the Hookers is great! Besides hanging out with Lisa, I've made lots of friends at school and love all my classes at Redwood High.*

Lisa's demands filled my afternoons. She wasn't interested in fostering a friendship; she only wanted me to serve her needs. Mealtime was the only time I had control over my inability to extricate myself from my hated task. The more Lisa consumed, the less I ate.

One evening at dinner, Mr. Hooker stared at Lisa and me as he slowly chewed his first bite. Immediately after swallowing, he raised his fist and slammed it down on the table, bouncing our plates and silverware. "I swear to Christ," he said, as he shifted his eyes between us. "One of you is gettin' fatter, or one of you is gettin' skinnier!"

Lisa pointed to me as she shoved a forkful of mashed potatoes into her mouth. "It's her . . . she never eats."

I had to admit; she was half right. But Lisa had easily gained far more than I'd lost. Whether or not it was a side effect from the little pink pill she took daily, she ate with abandon, grazing on leftovers and snacks after school and eating with gusto during dinner.

"Is it true?" he demanded. I wanted to say, yes, I'm skinny, but your daughter is working up an appetite from all the sex she's having upstairs with her boyfriend. But after Lisa gave me a swift kick to the shins underneath the table, I reconsidered and said nothing.

"Well, I want to see a clean plate tonight, young lady," Mr. Hooker announced. "Can't have Jim thinkin' I'm starvin' his daughter!"

After witnessing Mr. Hooker's volatile moods, I knew I'd stockpiled enough ammunition against Lisa, holding her afternoon trysts as ransom, to quit guard duty. No longer able to threaten me, she enjoyed making my life as miserable as possible, so I stayed as far from her as I could.

The school library became my second home, and I met students who, like me, enjoyed the safety and security of its quiet environment. One such student was a girl who was also in my American History class. Pale skinned, and as quiet and calm as I was loud and jittery, Mary McCrae possessed an enviable steadiness I found lacking in myself.

As embarrassed as I was about my shabby wardrobe, Mary, who could have afforded anything, preferred clothes from the thrift store—faded army pants, frayed-collared blouses, and oversized crewneck sweaters. With her vintage clothes, solemn expression, and cascade of thick, wavy, white-blonde hair parted down the middle, she looked as if she'd sprung from an old-time tin daguerreotype. More important than her dry sense of humor and forthrightness was her opinion that my life with the Hookers sucked.

"We've got plenty of room in our house. My parents won't mind," she told me. Mary had four siblings, but only she and her younger sister, Lacey, lived at home with their parents in the exclusive section of Kent Woodlands. I would've jumped at the chance to stay with a new family, but, considering the bad luck I'd had at the Hookers, I didn't want to jeopardize my friendship with Mary.

It was the middle of November when I received a letter from Pam and, to my surprise, a postcard from my father, mailed from Cartagena. *Heritage* had sailed along the northeastern coast of Panama to the San Blas Islands and had anchored at El Porvenir, one of the largest of the five habitable islands among the 365-island archipelago. After resting for the night, they'd sailed over to the two-and-a-half-acre island of Pidertupo and met the owners, Tom and Joan Moody, and their seven-year-old daughter, Marijo. The only *wagas* allowed to lease Cuna property, Tom and Joan had opened a ten-guest bush resort. I read how Nancy had taken a shine to the self-sufficient Marijo, who, Pam wrote, "can speak Cuna like a native and skippers her own tiny dinghy around the reef."

Whether it was an opportunity for my youngest sister to spend time with someone her age, or they all were enjoying hanging out with the Moodys, I learned they'd stayed five days before weighing anchor and sailing on to Cartagena.

According to the itinerary listed on my father's postcard, they would have sailed on to the ABC islands and reached the coast of Venezuela. My letter must have arrived in Cartagena after they'd departed, but I wondered why no one had written after they'd reached one of the ABCs. Maybe, I reasoned, they'd had engine trouble, or a major leak, or were too busy pressing on to Granada. I didn't want to consider a worse scenario, like sinking, or being lost at sea, or getting ransacked by pirates.

Pushing away my fears at night, I'd lay in bed and drift off, dreaming, as I'd done so many years earlier in our little apartment in Livermore, that I was sailing across a sapphire sea with my family aboard *Heritage*. Leaving them in Panama had ended this dream, but I'd always awake, overcome by a powerful yearning and an irresistible pull to pack my bags and return to them.

As the weeks passed, I slowly adjusted to land life. I was excelling at school, and with Mary's help, I made new friends. No longer relegated to eating lunch alone, I enjoyed sitting with other kids on Redwood High's grass quad. Even with the cultural and financial divide existing between me and most students, I could forget my status as "other." Life aboard *Heritage* had lent an air of mystery and I used my sailing trip as my golden pass, entertaining my classmates with colorful tales of danger and intrigue. No one needed to know my family was broke, and that I was hanging on by my fingernails with just enough money in my savings to make it through to graduation in June. As far as my friends were concerned, I'd lived an adventurous, swashbuckling life.

By the beginning of December, the days grew shorter and colder. With only a thin sweater to keep me warm and on a tight budget, I remembered the boxes of personal items and winter clothes my family had stored with friends.

After convincing a school friend to drive over to Oakland, I brought everything back to the Hookers. Besides several boxes of Pam's that she'd stored at her friend Cindy's house, which contained much needed sweaters and a winter coat, I'd also retrieved my grandmother's enormous black trunk from Germany. Opening it, I discovered, among many other items, my mother's fine china, all of our family albums, *Heritage's* boat plans, letters my father had written to my mother, my sisters' treasures, and folded carefully in tissue paper, on the very bottom, was Grandma's mink coat.

I pulled it out and buried my face in it, inhaling my grandmother's familiar scent, wishing she were here to stroke my forehead and tell me how much she loved me. Although I'd experienced love with a boy who'd cherished me, it ended when we started new lives. With Grandma, though, she'd promised her love would last forever. But when she died, it disappeared, swallowed by the sea and stars. I wrapped her coat around me, hoping by holding it close, I would find a way back to her.

Two weeks before Christmas, Mr. and Mrs. Hooker planned a weekend away in Mendocino. After dropping Lisa off with a friend and me at Mary's, they locked their house and headed up the coast.

Whenever Mary invited me for the weekend, it was like winning an all-inclusive stay at a country club. The McCraes' house in Kentfield was in one of the wealthiest enclaves in Marin County. Hidden from view, it sat at the end of a street, on two-and-a-quarter acres, bordered by a vast emerald lawn on one side, and a huge, organic garden, heated pool, and clay tennis court on the other side. They even had a full-time gardener, named Mr. Johnson, who could fix or grow anything and a housekeeper and cook, named Clara Mae, who was as loving and generous toward me as she was with Mary and Lacey.

I loved to slip down in the early morning before anyone else was awake to the McCraes' living room, where two baby grand pianos occupied opposite ends of the expansive, wood-beamed room and old books and items collected from their travels lined the walls. With Molly, their small sheepdog mix and George, their ancient, flatulent pointer, curled at my feet, I'd dig my toes into the plush carpet and stare out the window, dreaming of a different life.

But beyond the splendor of their property was the fact that, unlike the Hookers or my family, the McCraes were relaxed and easygoing. No one yelled during meals or demanded fealty or guard duty. And, at night, sprawled across my queen-sized bed in the guest room, I never failed to fall into a sound sleep.

So, it was not surprising that it took a minute to comprehend I wasn't dreaming when I felt a hand on my shoulder.

"Dear, wake up!"

"What time is it?" I asked, rubbing my eyes.

Mr. and Mrs. McCrae and Mary were standing next to my bed in their pajamas.

"It's three a.m.," Mrs. McCrae replied.

"What's going on?"

"I'm afraid we have some bad news."

Alarmed, I sat up. "My family?"

"No. It's the Hookers. They called to make sure you were safe," Mr. McCrae said, as Mrs. McCrae pulled the curtains apart.

I got out of bed and walked over to the window. In the distance, a bright orange line glowed against the dark sky.

"The hillside's on fire. It's the Santa Ana winds," Mr. McCrae said. "They're trying to save as many houses as they can, but the Hookers' house . . ." He hesitated. My heart pounded so loud in my chest I could barely hear the words, ". . . burned down."

An enormous lump formed in my throat, and I felt sick to my stomach. It was impossible to comprehend that what I'd considered home and everything dear to me was gone.

"Don't worry," Mr. McCrae said, as he put his hand on my shoulder. "You can stay right here with us."

Listening to the faint sounds of sirens in the distance, I watched the flames light up the sky.

# 29

# You Can't Go Home Again

## *Marin County, California*

**December 1971**

When the Hookers returned early from their weekend getaway, they'd called both Lisa and me to let us know we could come home if we wanted. I was perfectly happy to stay another day at the McCraes, and I knew Lisa was spending time with Randall. It was lucky we'd declined. The electrical fire that had started in the basement spread so rapidly there had been only enough time for the Hookers to jump out of bed, race down the stairs, and out the door before flames engulfed the entire house.

On the night of the fire, all I could think about as I watched the orange glow on Corte Madera's ridge grow brighter was that my existence and the little that defined me had been erased. If I could just get to the Hookers' house, I thought, I might find something, however small, that would connect me to my life.

The local news had reported the blaze was so intense that even the brick chimney had collapsed, tumbling down the hill and injuring Corte Madera's fire chief and one of his men. Hindered by the hairpin turn at the top of Chapman Drive, the fire truck lost valuable time, and firemen could only contain the blaze by hosing down the nearby houses. What they couldn't control were the soaring Santa Ana winds, which carried white-hot embers, igniting the rows of bone-dry eucalyptus along the ridge and torching rooftops down the hillside. If not for the rain starting in the predawn hours, the ridge and surrounding houses would've been destroyed.

The day after the fire, I convinced Mary I needed to see the damage for myself. Instead of heading off to school, we cut class and drove to Chapman Drive. When we reached the top of the hairpin turn, we checked for roaming patrol cars or signs of the Hookers' VW Beetle before parking and walking up to the remains. Bright yellow police tape cordoned off the cement carport and property line. The smell of smoke hung heavy in the air and a layer of ash carpeted the street. I looked around to make sure none of the neighbors were watching as we ducked under the tape and made our way up the steps, past the rubble, to the back terrace.

Looking down, it was hard to fathom a two-story house had stood there. Except for a rectangular-shaped lump near the far window that I recognized as my grandmother's trunk, what was once my bedroom was gone.

I slipped on a pair of heavy-duty gardening gloves, grabbed a garbage bag, and stepped gingerly onto the charred beams. When I reached the trunk, I brushed away the thick layer of wet ash and forced the lid open. The fire had burned the exterior, but the inside hadn't burned all the way through. I grabbed the only salvageable items, stuffing the soggy and charred photo albums and a single intact plate from my mother's china into the bag. Then I retraced my steps along the beams back to the terrace. Checking again to make sure no one was looking, Mary helped me drag the bag down the hill to her Jeep.

Back at the McCraes', I pulled the acrid and charred photographs apart and laid them edge to edge on a table to dry in the gardening shed. I picked up my mother's remaining plate, and as I traced my finger over its delicate rose pattern, I asked myself why hadn't I just left well enough alone? Even though my motive to move everything to the Hookers had been well intentioned, I couldn't help but think my family might feel otherwise.

Lisa stayed out of school the rest of the week, but I soldiered on, feeling the loss a second time as classmates whispered and averted their eyes when I passed them in the hallways or entered a classroom. Hunched over my desk, I felt raw and exposed. My loss was a stark reminder that, except for the clothes on my back, I had nothing. And the colorful stories and bravado I'd created to bridge the gap between what others had and I didn't, collapsed. All I saw when I looked down at my textbook was a future teetering on the edge of a dark, yawning abyss.

The weekend after the fire, the Hookers drove up to the house and sifted through the rubble. When Lisa returned to school the following Monday, she'd gloated about the stack of silver dollars she'd found, and I knew they were the ones Grandma had given me. But with no way to prove they were mine, I couldn't claim them.

While I could let go of the coins, I refused to surrender my new life. After less than a week at the McCraes, I knew I never wanted to go back.

I lobbied hard to stay at Mary's, presenting my plan to Mr. McCrae with an offer to pay rent and help with the housework or work in the garden. After listening to me, he leaned back in his chair and closed his eyes. Overwhelmed by anxiety, I sat on the edge of my chair and waited. Finally, he opened his eyes and addressed me.

"Well, I appreciate your offer, but I think we're doing fine here. As for gardening and housework, we have Mr. Johnson and Clara Mae."

Panic set in. I had nothing else to offer. Defeated, I got up. Mr. McCrae smiled and held up his hand to stop me from leaving. "So, the only thing left to do is call the Hookers and tell them you're staying with us for a while."

Relieved, and afraid I'd start crying, I blurted out "thank you" and rushed out of the room.

"You okay, honey?" Clara Mae asked, as she caught me swiping away my tears.

"I guess so," I said, crouching beside Molly and George, who were napping and stretched out on the kitchen floor.

"Have some lunch. You'll feel better."

I gave the dogs a last belly rub before I straightened up and walked over to Clara Mae.

She handed me a plate piled high with chips and a tuna-salad sandwich, with a dill pickle on the side. "Get yourself something to drink from the refrigerator."

While I sat at the table and ate, I watched Clara Mae move about the kitchen. She hummed as she cleaned the counters and dried the dishes. "Are you happy?" I asked, finishing up the last of my chips.

"As happy as anyone, I guess," she said, chuckling and shaking her head. "Why you askin'?"

"I dunno. Guess I'm just trying to figure out some things."

"Like what?"

"Why life is easier for some people and harder for others?"

"Only the good Lord knows the answer to that," she said.

"Seems to me He's a bit indiscriminate in doling out who gets what," I said.

She stood facing me, her hands resting on her ample hips. "You gotta have a little more faith, child. You got your whole life in front of you. Go on outside and get some fresh air. It'll clear that head of yours."

Instead of listening to Clara Mae's sage advice, I used the back stairs and hightailed it to my room. While I was grateful and relieved to stay with the McCraes until graduation, I lay on my bed, depressed, and mourning the loss of my things. I tried to remind myself what everyone said to me after hearing about the fire, "You're lucky you weren't there." It was true, there were fates far worse than losing possessions. I could be dead, like Joe Eklund, drowned and lying at the bottom of the sea, or burnt to a crisp, my bones a pile of ash in the cellar of the Hookers' house. Still, I couldn't stop feeling sorry for myself, especially since I had to sit down and write to my family about the fire. I could only think what a rotten Christmas present they'd receive when they reached Grenada—their own personal Scrooge sending a pile of ashes from sunny California.

While I waited to hear from them, a flurry of activity began in the McCrae household. Unlike my family, the McCraes embraced the holidays. The biggest fir tree I'd ever seen towered on one side of the living room, decorated with hundreds of lights and heirloom glass ornaments. Wreaths hung in every room and fir garlands wrapped around banisters and draped over mantles. The warm scent of orange and clove candles filled the rooms, and the delicious aroma from Clara Mae's baking wafted from the kitchen. Outside, strings of colored lights ran along the eaves, while life-sized wire deer, covered in tiny white lights, graced the lawn.

All during the holidays, as a revolving door of family, friends, and neighbors paraded through the house, Mrs. McCrae introduced me as her daughter's school friend who'd lost everything in a fire. I stood awkwardly next to her, as people expressed sympathy over my "terrible tragedy," and offered their deepest condolences as if someone had died. When I attempted to clarify the circumstances, their reaction confused me.

"Oh, so your *real* family is sailing on their yacht off the coast of South America? No problem then!"

I wanted to counter, "You got it all wrong. There's no daddy in yachting whites, smoking a pipe, with a fat checkbook, comforting me." But given their assumption I was privileged, how could I? Would they have believed me if I'd said I'd been on a trip from hell in a leaking boat, captained by a crazed father, and crewed by an addle-brained mother and seasick sisters? Caught in a false narrative, my only recourse was to smile, nod my head, and wish everyone a Merry Christmas.

A few days before the New Year, Clara Mae handed me mail from my family that had been forwarded from the Hookers. I ran up to my room and ripped the letters open, eager to find out if *Heritage* and her crew had reached Grenada. Each letter held several notes from my mother and sisters. In the first one, my mother had enclosed a $20 bill as my Christmas gift, and news they'd reached Isla Margarita's official port, Pampatar, off the Venezuelan coast. There was no mention of *Heritage's* voyage from Cartagena and the many anchorages between the Colombian port and Isla Margarita—including the ABC islands of Aruba, Curacao, and Bonaire, and stops along the Venezuelan coast, and Isla Tortuga. I could only assume the letters recounting those eight hundred miles were delayed or lost in the mail.

My mother wrote:

*I wanted to buy you and your sisters pearl necklaces because I'd read that Isla Margarita is called the "island of pearls." But since we've been here, there's not a single pearl in sight, and, if I'm being honest,*

*it's more like the "island of pigs and goats." They are everywhere! After*
*six days anchored here, we are all glad we're leaving tomorrow.*

When I'd read she'd included me alongside my sisters, I didn't care
that her gift hadn't materialized. What counted was the gesture, and it
made me hope she'd forgiven me for foiling her plans.

Following her last entry, she'd continued her note, dated a few days
later, explaining they'd departed the next morning, but had to turn back
when the engine overheated. Delayed another four days while my father
diagnosed and fixed the problem, she wrote about *Heritage*'s disgruntled
and impatient crew, except for my youngest sister, who, unperturbed
by the delay, happily camped out in the forepeak with her crayons and
tea set.

Ever the optimist, Nancy had sent me a note printed in large
bright-red block letters—"I am looking forward to the Virgin Islands!"—
and had made a drawing of a smiling stick-girl in front of a tiny cottage,
which she'd titled *Snow White and Her House.*

The second letter included more notes from my mother and Nancy,
but also notes from Pam and Gayle, who described *Heritage*'s second
attempt to reach Grenada.

Gayle wrote:

*Of course, we didn't make it—how could we possibly accomplish that?*
*I don't know what is wrong with us, but we're having a spell of bad*
*luck. To tell you the truth, I feel as though something drastic is about*
*to happen. Most important is that I don't believe I am going to leave*
*here by boat . . . I just can't go through it again . . . forty miles from*
*Grenada and we had to turn back!*

Pam had drawn a diagram detailing the circular path *Heritage* had
made, naming it "The Fantastic Voyage." She noted what day each disaster befell them—threatening trade winds, a current that drove them off
course, an electric bilge pump that shorted out, ocean swells that climbed
to twenty feet, a broken head, and a leaking propeller shaft that caused
life-threatening flooding—and how far off course they ended up before

their circular return to Isla Margarita's port, Juan Griego. After four tor-
tuous nights and five days, they ended up twenty miles farther west than
where they'd started.

The attempted leg from Isla Margarita to Grenada had been so brutal
and taxing that not only were my mother, Pam, and Gayle prepared to
give up, but, for the first time, my father voiced despair and doubts about
continuing.

Gayle wrote of her despondency after they'd returned and anchored
in Juan Griego.

*It's something I can't explain—a feeling over everybody, espe-
cially Dad.*

*He jokes about sailing into St. George's with a "for sale" sign painted
on each side of the hull in two-foot-high letters. We all have sea sores,
but Dad's are terrible, and he looks so tired and beat. I think this is
the biggest "down" I've been through. I just hope it passes, as I don't
know how much longer I can take it.*

And Pam admitted her own despair.

*Gayle and I have sworn not to continue and are planning a mutiny.*

Only Nancy had scrawled in crayon:

*I am having a good time. We turned back to Isla Margarita. We are
at Juan Griego.*

On the back of Nancy's note, my mother had scribbled,

*We're jealous of your life at the Hookers' warm house and the fresh-
water showers . . . consider yourself lucky. Make the best of everything
you have. We are having an adventure, but the experiences are sometimes sheer torture.*

*So, have a Merry Christmas!*

If I didn't think it was all so tragic, I'd have burst out laughing over my mother's misdirected envy.

I taped Nancy's drawing above my bed. As I drifted off, I thought if only we could all be like Snow White and sleep until awakened by a kiss to a wonderful life.

# 30

# Rising from the Ashes

## *Marin County, California*

**JANUARY 1–JUNE 17, 1972**

"You only need four more classes to graduate," Mr. Holbrook said, perusing my transcripts. "Why don't you pick up some extra credits at the junior college? I know you can handle it."

"Do you think I can?"

"Absolutely!" he said, smiling.

Unlike Skyline's hateful Mr. Bianchi, my guidance counselor at Redwood High was supportive and encouraging.

"Now, let's talk about colleges. Have you decided on any?"

I was too embarrassed to admit I didn't know the first thing about applying for college or where I was going to get the money to pay for it. If I'd been able to reach Pam, I would have asked for her help, but I hadn't heard from my family since Isla Margarita. So, I outright lied when I said, "It's hard to make a choice. There are so many."

"Well, what are your top two?" he asked.

I tossed out the first two I could think of—UC Berkeley and Macalester College. One was close to where I'd grown up and the other, in Minnesota, was where Pam had applied. But for now, any college was out of the question. I wasn't even sure how I was going to pay for the junior college courses Mr. Holbrook suggested I take. The plan to study hard, graduate, and apply to college had seemed so simple back in Panama, but without financing, its implementation was more complicated. The fire had stripped my reserve funds after I'd replaced clothes and essentials. Even with Mr. McCrae refusing to take rent money, I wasn't sure how I was going to make it to graduation. I knew I had to find an after-school job.

While I continued to scour the local paper for work, I worried about my family and where they might be. Had they attempted a third try to Grenada? And if they'd succeeded, did they receive the letter I'd sent? Maybe they'd written me off, concluding what I'd done as another colossal fuck-up. Overwhelmed by these intrusive thoughts, I was surprised when I returned home from school the next day by Clara Mae, who greeted me at the back door with a broad smile. "Looks like you got news from your folks," she said, as she handed me two letters. I threw my arms around her and then ran upstairs to my room to read them.

Postmarked from Isla Margarita, the first letter was from Pam.

*Just wanted you to know that Dad has scrapped plans for another attempt to Grenada and we are sailing south to Venezuela and following the coast until we reach Trinidad. As soon as we arrive, I'm flying to the States because, guess what? I've been accepted at Macalester College in St. Paul! I just need one little favor. Can you send the winter clothes I stored at Cindy's? Mail them to Aunt Ruth and Ethel's house, so I can have something warm to wear when I land.*

Unless St. George's port captain forwarded the letter to Trinidad, I'd have to write another one. But even if I mailed it in the morning, it wouldn't reach them before Pam left for the States. I felt terrible she'd discover the truth when she landed in St. Paul and hoped my parents would send her off with enough money to purchase a winter jacket.

Gayle's letter, postmarked from Trinidad, filled me in on what had happened from Isla Margarita to Trinidad. It had turned out worse than the attempted crossing to Grenada. After a smooth sail back to Venezuela's mainland, they'd anchored and spent the night. The next morning, combating rough seas and strong trade winds, they sailed along the coast, heading east. Passing their intended stop, they sailed on to Mejillones, where the anchorage was so untenable, they continued another sixty miles across the Bocas del Dragón straits.

*Just as we sighted a light off Trinidad, the first squall hit. Dad had the engine on full throttle to see if we could make it in before midnight, and then the steering mechanism failed. I had to hang over the stern just like I did off Big Sur. We would have been able to handle it, except for the terrible storm.*

By morning, after an exhausting night battling torrential rain and fifty-mile-an hour gusts, *Heritage* was still twenty-five miles off the coast. Jerry-rigged, *Heritage* inched forward, fighting opposing currents, worsening weather, and ship and freighter traffic. That was when, Gayle wrote, she noticed smoke pouring out of the engine manifold.

*When we lost power, Dad went below and sent out a mayday on the ship-to-shore radio. Finally, after waiting all day, and just before a huge fog bank started to roll in, the Trinidadian Coast Guard arrived and rescued us.*

*Everything was going okay until they started going faster and just like in Big Sur, we couldn't get them to slow down. Dad made us sit on the floor of the cockpit with our life jackets on under our float coats. We all thought* Heritage *would break apart. I've never been so scared in my entire life! We were exhausted by the time we made it to the Naval base.*

I set the letter on my nightstand. I thought about all that had happened to us on *Heritage* and how we'd encountered one challenge after another, without respite. Rather than uniting us, every disastrous encounter had increasingly separated us. Except for the handful of moments where happiness had been within our grasp, my father's promise that our lives would change for the better lay fallow and unrealized. And even though I was thousands of miles away in California, disaster had followed me as if I'd never left *Heritage*. How could it happen that the one house to burn down in all of Corte Madera would be the Hookers?

I recalled the story of the fisherman in Hemingway's *Old Man and the Sea* and wondered if we were also cursed and marked with *salão*, the worst form of unlucky. Were we destined, like the old man, to hook and catch a dream, only to watch something more powerful devour and tear it apart until nothing remained but the memory of what it once was?

Did the Hookers believe I'd brought them bad luck? Lisa must have because she hadn't spoken to me since the fire. I imagined she regretted my presence from the very start. She was an only child and used to being the center of attention. Sharing her family, home, and life must have been overwhelming. Maybe I'd been too harsh in my judgment after realizing she'd been a tyrant more out of necessity than spite.

The next morning, I called Macalester's main office and left my name and number. Within minutes, Pam called back. She'd been at school for a week. When my package didn't arrive, she'd been industrious enough to locate a few secondhand sweaters and an old parka. I told her all about the fire and how I ended up at the McCraes and she, in turn, revealed their disastrous trip to Trinidad was even worse than what Gayle had described.

"As soon as they towed us to Port of Spain's shipyard and we were dry-docked, I was never so glad to get on that plane and fly away," Pam said.

When I hung up, the tightness in my chest eased. If Pam could slog through snow and subzero temperatures wearing a few donated, dumpy hand-me-downs, existing on very little, and working twenty hours a week in the school office, I could hold my head up, live with what I had, and keep studying.

Walking home the next afternoon, I noticed a help-wanted sign in the window of the Chinese restaurant I passed every day to and from school and mustered the courage to walk in and apply.

"You work in Chinese restaurant before?" the owner asked, giving me an intense once over.

"No, but I'm a fast learner," I said.

"You need good memory. You take phone orders. Big menu. Many items."

"Try me out for a week without pay," I replied, hoping to seal the deal.

"Okay. You no work out, I no lose. You start tomorrow. Be here at four. You can learn to make wonton."

So began my job at Kentfield's only Chinese takeout and delivery. Mr. Wu greeted me the next afternoon with a grunt and led me to a table where two men sat, one younger and the other much older, whom I assumed might be Mr. Wu's father. A stack of pre-cut, triangular-shaped pieces of dough and a bowl filled with mashed meat were on the table.

"Pork for wonton," Mr. Wu said, noticing me staring into the bowl. "Sit. They show you."

I watched as the old man peeled off a triangle from the stack and then placed a spoonful of pork in the center. In a lightning quick move, he folded the dough over the meat, pinched the sides closed, and set it down on the metal oven sheet. Copying him, I peeled off a triangle of dough, folded it over the pork, and placed it on the sheet. "You need to do much faster!" Mr. Wu barked. "You do like that, take all night." This elicited guffaws and conversation I couldn't understand but obviously concerned my less-than-stellar performance.

Somehow, I muddled through and eventually got the hang of it. I was a better wonton maker than a phone order taker, though. It was hard to hear the phone orders over the din of Mr. Wu yelling at his cooks and delivery boys. Many times, I mixed up orders and sent off a container of moo shu pork instead of pork chow mein to some soon-to-be unhappy customer.

When I sat making wontons during the afternoons, Mr. Wu would pepper me with questions, most of the time not waiting for a reply as he boasted about his son in middle school and his daughter attending college.

When he discovered my family was on board a boat a continent away, and I'd bounced from one home to the next after being displaced by the fire, he exclaimed, "You like refugee." I had to agree. That was exactly how I felt. "You need to study hard, get good grades like my daughter . . . or you go nowhere," he warned. I nodded as I folded and pinched the dough.

After I received my first paycheck, I marched a half-mile down from the McCraes to the College of Marin and enrolled. Mr. Wu gave me Mondays off so I could attend my evening geography class. And on Tuesday and Thursday mornings, I'd race from my college English course to Redwood to make it in time for my third-period class.

Pam's weekly pep-talk calls kept me going and helped to keep despair at bay. Meanwhile, I put up a good front during dinners with the McCraes and even with Mary, who I knew couldn't understand the terror constantly nipping at my heels.

While the McCraes generously included me in their family outings and events, I was aware of the temporal nature of my situation and of the moments when the bounty of their lives overwhelmed me.

One evening, near the end of dinner, Mr. McCrae announced he had an interesting proposal.

"What do you have up your sleeve, Robert?" Mrs. McCrae teased.

"Who would like to spend three weeks living with the Inuits in Canada, where you'll learn to handle sled dogs, kayak around icebergs, and observe polar bears?"

My heart raced with excitement.

"Nah," Lacey replied. "Didya forget, I'm going to the Galapagos?"

"Yes, how could you forget?" Mrs. McCrae giggled, chiding her husband.

"Sorry, Dad, I'm spending the summer in Mexico," Mary replied.

Home from college, Mary's older sister Julie said, "This summer I don't want to go anywhere, except the pool."

I was dying to shout, "I'll go!" But I knew the offer was not meant for me. My temporary status was that of a spectator and not as a participant. In that moment, I hated Mary and her sisters for turning down an opportunity I'd never get to experience. As I pushed around the rest of my meal with my fork, I wondered what it would be like to go anywhere or do anything I desired.

Mr. McCrae smiled and sighed. "Can't say I didn't try," he said, pushing his chair back from the table. He glanced over at me and smiled. "And you, young lady, need to eat more. Either that, or you burn off calories faster than anyone I've ever seen."

Mrs. McCrae added, "I wish I had her metabolism."

As Mr. McCrae stood up, I wanted to stop and beg him to include me, but he walked away, and I felt the chance at the life I wanted slip away. Excusing myself, I returned to my room and curled up on my bed. As nice as the McCraes were, it was difficult to curb the envy that consumed me. They didn't feel the pervasive anxiousness I did. Making the next month's rent or affording groceries or where to lay one's head were non-issues for them.

And yet, I also understood wealth was not a guarantee that life was perfect or the answer to happiness. Mr. McCrae worked long hours; Mrs. McCrae, for all her outward cheeriness, was recovering from cancer; and I detected that at least one of Mary's siblings was depressed. Even when I thought back to the Frasers, things were not as they seemed, as Max dealt with a mutinous deckhand, a wife who lunched on Scotch, and a pot smoking daughter.

As I lay in bed, I realized the control I desired was illusory. While on the surface, it appeared as if I had it all together—all As, a job, and a beautiful place to live—underneath there was chaos. I'd wanted to disappear, and, without realizing, managed to accomplish it.

I knew my strict caloric intake had affected those around me, but it wasn't until I had to drop off a homework assignment to a school friend that I experienced its full effect. And what better way to do that than a face-off with a seven-year-old boy? Opening the door, the kid took one look at me and let out a blood-curdling scream. Racing down the hallway, he yelled, "There's a skeleton at our door!"

When my friend showed up, she was apologetic. "I'm so sorry. That was my stupid younger brother. Don't mind him."

"I'm sorry I scared you," I said, addressing the boy, who'd returned, and was hiding behind his sister.

"You're so white and skinny, I thought you were a ghost!" he said, peeking around and staring at me as if I were an apparition.

My friend's face turned beet red with embarrassment, and she apologized again before ordering her brother back up the stairs.

Back at the McCraes', I thought about the boy's reaction. I knew I was always hitching my jeans up and my appetite had dulled, but otherwise I felt fine. Maybe the kid was just being a smartass. I tried to laugh off the incident, yet I couldn't stop seeing his face.

Undressing in my room later, I caught my reflection in the bathroom mirror. Startled, I leaned in for a closer look. The girl who stared back was me, yet not me, as if I'd fallen, like Alice, down the rabbit hole and had drunk from the bottle labeled "drink me," shrinking and growing smaller. Replacing the strong sailor who'd scrambled up ratlines and sailed through storms was a pale, emaciated girl, who looked at me through dark, hollowed-out eyes. When she turned around, exposing her back, her shoulder blades jutted out from underneath her taut skin like tiny dragon wings. Matching her ribs and stick-like arms, bony hip bones sat atop a pair of scrawny legs. This was the girl everyone saw. While I'd assumed classmates and teachers had voiced concern because of the fire, it was now apparent it was because I was wasting away.

What had seemed like a game of revenge at the Hookers had turned into something more serious. I'd fallen overboard, and after treading water for a long time, I was tired and close to drowning. Ever since returning to California, and especially after the fire, it had been a constant struggle to quiet the panic. From the moment I opened my eyes in the morning until I shut them at night, I had to shove the fear deep down inside of me. My only lifeline was fragile, weakened, and frayed by fear and anger. I needed something stronger to help me hang on.

I'd never felt I belonged anywhere. Had I created this separateness or maybe it was simply fate and some of us were born under an unlucky star? How many times during downturns in my life had my mother joked I was born a "Wednesday's child?" Was I doomed to live a life full of woe? Or was I saddled with a family legacy of "otherness"?

Searching constantly for that one elusive port to shelter me, it was the barely detectable behavior of others that confirmed to me I had to keep moving to stay ahead of the storm. Why did I question everything? Why couldn't I be grateful the McCraes had given me my own bedroom, instead of noticing they also used it as a storage locker? I glanced over at the stack of large cardboard boxes filled with items belonging to Mary's older brother, who'd moved out years before. They'd taken up one-third of the room, and I wondered why no one had moved them to the other storage room down the hall? As I stared at them every night, I kept asking myself if their cardboard presence was a hint, reminding me I shouldn't get too comfortable. Wasn't it enough someone had offered me a place to lay my head? Why did I feel a need to make it my own?

Focusing outward, as I'd done with my family, friends, and even the Hookers and McCraes, in the hope I'd find security and safety and a sense of belonging, had proved the only way to have that was to count on myself and no one else. There was no point in wishing what might have been and what could be. To survive, I had to concentrate on the present and, instead of fearing the future, trust it was nothing more than just another day waiting to happen.

As the weeks flew by, Gayle wrote to me regularly. No longer adversaries as we'd been in Panama, her letters were revelatory, intimate, and friendly. *Heritage* had been dry-docked for several months and Gayle wrote about how she'd helped repair the damage incurred after leaving Panama and also about her life in Trinidad. I felt guilty I'd left her to shoulder all the work, but she professed to enjoy it. And by her account, the captain had changed for the better. Instead of ordering her around as he'd done with me, he'd sought her opinion and respected her suggestions:

*You know how his word was always dead final and how much more superior he always acted? Well, somehow that all changed. It's hard to explain, but I feel more equal. He realizes how much he needs me.*

*I don't exactly talk back to him, but if he watches over my work and makes too many comments, I turn around and give him a look. So, he backs off and says, ok, ok, ok, and leaves . . .*

I admired her tenacity and willingness to put in the hard labor to ready *Heritage* for cruising. She'd helped my father scrape a layer of barnacles off the hull, burn off the bottom paint, chop out the rotten wood under the topside, rip off the bulwarks and teak toe rail and rebuild them, caulk the decks, replace the underwater bearing for the propeller shaft, and repaint the hull and cabin from top to bottom.

Along with hanging out with new friends, she wrote about how much she loved time spent alone.

*It's so nice to have the boat to myself. As soon as they're gone, I light a candle and put on Mungo Jerry and . . .*

Reading that, I imagined her singing along to her favorite song, "In the Summertime." It reminded me of our banana boat adventure and dinner with the drunken officers, where she sprayed fried rice over everyone. What a bag of shit I gave her for doing that. If I got the chance, I vowed to be a better friend and sister. And I hoped the time spent away from them had also made me a better daughter, so maybe, as my father had with Gayle, he would behave the same with me.

If I returned, I might have the trip I still dreamed about.

It was now May and spring was in full bloom in Marin. Whenever I wasn't studying or making wontons, Mary and I would drive in her Jeep to the base of Mount Tamalpais and hike up to my favorite outlooks on Trojan Point or the East Peak. Enjoying the incredible sights of San Francisco Bay and beyond or the Pacific Ocean toward Point Reyes, it was one of the few places where my thoughts slowed enough to where I had no desire to look behind or forward but to just enjoy the view.

A few weeks before graduation, Pam forewarned me of our grandparents' plan to attend the ceremony. I couldn't understand why they wanted to take the time to drive all the way from Burbank, when they'd constantly complained during our trip about how much we'd inconvenienced them and how much time it had taken to manage our affairs.

I harbored a grudge toward them, convinced their disapproval, communicated in every letter they'd sent, had affected my father and helped sour our chance at happiness. If we'd left with their approval and support, I believe my father would have handled the challenges we encountered with less doubt and uncertainty.

"Are you sure they're not just showing up to see if I'm actually graduating?" I asked.

"Who knows why they do what they do?" she replied. Pam was far more philosophical than I. "Why worry? They'll be gone before you know it."

"I'm going to have to give an Oscar-worthy performance," I said. "Because what I'd really like to do is tell them to go to hell."

"There's no point," Pam said. "By the way, I had to give them the McCraes' number, so expect a call from them."

As I was rushing out of the house a week later to make it to my Monday night class, Mrs. McCrae stopped me and told me she'd received a call from my grandparents. Embarrassed, I asked her what they'd said.

"They wanted to know about accommodations. Of course, dear, I told them with family coming for Mary's graduation, we couldn't extend an invitation."

"Of . . . course . . . not," I stammered. How could my grandparents even entertain that thought? I wanted to murder them.

"I gave them a few names of accommodations nearby. Maybe you can call and help them with that," she said.

I nodded and ran out the door. As I fled down the street, I couldn't stop the thoughts swirling in my head. I knew it wasn't Mrs. McCrae's fault, but I always felt like an unwelcome guest in her presence. It wasn't what she said, but rather, what was left unsaid. All it took was a perceived slight to land me back at Porter Elementary or Montera Junior High, where I was the misfit and outcast.

I thought about the stupid boxes piled up in my room and recalled the sweater I'd picked from the box of clothes Mrs. McCrae had slated for the Goodwill. I couldn't shake the feeling she looked unhappy whenever I wore it. Unlike Mr. McCrae, she asked what my plans were for the summer. I knew she felt my time staying with them had ended. For her, five months had been long enough. And who could blame her? I knew I had to figure out my next plan of action and where I was going to go.

Pam was going back to Trinidad as soon as her classes at Macalester finished at the end of the month, and I wondered if I should do the same. *Heritage* had been dry-docked for over three-and-a-half months and was almost ready to go back in the water. The plan, Pam told me, was to have someone help them sail up to Grenada and then, if needed, find people along the way to crew the seven hundred miles to the Virgin Islands.

The day before graduation, my grandparents pulled into the McCraes' driveway. When I walked out to greet them, my grandfather got out and said, "Mother and I drove straight here . . . didn't even stop to check in at the motel." He looked around and said, "Mighty nice house you're stayin' at."

Mrs. McCrae invited them in and offered them a snack by the pool. That was all it took for my grandparents to be gobstruck. After lunch, Mrs. McCrae took them on a personal tour of the house and grounds. I wondered if they'd ever leave or just ask to move in. I told them I needed to pick up my cap and gown early the next morning, hoping they'd take the hint and leave. Finally, they pulled out of the driveway right before dinner.

That night I lay in bed and thought about the day's events. Turning toward the wall, I stared at the stack of boxes and realized someone had added more of them, making it seem as if they were slowly encroaching and crowding me out. I leapt up, and, with a couple of savage kicks, toppled them. Then, I climbed back into bed and enjoyed the best night's rest I'd had in weeks.

Refreshed and ready to embrace the day, I awoke on graduation morning to blue skies and the sound of birds singing through my open window. I dressed and threw my cap and gown over my clothes before going downstairs, where Mary was waiting in her Jeep to drive us to the Cushing Memorial Theater at Mount Tamalpais State Park.

When we arrived, I looked out at the Greek-styled amphitheater with its rock hard, carved-stone seating and wondered how my grandparents would fare sitting for a couple of hours. I hoped, for the sake of their bony backsides, they'd brought cushions.

As I looked around at the sea of scarlet caps and gowns, it occurred to me that out of the five-hundred-plus graduating seniors, I only knew two, and one of them no longer spoke to me. I wondered if that said something about me. Had I spent too much time worrying about surviving and the challenges that lay ahead, instead of just enjoying being the teen I'd hoped to be by returning to California? To the majority, I was a ghost who had floated through class and campus, a girl so thin she'd been mistaken for a skeleton.

By the time I strode across the stage to shake the principal's hand and receive my diploma, the summer heat had soaked everything underneath my gown. As I walked back to my seat, I scanned the audience. There were still 135 students waiting to graduate, and I imagined my grandparents melting under the blistering sun.

After the last name was called, everyone flung their caps in the air and rushed to their families. I found my grandparents fanning themselves near the far side of the theater. Instead of congratulating me, my grandfather grunted and said, "Good to see one of you gals is finally gettin' your diploma." I wasn't sure what he meant. Pam had graduated high school with honors before the trip started and was now attending Macalester on scholarship, and Gayle, who was a junior, was smarter than Pam and I put together. Even Nancy was reading years ahead of her peers. I wanted to shout in his face, "Screw you! We're all smarter than *you'll* ever be."

I could hear Pam's voice of reason, "They'll be gone before you know it," and held my tongue.

"You comin' back with us?" my grandfather asked. I hadn't planned on driving with them, but I couldn't find Mary, so I nodded yes. We made our way back to the car and drove the winding, eighteen-and-a-half-mile, fifty-three-minute drive back to the McCraes. When we arrived, everyone was already seated at the table, where Clara Mae had set out plates piled high with cold cuts, potato salad, several fresh pastas, a baked ham, and a huge cheese plate.

I held my breath throughout lunch, worried my grandfather might crack one of his racist "colored" or "jungle bunny" jokes and shame me for all eternity. But he and my grandmother were on their best behavior. The worst I could accuse them of was their nonstop fawning over the McCraes' house and what my grandfather described as their "stylish furnishings." While my grandparents would never win awards for their interior decorating skills, the property they owned, which included their house and two adjacent apartments, sat on a valuable piece of land near downtown Burbank. It wasn't as if they lived in a rundown trailer, but their oohing and aahing made it seem that way. And observing Mrs.

McCrae's bemused expression as she listened to them blathering on made it even more apparent.

While I'd harbored my own envy over the McCraes' lifestyle, it was not their things I yearned for, but the sense of belonging and security they exuded. My grandparents, however, had never concerned themselves with creating a warm, loving environment for their children or grandchildren. To them, success was measured not by love or encouragement, but by how much one could acquire. In that, my father failed as he'd thrown away his job and home for a "foolish dream."

I knew we weren't the perfect family. My father was a bastard, my mother, a wimp, my sisters, competitors, and me, self-involved, resentful, and angry, but I believed other families worse than us had suffered less. And even though we'd failed in some things, we'd succeeded in others. Like Ahab's *Pequod*, we'd chased the elusive prize, sailing from port to port, hoping to one day close in and capture it. But, unlike the old whaling captain who met his watery death, those fleeting glimpses of happiness offered a lifeline to a life different from the one I'd known. It was those thoughts I'd entertained as I looked out the McCraes' living room window in the early mornings with Molly and George at my feet. Wealth might have made it easier for the Frasers and McCraes of the world, but I'd learned that every family, including us, deserved a chance at a better and happier life.

After spending the past two days with my grandparents, I concluded I'd wasted an inordinate amount of time despising them. They were just two old, cranky, unsophisticated people who happened to be related to me. Why couldn't my father see how petty and pedestrian they were? They'd never understand giving up everything to pursue something far greater. Because of that, they'd stood in judgment of him. How could I, at eighteen, understand this when my father, in his forties, was still trying to impress them? Why had he invested so much of himself in getting their approval? Didn't he realize he'd outgrown them long ago, and that his achievements had carried him far beyond anything they'd ever accomplished?

As the afternoon wore on and I watched Mrs. McCrae tire, it was apparent my grandparents had overstayed their welcome. Urging my guests to get on the road before dusk, I walked them to their car. After promising to write and giving each a quick hug, I watched them drive off. Just as they disappeared down the road, Mary ran out and said, "Your dad's on the line."

I ran back into the house and picked up the phone. "You just missed Grandpa and Grandma. I got my diploma, Dad!"

I waited, but instead of congratulating me, he said, "I'm afraid to tell you the bad news." He paused and then cleared his throat. "It happened last week, but we didn't want to spoil your day."

"What happened?" I asked.

"*Heritage*. . . ." My father's voice faltered. "She's gone."

"What do you mean, gone?"

"The crane dropped her."

"Where?"

"Just before she got to the water."

I pressed the phone to my ear, unable to speak.

"It's alright. There's nothing to say, Sport." He hadn't called me that in a long time. His voice caught when he said, "And the shame is she was a better boat than when we first launched her."

I swallowed hard, trying not to cry.

"Think about joining us here in Trinidad. There's an oil barge captain I befriended who's promised to put *Heritage*'s remains in a container on his next run to the States. We can start over and make her better than ever." Before I could reply, he said he had to go and hung up.

I leaned against the wall knowing I had to face the McCraes, who were gathered around the patio next to the pool, but I didn't know if I'd be able to collect myself enough to do so. I stood in the hallway for another minute and then walked out.

"Oh, dear! You look as if you've seen a ghost," Mrs. McCrae said.

I took a deep breath. "There was an accident. . . . " Avoiding their gaze, I let the words tumble out, "and our boat was destroyed."

"You have insurance, of course?" Mrs. McCrae innocently asked.

I stood there, not knowing how to react. I could see that she'd assumed *Heritage* was insured and replaceable. How could I explain buying insurance from Lloyds of London, the only marine insurer of private yachts, had been completely beyond our budget? Would she even understand that it wasn't just that *Heritage* was destroyed, but that a significant part of my life spent building, caring, maintaining, and living on her was also gone? I wanted to laugh but instead brushed aside her question with the excuse I suddenly wasn't feeling well. As I backed out of the patio and walked slowly through the house, I thought about Mrs. McCrae's response and my father's call. For them, it was a simple replace or rebuild. But for me, *Heritage* and the dream I'd carried for so many years had died. I didn't want to spend another ten years rebuilding her and there was no replacing her. I didn't want to start over. I'd begun to have new dreams, dreams that were mine and not my father's. It was in that moment I knew I would not rejoin my family in Trinidad.

When I returned to my room, I lay on my bed, listening to the sound of my heartbeat. It was slow and steady. I closed my eyes and remembered my father and me diving to the coral reef in Isla Secas, as schools of brightly colored parrot fish surrounded us, and a sea turtle lazily swam in the distance. And later, near sunset, gathering driftwood for a campfire on the beach. But most of all, I remembered *Heritage* and how, at night, sitting in her cockpit, I'd realized that the sea and sky were the same: the Milky Way, with its swath of a hundred billion stars glittering in the black night and the ocean's dark, underwater cosmos, lit by infinite swirls of shimmering bioluminescence below. We'd lived in both worlds, but only *Heritage* marked the boundary between the two—her upper half facing the sky, her lower half embracing the sea. She'd protected us from both worlds as she navigated her way through fog, storms, rogue waves, flat seas, frigid cold, and oppressive heat, transporting her ragged crew toward their next anchorage, be it rolling roadstead, or pristine cove, or protected bay. Despite her demanding facade, uncomfortable quarters, and leaking bilge, she'd delivered.

My father had built her to escape, and I'd escaped from her to live, but even with her gone, I knew she'd remain as much a part of us as we'd been a part of her. After a voyage of over seven thousand miles, *Heritage* had been a testimony to stamina and perseverance. So it had been for my father, as I now realized, it had been for me. But it was time to let go, even as my father continued to dream.

I wasn't sure where I'd go or where life would take me, but I knew I'd be okay. Something far stronger had replaced the frayed and worn line that I had been holding onto for so long. Not only was the new line stronger, but I had also gained a newfound strength. I'd learned that one's true worth was measured not by where one landed or by the opinion of others, but in the attempt to get somewhere better than where one started. In that, *Heritage* had succeeded, and by default, so had I.

I learned the outcome is never guaranteed. Sometimes not even the journey is a sure thing. We break down, spring leaks, veer off course, run scared, wound others, lose our way. But in those moments, we discover resiliency, and strength, and most of all, forgiveness. When that happens, the storm clouds break, and we find we are buoyed and connected once again by the power and beauty of the ocean and the sky and the smell of earth.

# Author's Notes

I was asked how I could remember minute details and the seemingly verbatim dialogue after so many decades, and the answer is twofold. I spent months researching the numerous towns, harbors, and coastlines from San Francisco to Trinidad and how they appeared during the late '60s and early '70s. My research also included our ship's log and port entry papers, my teenage journals, and family letters. Many conversations come directly from decades of family reunions, when my sisters, mother, and I would sit around the dinner table recalling, word for word, what had transpired during our two-year voyage aboard *Heritage*. This oral history helped keep the memories fresh, alive, and accessible.

While I'm fortunate to have had the blessings of my mother before she passed away, permission from two of the most fabulous, supportive siblings, and the green light from certain individuals whose names remained unchanged, some names and identifying details of people described in this book have been altered to protect their privacy. Names of certain landmarks and harbors have been altered and/or have been renamed over the years, either through tourist development or political change, such as the renaming of the Thatcher Ferry Bridge to the Bridge of the Americas, or The Friars, now commonly referred to as El Arco de Cabo San Lucas or The Arch at Land's End.

For all my non-sailor readers, I have included a sailing glossary at the end of the book for reference.

I have made every effort to maintain the utmost accuracy in telling my story, not only onboard *Heritage* but also when I returned to California. I shall forever be grateful to the two families I lived with during my last year in high school, and I recognize that their memories of the events described may differ from mine. Without their generosity, I would have found myself homeless and wandering the streets.

If there are viewpoints or dialogue in my story that some might consider personally or culturally offensive, please bear in mind that it is a memoir and, as such, reflects the sign of the times and not the author's current perspective.

I would like to clarify a few things about my high school drama teacher, Mr. Farnsworth, who rose to acclaim when he was famously outed by Tom Hanks during Hanks's 1994 Academy Award win. Holding up his Oscar after winning best actor for the film *Philadelphia*, Hanks credited his love of acting to having "had the good fortune to be associated with, to fall under [Farnsworth's] inspiration at such a young age." Hanks continued to express admiration for his high school teacher by generously contributing to the $400,000 renovation of Skyline High's thirty-five-year-old theater, renamed the Rawley T. Farnsworth Theater. He also helped establish the creation of The Farnsworth Fellowship with ACT (American Conservatory Theater) in San Francisco, which places teaching artists in schools located in disadvantaged areas. Without a doubt, Mr. Farnsworth, who passed away in 2013, has earned his place in history. My impression of him was simply that of a self-conscious, sensitive sixteen-year-old-girl who took a teacher's stinging criticism to heart. Nonetheless, I can say now, after all these years, that although he failed to impart to me the sage advice he gave to Hanks, to "act well the part, there all the glory lies," I have discovered that those words ring true for any endeavor that one pursues.

Likewise, my impressions and observations of Lin and Larry Pardey were made when I was a teen and, although true to my experience, are in no way meant to malign or defame. The Pardeys went on to become one of the yachting world's most renowned sailing couples, spending the next five decades together, sailing over 200,000 miles, until Larry's death in 2020. Lin still sails and will soon be, along with Larry, inducted into the National Sailing Hall of Fame.

Although Mark and I pursued different lives, I remained in touch for many years with Mr. Darden, exchanging letters every Christmas.

For years afterward, we'd laugh about his "visit" to *Heritage* and my guest appearance at dinner.

I have written unsparingly about myself and others, hopefully tempering the truth with humor, to show we are all flawed in some way, and by revealing that, we can recognize our humanity and connectedness.

# ACKNOWLEDGMENTS

A very special thank you to my agent extraordinaire, Adam Chromy, whose towering presence and shoot-from-the-hip style makes me yearn for the years I spent in New York City, for your guidance, coaching, and support. My life has been forever changed, as I can now proudly state I'm not only a writer, but an author. You made it happen.

I would like to thank everyone at Lyons Press, first and foremost, my editor, Rick Rinehart, who, against all odds, took a chance with a first-time author. Your belief in me pushed me beyond my limitations to help deliver a manuscript that met your expectations. My appreciation to Brittany Stoner, for guiding me through the necessary steps to publication; Meredith Dias for overseeing the production and review of my manuscript; Joshua Rosenberg for copy-editing and saving me from embarrassment by correcting punctuation and spelling. Also, a thank you to Jen Huppert for the beautiful cover design, Virginia Bridges for proofreading, and Alyssa Griffin in marketing.

I was so fortunate to have had the opportunity to not only work with but become friends with the talented developmental editor Michele Matrisciani. Thank you, Michele. Without your keen sense of narrative and story arc, which helped shape my memoir, and suggested cuts that you delivered with a gentle touch, I would not have the book I have today.

Thank you, Michael Neff, founder and director of Algonkian Writers Conference, for pulling me aside during the St. Augustine Author-Mentor Workshop to reassure me that swear words were perfectly acceptable and germane to my story; and to Paula Munier, best-selling author, agent, and Author-Mentor Workshop codirector, you were spot on for giving me the painful but ultimately wise advice to drop the first nine chapters.

My deepest thanks to the Darden family for allowing me the freedom to write as I remembered. A special thank you to Beth Darden McElvain for taking the time to send her recollections of me when I lived in the Canal Zone, and to Mark Darden for your trust in me. Thank you to the Hookers and McCraes, and fellow cruisers and boating community—especially the Soules, Duffs, Frasers, Pardeys, and Kennedys—for being part of my story.

Thank you to Peter Bricklebank, creative nonfiction professor at New York University, whose unbridled enthusiasm and belief that my story was worth telling; to Michael Zam, screenwriting and playwrighting professor at NYU, who taught me the importance of dialogue, pacing, and character development, and how to approach storytelling cinematically; and to my advisor, Kate Falvey, whose unrelenting persistence made me overcome my fear of public speaking, allowing me to stand before NYU's graduating class of 2000 as class speaker to deliver a message that it's never too late to pursue a dream.

I am grateful for my writing groups. In the first one, led by Peter Bricklebank postgraduation, I learned the importance of a judgment-free zone, surrounded by open and receptive fellow writers. Among them I owe a special thank you to Deborah Unger, who urged me to keep writing. I am grateful for all the women in my current writing group, especially Karen Brandin, Susan Reynolds, and Janis Robinson Daly.

To my non-writer friends, your support has meant so much: Terri Bailey, who has been a faithful friend and constant supporter; Carrie Otto and Tami Albritton, who listened to my blow-by-blow progress during weekly treks to the top of St. Augustine's Lighthouse; and Dawn Broun, who voiced her belief and conviction when I had none.

A special thank you to Shane Ann Younts, a sister by choice, for decades of cheerleading, support, and willingness to read numerous drafts, and standing by me as I pursued one crazy endeavor after another. To Shawn Ehlers, an incredible artist and friend, for praising me more than I deserve and taking the time to read my original tome.

Thank you to my readers, some of you who are family—Leonard Fricke, strictly a reader of military history, who nonetheless sat down and read from start to finish a book about a rebellious teenage girl; Stuart

Fricke, professed fan of audiobooks, and his wife Amy Fricke, adventure seeker, who waded through my first 750-page draft; Allison Bryant, bonafide Aussie from Down Under, who took time out of her busy life as a young, working mother to read her aunt's book; and to Al Fricke, expert sailor and nautical checker, for his input and welcome corrections. Thank you to Rodney Clark, practitioner of less is more, for even attempting to read my meandering, wordy first draft.

To Ian McCluskey, who will always remain my brother-in-law, thank you for your encouragement, support, and most significantly, for the love and care you gave to my sister Gayle.

I'm grateful to my cousins, Susan Taylor and Teri Lockwood, and their parents, June and Charles Roessl, for being part of the story.

Thank you to my other readers, Wendy Ward, Elizabeth Willis, Linda Saxton, and Cindy Schwarz for your enthusiastic support.

To Peggy Gelfond, Kati Garcia-Renart, Marie-Janine and Simon Prebble, Charissa Craig, Gloria Ros, Visnja Clayton, Simon Rogers, Tony Wise, Mike Wise, and Theresa and Louis Krzemien, my heartfelt thanks for simply being there.

I can't forget to mention my writing teacher, Mrs. Buehler, who planted the first seeds in me during summer school in the Canal Zone, that perhaps I could actually write.

Lastly and most importantly, I would like to thank my family. Without their love, support, and encouragement, there would be no book.

I owe a debt of gratitude that I can never repay to my sisters. My sister Pam Fricke, for being my accountability partner, and for being there every step of the way from that long, rough early first draft to the final manuscript. You were selfless with your time and memories and gave me carte blanche to write about our family's adventure. My sister Cate Clark, for focusing her discerning artist's eye on detail, and her keen insight, which helped me to discover the ending to my book. You will remain forever, Nancy, the little green-eyed sprite who brought hope and light to my story. And finally to my sister Gayle, whose memory I hold dear, who made me a better person.

To my amazing daughter, Vivien, who has been more patient than any child should ever have to be, I thank you for giving me time to write my story. I hope the immense love I have for you will give you the security and freedom to spread your wings and fly as far and as fast as you desire. If you ever need somewhere to rest, you won't have to land and skip like a frigate bird, because I will always be there, waiting with open arms to catch you.

To Peter, my saint of a husband, who shouldered parent and home duty while I sat holed up for months writing draft after draft, I promise to follow Steven King's writing advice and disappear for only four hours a day. It's time to get some sun on my face, reenter the living, and assume dishwashing and dinner duty. I'll even throw in laundry duty. Thank you for being my rock and encouraging me to follow a dream, and most of all, for your unconditional love.

My father and mother, my sister Gayle, and my beloved grandma have also been with me on this journey. During moments of despair, I have felt their presence, whispering over my shoulder and urging me to carry on. Then I remember that all I have to do is gaze up at the star-studded night sky and follow the second star to the right. I know, one day, I'll find them there.

# SAILING GLOSSARY

**Aboard:** on or in a vessel; synonymous with "on board."

**Aft:** toward the stern.

**Aground:** resting on or touching the ground or bottom.

**Ahoy:** a cry to draw attention. Used to hail a boat or a ship.

**Anchor watch:** while anchored, crew members are assigned to ensure that the anchor holds in rough weather or when the captain isn't sure the anchor will hold.

**Anchor:** a heavy metal hook designed to prevent or slow the drift of a boat, attached by a chain.

**Anchorage:** a designated place for boats to anchor.

**Astern:** back of the boat or opposite of ahead.

**Bail:** to throw out seawater or rainwater that has collected in a vessel.

**Ballast:** weight placed in the bottom of a boat to give it stability.

**Bare poles:** with all the sails down.

**Beam:** the widest point of the boat. *Heritage* had a ten-foot beam.

**Belay:** to fix (a running rope) around a cleat, rock, pin, or other object, to secure it.

**Berth:** a bed on a boat, or a space in a port or harbor where a boat can tie up.

**Bilge:** the compartment at the bottom of the boat's hull, where water collects to be pumped out later.

**Binnacle:** the stand on which the ship's compass is mounted.

**Bitt:** the post mounted on the ship's bow to attach a line either to tie to a dock or to be towed.

**Block:** a nautical pulley.

**Boat hook:** a pole with a hook on one end designed to grab anything beyond reach, or to fend off another vessel.

**Boatswain or Bosun:** the senior crewman of the deck, responsible for the ship's hull and all its components, including its rigging, anchors, cables, sails, deck maintenance, and small boat operations (as in manning the dinghy!).

**Boom:** a spar to support the foot of a fore-and-aft-sail.

**Boot top:** the part of a ship's hull that is between the load line and the waterline when the ship is not loaded.

**Bosun's chair:** a swath of canvas, used to suspend a person from a rope to perform work aloft.

**Bow:** the front of the boat.

**Bowline:** the rope that's tied onto the bow (front) that stops the vessel from moving sideways when moored.

**Bowsprit:** a spar (wooden pole) projecting from the bow to support the forestay and other rigging.

**Broach:** when the boat is crosswise to the waves and water starts to come over the side, coming close to or actually capsizing.

**Bulkhead:** vertical wall or partition separating areas or compartments on a boat.

**Bulwark:** the ship's side that extends above the hull.

**Buoy:** anchored float.

**Cast off:** to let go of a line when leaving the dock or mooring.

**Cleat:** a metal or wooden device to secure a line on a boat or a dock.

**Coaming:** the raised protection around a cockpit.

**Cockpit:** the location from which the boat is steered, usually in the stern. This is where the seating is as well.

**Companionway:** a raised hatch with a ladder leading below deck.

**Compass:** the navigational instrument that shows north, south, east, and west directions.

**Course:** direction to which the boat is steered.

**Cutter:** a sailing vessel with one mast and two headsails.

**Danforth:** a lightweight, versatile, and high-efficiency fluke-style anchor, preferably used in easy, penetrable seabeds, except very fine sand.

**Deckhand:** a member of a ship's crew whose duties involve the maintenance of a boat or ship.

**Dinghy:** a small open boat carried aboard a yacht for taking the crew ashore.

**Dodger:** the canvas awning that provides some shelter to the cockpit and companionway.

**Draft:** the depth of a ship's keel below the waterline.

**Dragging anchor:** when the vessel drifts without holding power in spite of being anchored.

**Dry-dock:** a term used for repairs or when a ship is taken to dry land (boatyard) so that the submerged portions of the hull can be cleaned or inspected.

**Ebbing tide:** the period between high tide and low tide during which water flows away from the shore.

**Fathom:** a nautical measure of depth or distance equal to six feet.

**Fender:** a bumper used in boating to keep boats from banging into docks or each other.

**Finger slip:** a flat slender walkway that branches out from a dock and divides two slips.

**Float coat:** a jacket that provides the flotation you need to keep from drowning.

**Fo'c'sle:** living quarters in the bow of a ship, usually consisting of two bunks on either side of the foremast and offering access to the anchor locker.

**Following sea:** wave action that is traveling in the same direction as the boat.

**Fore and aft:** in the direction of the keel, from front to back.

**Foremast:** the most forward mast of a sailboat having two or more masts.

**Forepeak:** the part in the cabin between the foremast and the bow, usually a cramped space.

**Foresail:** the lowest sail set on the foremast of a square-rigged ship or schooner.

**Fouled:** entangled or clogged.

**Gaff:** the spar that holds the upper edge of a fore-and-aft sail.

**Gaff jaw:** fits around the mast's lower end, thus allowing it to slew sideways or be topped up or down.

**Galley:** the boat's kitchen.

**Genoa:** a type of large jib or staysail that extends past the mast, overlapping the main sail when viewed from the side, used in moderate or light winds.

**Grommet:** a metal ring fastened in a sail.

**Halyard:** the line, or rope, used to raise or lower sails.

**Hard aground:** a vessel that has gone aground and is incapable of refloating under her own power.

**Hatch:** an opening between the deck and the cabin, protected with a hatch cover.

**Head:** the boat's bathroom.

**Heave to:** to stop a boat by turning the bow to the wind and holding it there. A boat stopped this way is hove to.

**Heeling:** the lean caused by the wind's force against the sails.

**Helm:** the steering mechanism controlling the rudder.

**Hoist:** to haul aloft.

**Hull:** the main body of a boat.

**Jib:** a triangular sail at the front of the boat.

**Jibe:** turning the boat so that the wind changes from one side to the other. It can swing the boom violently from one side to the other.

**Jury rig:** a makeshift repair.

**Keel:** the weighted fin filled with lead ballast below the hull that helps to keep the boat upright.

**Ketch:** a sailing vessel rigged fore and aft on two masts, the larger, forward one being the mainmast and the after one, stepped forward of the rudderpost, being the mizzen or jigger.

**Knot:** a nautical unit of speed: 6,076 feet or one nautical mile per hour.

**Lee rail:** the boat rail on the downwind side of the boat. The low rail.

**Leeward:** the side of the boat sheltered from the wind. When heeling over this will always be the low side.

**Lifeline:** on the deck of a boat, a line to which one can attach oneself to stay aboard on rough seas.

**Lines:** on board a boat, this is what you call ropes.

**Logline:** the line by which the log is trailed from a ship to determine its speed.

**Luff:** the forward most section of a sail.

**Mainmast:** the principal mast of a sailboat.

**Mainsail:** the large sail just aft of the mainmast. As the name suggests it is a sailboat's largest and most important sail. Along its bottom edge, the sail is fasted to a thick pole called a boom.

**Midship(s):** area of the ship in equal distance between the bow and stern.

**Monkey fist:** a ball woven out of line used to provide heft to heave the line to another boat or dock.

**Moor:** to attach a boat to a mooring buoy or post.

**Mooring:** putting the boat in a fixed position with a mooring ball secured to the sea floor.

**Nautical mile:** a unit used to measure distance at sea (approximately 2,025 yards).

**Navigation:** steering a boat safely from one area to another aided by charts, radar, GPS, and dead reckoning.

**Open roadstead:** an anchorage that is in the lee of the land, but otherwise unprotected, so is subject to changing wind conditions and swells.

**Painter:** a small diameter line attached to the bow of a dinghy.

**Payed out:** to let out a rope or cable by slacking.

**Peak and throat halyards:** the peak halyard (or peak for short) is a line that raises the end of a gaff that is farther from the mast; the throat halyard raises the end and is nearer to the mast. Such rigging was normal in classic gaff-rigged schooners and in other ships with fore-and-aft rigging.

**Plow anchor:** is an anchor shaped like a farmer's plow, with a long shank ending in two curved flukes. It performs well in sand, gravel, rocks, and coral, but not so well in soft mud or clay, where its smaller surface area may not provide adequate resistance.

**Port:** the left side of the boat facing forward.

**Quarter berth:** a single bunk tucked under the cockpit.

**Rail:** the outer edge of the deck.

**Ratlines:** rope ladders rigged from bulwarks to the topmast to enable easier access aloft.

**Reef:** to temporarily reduce the area of the sail exposed to the wind.

**Rolly:** an anchorage with a strong swell that causes the boat to roll from side to side as much as twenty degrees is called rolly. Often found at open roadsteads.

**Rudder:** located beneath the stern of the boat, the rudder is attached to the steering mechanism (wheel).

**Running lights:** required lights affixed to the craft that display the aspect of the vessel.

**Schooner:** a sailboat with fore-and-aft rigging on all of two or more masts. On two-masted schooners, the mainmast is typically longer than the foremast.

**Seaworthy:** when a boat can handle the conditions of the sea and is capable of safely sailing at sea.

**Secure:** to stow equipment and keep it from moving about the boat.

**Shackle:** a U-shaped piece of metal with eyes in the end, connecting items together by a pin, spring, or bolt. Used in boating to secure an anchor, hold lines in place, etc.

**Shakedown:** a cruise performed during which the ship and her crew are tested under working conditions.

**Sheet:** the line, or rope, that controls the horizontal movement of the sail.

**Shrouds:** vertical wires that hold the mast upright.

**Sloop:** a one-masted sailboat with a fore-and-aft mainsail and a jib.

**Sounding:** a unit of measurement for the depth of the water.

**Spreaders:** struts attached to the sides of a mast to hold away the shrouds and increase the angle at which they meet the mast.

**Springlines:** lines are additional mooring lines, which prevent the boat from moving forward or aft.

**Squall:** a brief, sometimes violent storm that arrives suddenly.

**Stanchion:** a vertical pipe or beam that supports the rails on the deck.

**Starboard:** the right side of the boat facing forward.

**Stern:** the rear part of the boat.

**Tack:** to change course by passing into the wind.

**Taffrail:** the rail around the stern of a ship.

**Transom:** the surface at the stern of the boat, where the boat's name and port of origin are displayed.

**Underway:** when a craft is not moored, anchored, or docked but en route.

**Wake:** a track in the water left by the movement of the boat.

**Watch:** a period during which a crew member is on duty. We generally had four-hour watches on *Heritage*, except when the weather was bad or someone was sick.

**Waterline:** a line painted on the hull of the boat where the boat meets the water.

**Winch:** the mechanism, usually in the cockpit, that you use to tighten the sheets.

**Windlass:** a mechanism with gears and a handle, mounted at the bow to give a mechanical advantage to raising an anchor.

**Windward:** the side or direction that the wind is coming from.

**Wing and wing:** with a sail extended on each side, as with the foresail out on one side and the mainsail out on the other.